PENGUIN BOOKS

WAR ON THE MIDDLE CLASS

Lou Dobbs is the anchor and managing editor of CNN's *Lou Dobbs Tonight*. He has received the Peabody Award, the Luminary Award by the *Business Journalism Review*, and the Horatio Alger Association Award for Distinguished Americans, as well as an Emmy Lifetime Achievement Award.

LOU DOBBS

WAR ON THE MIDDLE CLASS

How the Government,

Big Business, and Special Interest Groups

Are Waging War on the American Dream and

HOW TO FIGHT BACK

PENGUIN BOOKS

PENGUIN BOOKS

Published by the Penguin Group
Penguin Group (USA) Inc., 375 Hudson Street, New York, New York 10014, U.S.A.
Penguin Group (Canada), 90 Eglinton Avenue East, Suite 700, Toronto,
Ontario, Canada M4P 2Y3 (a division of Pearson Penguin Canada Inc.)
Penguin Books Ltd, 80 Strand, London WC2R 0RL, England
Penguin Ireland, 25 St Stephen's Green, Dublin 2, Ireland (a division of Penguin Books Ltd)
Penguin Group (Australia), 250 Camberwell Road, Camberwell,
Victoria 3124, Australia (a division of Pearson Australia Group Pty Ltd)
Penguin Books India Pvt Ltd, 11 Community Centre, Panchsheel Park, New Delhi – 110 017, India
Penguin Group (NZ), 67 Apollo Drive, Rosedale, North Shore 0745,
Auckland, New Zealand (a division of Pearson New Zealand Ltd)
Penguin Books (South Africa) (Pty) Ltd, 24 Sturdee Avenue,
Rosebank, Johannesburg 2196, South Africa

Penguin Books Ltd, Registered Offices:
80 Strand, London WC2R 0RL, England

First published in the United States of America by Viking Penguin,
a member of Penguin Group (USA) Inc. 2006
Published in Penguin Books 2007

10 9 8 7 6 5 4 3 2 1

ISBN 0-670-03792-3 (hc.)
ISBN 978-0-14-311252-5 (pbk.)
CIP data available

Printed in the United States of America
Designed by Carla Bolte • Set in Dante

To my wife, Debi, and the kids:

Chance, Buffie, Jason, Michelle, Heather, and Hillary

ACKNOWLEDGMENTS

First and always, thanks to my wonderful family for their love and support, and for putting up with me. Thanks also to a great team of journalists, who, yes, also put up with me, and each weekday evening produce *Lou Dobbs Tonight* and work tirelessly and diligently to report the events and issues that are shaping the lives of all Americans.

Together, we've been reporting for the past two years on what has become an undeclared war on the mainstay and bedrock of American society, our middle class. Our great group of journalists has researched and reported on a wide array of events and developments that have appeared to many, including us at the outset, to be independent and unrelated in any way to one another. But over time, those events became social, economic, and political trends that are demonstrably connected and, in many instances, orchestrated by the same forces and groups within our political economy.

Whether the issue is failing public education, corruption in Washington, rampant illegal immigration, the outsourcing of jobs to cheap foreign labor markets, massive U.S. budget and trade deficits, a crumbling national infrastructure, voter fraud, or runaway costs of energy and health care, the principal victim is the same: hardworking, taxpaying middle-class Americans and their families and those who aspire to be part of the middle class. Over time, we've managed to report the relationship among politicians of both parties, corporate and special interests, and lobbyists and the roles they are playing in attacking, often consciously and without conscience, the very people who make up the foundation of our great country, the middle class. Thanks to my colleagues Jim McGinnis, Kevin Burke, Leslie Bella-Henry, Dierdre Hughes, Chris Billante, Deborah Davis, Kitty Pilgrim, Casey Wian, Bill Tucker, Christine Romans, Lisa Sylvester, Louise Schiavone, Peter Viles, Claudine Hutton, Philippa Holland, Adrienne Klein, Rene Brinkley, Nickie Bonner, Jessica Rosgaard, Jill Billante, Tom Evans, David Brandt, Lisa Dilallo, Paul Vitale, Marci Starzec, Kimberly Cardinal, Nicole Duignan, Vandana Agrawal, Jessie Anderson, Angela Ramos, Stacy Curtin, April Harris, Richard Dool, Diane Saltzman, Kaleigh Mountain, and Kathleen Goldrick.

My thanks to CNN News Group President Jim Walton for unstinting encouragement and support, and to Time Warner Chairman and CEO Dick Parsons and President Jeffrey Bewkes for their commitment to world-class journalism.

My thanks also to my friend and counselor Wayne Kabak of William Morris Agency for urging me to write this book, to Viking's Richard Kot, who both encouraged me and skillfully edited the book, and to my friend and compadre H. P. Newquist, whose talent, energy, and humor made this third book in six years possible. My gratitude as well to my colleague Slade Sohmer for editorial research and always helpful suggestions, to Lisa Lee for her research, and finally, to Arlene Forman and Mario Spagnola for their daily efforts to assist me in countless ways, and yes, also for putting up with me.

CONTENTS

Introduction

George W. Bush claimed through two presidential campaigns that America has become the "ownership society." I couldn't agree more. America has become a society owned by corporations and a political system dominated by corporate and special interests, and directed by elites who are hostile—or at best indifferent—to the interests of working men and women of the middle class and their families.

Corporate America holds dominion over the Republican and Democratic parties through campaign contributions, armies of lobbyists that have swamped Washington, and control of political and economic think tanks and media. What was for almost two hundred years a government of the people has become a government of corporations, and the consent of the governed is now little more than a quaint rubric of our Declaration of Independence, honored as a perfunctory exercise in artifice, and practiced every two to four years in midterm and presidential elections in which only about half of our eligible voters go to the polls.

We stand on the brink of being judged by future historians as the generation that failed to heed Abraham Lincoln's call to assure that the "government of the people, by the people, for the people, shall not perish from the earth."

There is almost no countervailing influence in our society to mitigate, even at the margins, the awesome and all but total corporate ownership of our political system. Labor unions are nearing extinction, and those that survive are in the midst of internal leadership struggles to find relevance in our economy and our society. Most of our universities are rarely, if ever, bastions of independent thinking, social scholarship, and activism. Instead they are dependent and rely upon either the federal government or the favor of corporations and the wealthy for funding their very existences. Our churches are in decline and tend to expend their political energy on issues such as gay marriage and highly amorphous "family values" rather than on the relevent causes of our time, including the preservation of our traditional national values of independence, equality, personal freedom, the common good, and our national interest. Isn't preserving the American Dream, and fighting back against those forces that would diminish or destroy it, a worthy cause for our traditional institutions and to all of us who care deeply about our great democracy and way of life?

Most alarmingly, our federal government has become so dysfunctional that it no longer serves well the needs of the people, nor do our elected officials assert the common good against the power of money and capital.

No one believes more strongly than I do in our free enterprise democracy, or in the importance of capitalism as the driving force of our economy. At the same time, I also strongly reject unfettered capitalism, and those forces that now rampant corporatism has arrayed against our middle class and those who aspire to be part of it.

The title of this book reflects an evolution in my understanding of our failed public policies, business practices, and politics over the past five years, and of their disastrous impact on the single largest group of people in this country—our middle class. My understanding has, admittedly, evolved far too slowly, and occasionally only haltingly—especially when I consider that the result of those failed policies, practices, and politics are now so painfully obvious: Middle-class working men and women and their families have been devastated.

In this conflict, the middle class is not collateral damage. Working men and women are not innocent bystanders in a great national accident. Our political, business, and academic elites are waging an outright war on Americans, and I doubt the middle class can survive the continued assault by forces unleashed over the past five years if they go on unchecked.

Whether the issue is a total lack of border security, an illegal immigration crisis, taxation, education, or jobs, big business and big government are unchecked in their attacks on the common good. Most of our elected officials, whether Democrat or Republican, have been bought and paid for through campaign donations from corporate lobbyists and other special interest groups. We've reached a stage where lobbyists no longer merely influence legislation but write the actual language of what becomes law.

The Bankruptcy Abuse Prevention and Consumer Protection Act of 2005 is only one such example. Credit card, banking, and other financial institutions all but wrote this measure. As a law, it now means that many middle-class families cannot turn to the protection of bankruptcy—even though the leading cause of personal bankruptcy is the medical and health care costs incurred by catastrophic illness.

In conjunction with the Bush administration's unwavering commitment to faith-based economics and free trade at any cost, the effect of its failed public policies has been draconian. Our unrepresentative Congress has actually cheered on corporate America's business practices—practices that have destroyed millions of well-paying middle-class jobs, and continue to do so. We are witnessing something that would have been unimaginable a quarter century ago: the emergence of a House of Representatives and a Senate that ignore the will of the majority of Americans, the middle class. Politicians have become viciously and vacuously partisan, and contemptuous of their constituencies. These forces are committed to a world order that views national sovereignty and borders as inconvenient impediments to trade and commerce, and our citizens as nothing more than consumers or units of labor in a global marketplace. That ideology has damaged, perhaps irreversibly, our manufacturing base as a result of the corporate offshoring of production facilities and the outsourcing of jobs to overseas cheap labor markets.

Each night, as I conclude my nightly broadcast on CNN, I have the gut-sick feeling that we have chronicled another twenty-four hours in the decline of our great democratic republic and the bankrupting of our free enterprise economy. Almost every night it seems we report on the erosion of individual rights and individual liberty, on ever bolder attempts by political and business elites to define what America now means, and on actions of elected officials, corporate leaders, and special interests who seemingly are determined to deny millions of Americans the same economic and educational opportunities that previous generations enjoyed.

A few years ago, on *Lou Dobbs Tonight,* we began reporting on the economic challenges facing most Americans in a series called "The Middle-Class Squeeze," which initially focused on health care, job losses in manufacturing, and the corporate outsourcing of jobs. In 2004, the Kerry campaign even adopted "The Middle-Class Squeeze" as a designation for some of the senator's policy positions. By the end of that election year, we had escalated our coverage, and changed the title of the series to "Assault on the Middle Class." The economy had finally started creating jobs, but they were low-paying ones; middle-class jobs were still being shipped overseas. Those who lost their positions were finding new work, but slowly, and they were forced to accept 20 to 25 percent less in wages or salary. At the same time, public education, despite the No

Child Left Behind Act (or perhaps because of it, as critics maintain), was failing millions of our students.

By now it had become evident to me that the problems beleaguering the middle class were about more than the erosion of jobs and pay, health care, and education. The issue was bigger than any of us could have imagined. When the realization that that was the case finally took hold last year, the title of our ongoing series was changed to "War on the Middle Class."

Make no mistake: This *is* an outright war. To call it anything less is a disservice to the truth and to the American people. The mass capitulation of most Americans to political correctness over the past two decades has frequently provoked me to forgo gentle and indirect language in favor of simpler and more direct statements of meaning. I'm biased in my preference for direct language, but I'm convinced there is no other way to address the most critical issues facing the country.

I've found out the hard way that being direct and straightforward on my nightly broadcast is not always pleasing to those people trying to control the national agenda, define issues in their own narrow terms, and obfuscate their vested interests and motives. I was surprised early on that a discussion of something so seemingly boring as international trade and corporate business practices could be met with vicious personal attacks. These came by way of some of the country's leading political figures and news columnists, who assailed me and the broadcast because we were reporting facts, analysis, and conclusions that contradicted, or were inconsistent with, their particular political or economic beliefs.

For instance, I told my audience in 2002 that the Bush administration was mistaken in calling our global war on terrorists simply a "war on terror." I strongly believed then, as now, that we are fighting a global war not against terror, but against radical Islamist terrorists. I questioned, and still do, whether we can effectively fight a war in which we are constrained by some bizarre construction of political correctness to name our enemy.

So I named the enemy. A lot of people didn't like this. Ibrahim Hooper, a spokesman for the Council on American-Islamic Relations, said that I had "taken the definition of Islamist from bigots and [was] trying to apply it to the war on terror." The American-Arab Anti-Discrimination Committee likewise took issue with me, and James Zogby, head of the Arab American Institute, said, "I think he has really added to the confusion."

The Bush White House press office went nuts. A White House press aide, Adam Levine, declared that I would not be permitted interviews with then secretary of state Colin Powell and former national security adviser Condoleezza Rice—in fact, with anyone at the White House. (Rice, by the way, has in fact declined interview requests by *Lou Dobbs Tonight* for the past four years. Knowing now the way this administration works, I doubt my audience will ever see her sitting comfortably across the desk from me in our New York studios.)

To their credit, Veterans Affairs secretary Jim Nicholson, now former trade representative Rob Portman, and UN ambassador John Bolton have all had the courage of intellect and character to come on the show to debate and discuss important issues and policies with me. And White House press secretary Tony Snow broke the four-year embargo that kept White House staffers from appearing on my show when he and I sat down on May 24, 2006, for his first prime-time interview. Snow was candid and engaging, something I appreciate in light of the way the Bush administration typically handles questions from journalists. Still, Snow is the exception in this otherwise insular administration, which absolutely will not tolerate public criticism of its policies and pursuits.

Four years ago I declared on my broadcast that the U.S. Justice Department's decision to indict the Enron auditing firm of Arthur

Andersen was a catastrophic mistake of judgment. Indicting the corporation rather than the culpable executives would needlessly destroy twenty-eight thousand jobs in this country. While some of my colleagues in the national press chose to construe my opinion as defending the firm of Arthur Andersen, I was in fact defending twenty-eight thousand innocent employees who ultimately were put out of work because the Justice Department would not indict the specific individuals who were responsible for any obstruction of justice in the federal investigation of Enron.

To this day I hear almost weekly from a few of the thousands of ex-employees of Andersen who thank me for our coverage and my defense of their jobs. Their gratitude over these years has been more than enough to make me firmly believe I was right in the position I took on the issue. It is also satisfying to note that since its wrongheaded indictment of Arthur Andersen as a firm, the Justice Department has adopted a policy of indicting individuals instead of corporations. My position on the issue was absolutely vindicated when in the case of *Arthur Andersen LLP v. The United States* the U.S. Supreme Court voted to overturn the firm's conviction on May 31, 2005. Nonetheless, all these years later, not a single Arthur Andersen executive involved in the fraud has served a single day in jail.

When I began criticizing corporate America over the issue of outsourcing American jobs to cheap overseas labor markets, I was again besieged by personal criticism. John Castellani, the executive director of the Business Roundtable, couldn't believe that I would speak out against outsourcing, especially since I'm a lifelong Republican and a strong believer in free enterprise. In a speech, Castellani said, "It's as if whatever made Linda Blair's head spin around in *The Exorcist* has invaded the body of Lou Dobbs and left him with the brain of [Democratic presidential candidate] Dennis Kucinich."

It didn't stop there. Gerard Baker of the *Financial Times* called me the "high priest of demotic sensationalism," while James Glassman of the *Washington Post* said, "Once a sensible, if self-important and sycophantic, CNN anchor, he has suddenly become a table-thumping protectionist."

Over the years I've grown accustomed to nasty personal reactions whenever I take a stand against the increasingly entrenched establishment that runs this country. Our privileged elites, along with the orthodoxies of the left and right, demand that they alone will determine our nation's future, and they are dismissive of anyone who would have the temerity to raise his or her voice and speak directly and critically against those in power. I've learned hard lessons along the way, and my skin has thickened, and I will never fail to take strong positions on issues I believe to be critically important to the well-being of working men and women in this country, and to our common good. While columnist Michael Kinsley of the *Washington Post* may describe me as a "raving populist xenophobe," I make no apologies for having more confidence in our middle class than in our elites, or for calling for higher levels of legal immigration, while at the same time demanding the government secure our borders and stop illegal immigration.

Pulitzer Prize–winning *New York Times* columnist Thomas Friedman calls me "a blithering idiot." Columnist Andres Oppenheimer of the *Miami Herald* calls me part of some "isolationist media brotherhood." The ad hominem attacks on me in this debate reveal far more about my critics' reasoning than the issue we're debating.

We open our nightly broadcast announcing an hour of news, debate, and opinion. My commitment is to getting to the facts and the truth whenever and wherever possible. That's what my audience expects, and my audience also expects to hear my opinion on the events and issues that matter most to them. I don't do "fair and balanced," as some would have it, and I don't do the dominant brand of "he says, she says" journalism.

Much of what passes for journalism in this country allows the elites in government and big business to promote their agendas without investigating underlying facts and motivations. By forsaking its role as the institution entrusted by the public to present the truth, the media has become complicit in the war on the middle class. The truth is no longer its goal; meeting deadlines and achieving profitability are now the sacrosanct objectives of news reporting. I truly believe that he says, she says journalism is nothing more than a rationalization for a news organization's failure to commit its journalists and resources to an independent search for the facts and the admittedly elusive truth. When a newspaper, magazine, or news network presents a Republican's view along with that of a Democrat, and passes off such fair and balanced reporting as the truth, it involves a lot less mental heavy lifting for journalists; it's a way for the news organization to avoid the costly, time-and-resource-consuming demands of gathering data and analyzing it before reporting a story. It may even be somewhat satisfying for a reader, viewer, or listener who gets to see or hear his own partisan view expressed for as much as one half of the report. Unfortunately, the result of that approach is that the media usually doesn't even manage to produce half-truths.

He says, she says journalism is a poor substitute for the investigative groundwork, analysis—and yes, opinion—that aims to offer a nonpartisan, independent reality. The truth is seldom fair and balanced, and rarely captured by simply balancing a Democratic view against a Republican view. I have no interest in being objective in my practice of journalism if objectivity can only be achieved through neutrality. I'm never neutral on any issue that affects the common good, our national interest, and the working men and women of this country.

If ever there were a time for truth in America, it is now. For more than two hundred years, the American middle class has been the core of a work ethic, a tradition of values, and a belief that every citizen is an important part of a greater good. This heritage has made the United States a unique nation with shared goals and ideals. Our middle class is America's foundation, and it is in its hearts and minds that the ideal of America is held strongest and brightest.

But ours is becoming increasingly a divided society—a society of haves and have-nots, educated and uneducated, rich and poor. The rich have gotten richer while working people have gotten poorer. We must also recognize that our public education system is failing, that there are far fewer well-paying jobs for our workers, that the middle class is hardly represented in government, and that our community and national values are increasingly challenged by corporatism, consumerism, and ethnocentric multiculturalism.

At a time when our nation should be investing strongly in our middle class, dramatically improving poor schools, rebuilding our manufacturing base, and restoring and refurbishing our infrastructure throughout the country, we are allowing our biggest businesses to ignore their social responsibilities and our federal government to squander hundreds of billions of dollars and accumulate enormous debts—debts that will fall upon our children. While corporations are paying lower taxes than ever before, and tax breaks for the wealthy are expanded, the middle class is forced to shoulder ever more of the tax burden—even as American working men and women are working harder than ever simply to keep their jobs, and they are working longer hours at reduced pay with fewer benefits.

The people who built this country find themselves employed by companies that seem hell-bent on sending their jobs overseas to cut costs and payroll, and electing those representatives who ignore failing public schools and ever more expensive health care. They are, in short, becoming a class of people with uncertain job prospects, insecure financial futures, and the likelihood of a severely reduced standard of living. Making matters worse is the fact that, as a nation, we seem to be in the grip of a national ennui, a numb and passive acceptance of the status quo.

In my opinion we are on the verge of not only losing our government of the people, for the people, and by the people, but also standing idly by while the American Dream becomes a national nightmare for all of us.

Our nation was built by working people who are at once the producers, the consumers, the taxpayers, and the electorate. They are individual contributors to our economy and have always cherished the principle that is the bedrock of democracy, the principle that every single vote counts. Individual rights and responsibilities are the core of America, both two hundred years ago when we were a country of only four million people and today, when we're three hundred million strong. But today we live in a postmodern society in which we've allowed interdependence to overpower individualism. The essential respect for the importance of the rights of the individual is eroding in America.

Americans are still the richest—in every sense of the word—people on Earth, with more guaranteed freedoms, more wealth, and more opportunity than anywhere else on the planet. Yet, in the past four decades, I think many of us have lost sight not only of who we are, but also of the powerful ideas that are the source of our traditions and our values. We have allowed the elites to subvert the principles of free markets and a democratic society, and to establish the lie that the unfettered growth of our economic system is far more important than the preservation of our political system.

I believe our middle class has suffered in silence for far too long, and it simply cannot afford to suffer or be silent for much longer. Hardworking Americans have not spoken out about their increasingly marginalized role in this society, and as a consequence they've all but lost their voice. Without that strong, clear, and vibrant voice, all the major decisions about America and our future will be made by the elites of government, big business, and special interests. Those elites treasure your silence, as it enables them to claim America's future for their own.

If we are to have the America you and I want, and the one we and our children deserve, we must resolutely face these challenges to our way of life. And we must do so now.

— Chapter 1 —

War on the Middle Class

I cannot imagine what the men who wrote these words would think of America today:

> We hold these Truths to be self-evident, that all men are created equal, that they are endowed by their Creator with certain unalienable Rights, that among these are Life, Liberty and the pursuit of Happiness. That to secure these rights, Governments are instituted among Men, deriving their just powers from the consent of the governed.

I don't know about you, but I haven't consented to much of what government has done in the past twenty years.

Our declaration states unequivocally that all men are created equal, and that governments derive their just powers from the consent of the governed. Our country was founded with the intent that class distinction and rigid social structure were things left behind in the old world and had no place in the new. The American Dream was, from the beginning, the promise of political democracy, a wide range of civil liberties, and the opportunity for economic prosperity . . . for each and every citizen.

The men who signed our Declaration of Independence were a mixture of the wealthy and the poor, the well educated and the uneducated. Revisionist history would have us believe that our nation's founders were uniformly elitists, wealthy and entitled men who were the only individuals capable of grasping the enormity of what it took to govern a new country. This was born of a very European notion that the aristocrats were born, or entitled, to public service. They point to Thomas Jefferson, a landowner with extensive holdings. Or John Hancock, who inherited one of the largest estates in the colonies. Or Samuel Adams, owner of a brewery. They rarely cite the fact that Benjamin Franklin was one of seventeen children of a candle maker, and spent much of his youth as an indentured printer's apprentice and clerk. Or that George Taylor worked in an iron mill. Or that William Whipple was a merchant seaman. Or that George Walton was an orphan who apprenticed as a carpenter.

The fifty-six men who signed the declaration were a diverse group, consisting of doctors, lawyers, soldiers, farmers, and merchants. Their backgrounds were varied. Some were born in one of the colonies, others came from disparate parts of Britain. Some went to Harvard, some went to Yale, some were schooled in England, some were schooled at home, others were entirely self-taught. Together these men forged a collective understanding of the needs and desires of the entire country, not of a few select and special interests.

Today the politically powerful and wealthy dominate our society, economy, and government. Never has social class been more distinct or disturbing in American society than it is now. As well as having become a nation sharply divided by partisan politics, race, religion, culture, and age, we are divided by what we do and what we have—or don't have. Our social, economic, and political divisions are all the more troubling because we Americans, or at least the vast majority of us, still truly believe in the democratic principles that have defined our nation from its founding: equality, individual freedom and responsibility, and economic opportunity.

Now a new reality is being forced upon us, a reality that is being shaped by elites who care little for the common good and the success of the great American experiment as it's been defined for two hundred years. Political, business, and academic elites have embraced a vision of the world that supersedes our mere nation, and what they apparently consider to be quaint notions of citizenship. Those making the rules, and often breaking them, are less representative of our country than at any time in our history. Elites are not interested in working people. They are dedicated to attaining power and money, and in the process deprive the middle class of economic opportunity, fair wages, and a voice in Washington. The arrogance and indifference of our elites not only give lie to the notion of America as a nation without class distinction, but their abuse of power has actually brought class division in America into stark relief. We ignore the clash between classes at our own peril.

Our reluctance to address the reality of what has become a class structure in the United States is born in part of our long-standing ideals of American society. Interestingly, the U.S. Census Bureau makes no mention of class but simply divides the population into five groups, in descending order of income. While the census's top quintile is comprised of families who make an average of more than $150,000 a year, for the purposes of this discussion let's consider our upper class as consisting of the top 1 percent of income earners, those making more than $400,000. The top 1 percent of our population earns, on average, more than $1 million per year, and is a heterogeneous group, including CEOs, Wall Street bankers and brokers, a lot of Hollywood actors and actresses, entertainers, professional athletes, and entrepreneurs.

The bottom 20 percent, or our lower class, includes families scraping by on just over ten thousand dollars a year. They are called the working poor, and barely survive.

The remaining three quintiles make up what is commonly understood to be our middle class, making between $26,000 and $150,000 per year. In purely economic terms, it's the people in the middle income brackets, between the richest 20 percent and the poorest 20 percent, who make up our middle class. The average U.S. income, interestingly, is $60,529, due to the fact that people making millions of dollars dramatically offset the income of those at the poverty level. In actuality, half of all Americans make more than $44,000, and half make less.

I would argue that the middle class includes Americans from all walks of life, working at almost every kind of job, and includes all but the very rich and the very poor. Most people in the middle class are from families in which one or both parents worked and strived for the best possible lives for their children. For generations, middle-class families have been able to rely on public schools to be the great equalizer. Even the poorest people in our country could rely on that same public education system—where intelligence and talent were often discovered and nurtured.

The breakdown in the public education system means that the meritocracy in our society has been compromised, and in some instances eradicated. And without a strong public school system that serves all of us regardless of wealth or poverty, a class system will become ever more firmly entrenched.

Some critics believe that money should not be the only index of class distinctions, and have proposed other definitions. Elizabeth Warren, a law professor at Harvard who has done extensive research on the issue, argues that finances alone don't provide enough information, and that using a scale that divides the population into fifths is too confining and doesn't take into account that some people move freely between those various quintiles. Instead, she's developed this baseline criteria for membership in the middle class: property ownership, higher education, and occupational prestige. People in the middle class have been to college, but have not necessarily graduated. They have, or have had, a "good job"—a job in the upper 80 percent of occupational prestige scores. And they have bought a home.

A recent comprehensive series on class by the *New York Times* identified occupation, income, education, and wealth as four criteria that—when viewed in various combinations—determine class status. Moving up the class ladder, according to the *Times* series, can be achieved by overcoming shortcomings in one area with strong showings in others. For instance, too little wealth can be offset by a superior education, while too little education can be offset by a prestigious job. Think Bill Clinton in the former case (poor upbringing in Arkansas offset by an education at Yale and Oxford), Steve Jobs in the latter (dropping out of college offset by founding Apple).

In addition to income, education, and occupation, mobility is another factor that economists and sociologists take into account when examining America's class structure. Mobility, of course, is the ability of people to move between income groups. Being American once meant being "upwardly mobile": using energy and talent to improve our lot in life. Unfortunately, a rapidly changing postmodern economy is less uplifting, and is putting more downward pressure on millions of our fellow Americans. For the first time in our history, Americans aren't dreaming of a better life for their children—they're desperately hoping that their children won't be forced into a *lower* standard of living and lower quality of life.

If you have a couple of kids, a couple of cars, and you're still married, then it's likely that you and your spouse both work, and your family never has enough time because you're all busy just trying to catch up in this hyperactive, overwrought, consumer society that we've created. No matter what your personal circumstance, there is never enough time, never enough money, never enough sleep, and never enough opportunities to reflect on the America we've created.

As a practical matter the America we've created has become so culturally, socially, and economically diverse that class distinction has become a little like art: We know it when we see it. And as Americans we cringe when we see its manifestation in our society. Nonetheless, most people consider themselves to be part of the middle class. They base this personal assessment on yet other criteria: their upbringing, or their financial situation, or where they live.

While we can debate and define forever those elements that make us part of a given class, big government, big business, and big media have already done the slicing and dicing, categorizing the middle class by its consumption habits, by statistics, and by demographics. Big business looks at you as either a unit of labor or a consumer. Big media sees you as a consumer, and as a unit of audience measurement for whatever message it is bombarding us with. And government? If you're in the middle class, you're just a taxpayer. Every ten years, however, you become yet another unit of measurement, when the bureaucracy takes an official count of the population of the state you live in to determine how many congressional seats that state gets. Those estimates are usually wrong—but usually close enough for government work.

The middle class finds itself in the enviable position of being the largest segment of society, but unfortunately, it is also the least well served by big business and big government. While the middle class contains the largest number of citizens and voters, it has the least effective representation in Washington. I've asked a number of senators and congressmen over the past year to name even a single piece of legislation that they've enacted on behalf of working men and women. Their response has typically been a blank stare, followed by some stammering, and not one example came to their minds. As a matter of fact, it was clear that each of them was surprised that I would even pose such a silly, offbeat question. A few of our legislators offered, "What about the Bush tax cuts? Those helped the middle class." In fairness, they did help, indirectly. In reality, however, they were designed to accommodate the very wealthy. And the very wealthy derived more than three times as much benefit from them as did the middle class that, incidentally, pays the largest amount of taxes.

We are increasingly at the mercy of institutions that only appear to be serving our interests. In reality, these institutions are the breeding ground for a new type of upper class, made up of those who simply want to enrich themselves at the expense of the people who work for them or vote for them. These people, and their institutions, are the commanders in a type of class warfare never before seen in America. To them, the middle class is a target.

Warren Buffett is not only one of the richest men in the world, he is also one of the smartest. He has chosen to live in the heart of America. Warren said to me almost two years ago, regarding recent economic measures, "This is class warfare," and, he added, "My class is winning, but they shouldn't be." By winning, Buffett was referring to the efforts to roll back the estate tax for wealthy Americans, to the calls for tougher bankruptcy laws, to the lower taxes on capital, and to the disproportionately higher taxes on labor.

The legislation to roll back the estate tax still sticks in Buffett's craw. The estate tax affects barely 2 percent of the American population, but it accounts for more than $20 billion a year in taxes. Those who are helping to fund the effort to overturn it include the very rich corporate families behind Gallo wines, Campbell's soup, and Mars candies. If they wind up paying less taxes, you will most assuredly pay more. And if you don't, your children will. In other words, the resulting huge federal budget deficits will effectively function as an estate tax on the middle class and their children.

Over the last twenty-five years, median family income has risen by 18 percent while the income of the top 1 percent—the very wealthiest families—has gone up by 200 percent. In 1996, the organization United for a Fair Economy looked at the Forbes 400 list, an annual ranking of the four hundred richest people in the United States. It found that approximately 43 percent of the individuals on the list had inherited enough money outright to qualify for inclusion. Nearly 7 percent had originally inherited more than $50 million, which they subsequently used to build more wealth (thereby gaining inclusion to the top four hundred). Another 6 percent had inherited more than $1 million but less than $50 million; 14 percent were raised in wealthy or upper-class homes, but did not initially have assets in excess of $1 million. Only 30 percent of the richest people came from families who did not have great wealth or own a small business. That means that less than a third of the richest people in the United States started out their lives in the middle or lower classes on the economic scale. If you have any doubts about whether our classless American society is firmly in the grip of a class structure, remember that the best way to have money in this society is still to be born into wealth.

In recent years, the ranks of the upper class have changed; they have swelled with a new kind of wealth. Highly paid CEOs and company founders with millions of dollars in stock have become rich based on the performance of their businesses. To that end, they are willing to do almost anything to protect their companies. It is this group of people, along with their compatriots in the government and the media, who are using their newfound status to keep the interests of the middle class from getting in the way of their own.

It is the members of this business elite, this new upper class, that pose the greatest danger to our American way of life. They are the ones who've bought and paid for members of both political parties, and who pursue so-called free trade policies for the benefit of U.S. multinationals that remain uncompetitive in the global marketplace. They have put American middle-class workers in direct competition with the world's poorest workers. And they have the temerity to blame America's lack of competitiveness on the poor education of working Americans, while having done nothing to improve our educational system. In fact, their greed in pressing for tax cuts has exacerbated the decline of our public schools.

Instead of leadership from big business on the nation's paramount need to address the decline in public education, they have offered only inaction and neglect. There was a time when we could count on the great leaders of business for philanthropy, for seeing to the needs and well-being of the American people. George Peabody established schools and museums; Andrew Carnegie funded schools and public libraries; Milton Hershey built schools and roads. Today we are confronted by a business establishment that is far more concerned with big compensation packages, restricted stock options, and claiming a share of the global marketplace. And while the pay of CEOs skyrockets, the average worker's wages stagnate.

Greed and self-interest in the nation's executive suites and boardrooms are major weapons in the war on our middle class, and have often led to outright criminality. Tyco chief executive Dennis Kozlowski, WorldCom founder Bernie Ebbers, and Enron CFO Andrew Fastow are only some of the executives sentenced to prison in the corruption scandals of the early twenty-first century. They all claimed they were just doing business as usual, and in too many cases, they're exactly right: They had no qualms about cooking the books, lying to their colleagues and friends, and defrauding investors.

While the vast majority of business executives in this country are honest, they are also frequently monomaniacal, and serve their own personal financial interests. They are quick to become defensive and cloak themselves in the colors of capitalism and their corporate responsibilities. When was the last time you heard an American business leader talk about the civic and community responsibilities of a corporation? When was the last time you heard the phrase "good corporate citizen"? What you do hear is the former CEO of Hewlett-Packard, Carly Fiorina, declaring that "no American has a God-given right to a job." You hear Google executives speak proudly of cooperating with government censorship in communist China. And you see the executives of Northwest Airlines increase their compensation by $2.5 million while the financially beleaguered airline attempts to slash the pay of its pilots, flight attendants, mechanics, and baggage handlers.

Unfortunately for all of us, the CEOs, COOs, and CFOs of corporate America are not joined by chief courage officers, as an IBM commercial famously put it. The shame is that in corporate America today, it requires great courage to constrain self-interest and commit to the good of the nation.

— *Chapter 2* —

Class Warfare

Even writing the words "class warfare" makes me uncomfortable. But as I've explained, I like direct language—and the reality is that Americans today are caught in a class war. I grew up truly believing that the United States was a classless society, and the idea that any of us would look at another American and not want for that person the same opportunities that have been given to us is distinctly un-American. We can't guarantee anyone success, or riches, or happiness, but we can sure as hell provide the opportunity to succeed or fail, to have a fair shot at doing the best our God-given talents and abilities will allow. I don't know anyone who wants more than that, and no American deserves less.

There was a time when Americans respected work, no matter how menial, no matter how low the pay, whether it was digging a ditch, picking strawberries, cleaning a restroom, or collecting garbage. I'm afraid there's too much evidence that this is no longer the case.

We have a president who blithely refers to work that "Americans won't do" when he talks about illegal immigration. That's a shame. Senator John McCain went further, telling a gathering of the AFL-CIO that not only wouldn't Americans work for fifty dollars an hour picking produce, but that they *couldn't* physically do it for a whole season. He even offered that rate to anyone who would go to Arizona and pick lettuce. The workers in attendance jeered the good senator, and tried to take him up on his offer. McCain responded simply, "You can't do it, my friends."

I became so concerned about our rising lack of respect for work that I started a segment on my show called "America Works," in which we feature men and women who have jobs that are neither glamorous nor high paying, but which they do because it provides for them and their families. That segment has featured some of the best stories we've told: a Milwaukee waitress and her firefighter husband working to support their young daughter; a Santa Ana trash hauler and his wife, a school-bus driver, raising two kids; and a woman in New York who has been cleaning hotel rooms for thirty-three years—but is now concerned that illegal immigrants might take her job. At the same time that we have lost respect for people who work hard, and work for the barest of pay, our society has increasingly come to adulate and glorify many of the wealthiest people in the country, irrespective of the values and the principles they represent. Too often, those values are greed and callowness. Schoolteachers are no longer as exalted in our society as they once were, and we reserve our honor instead for entertainers, professional athletes, and CEOs.

The full emergence of a class structure is nowhere more evident than in the differential in pay of corporate CEOs and average workers. CEOs have always been paid better than the average employee in this country, but over the past decade the disparity between the two has become even more stark. The average CEO's pay went from being forty-two times that of the average blue-collar worker's pay in 1980, to eighty-four times that worker's pay by the end of the decade. While the gulf in compensation widened dramatically in that decade, the next fifteen years saw the pay ratio between CEO and average worker rise to 431 to 1.

Median CEO compensation went from $1.8 million in 1992 to

$6.1 million in 2000. CEO pay increased 340 percent from 1992 to 2002, while compensation pay for rank-and-file employees increased a mere 36 percent. By 2004, the average CEO pay was $9.6 million, with one hundred CEOs making more than $10 million and forty making more than $20 million. In 2005, the median pay for CEOs in the one hundred largest U.S. companies increased to $17.9 million—an increase of 25 percent from the year before. (The average employee, by the way, got a raise of 3.1 percent during the same time period.)

In the past few years, we've seen levels of pay for individual CEOs that is beyond most people's comprehension—money that sounds as if it belongs in a company's revenue column rather than on a paycheck. In 2004, Terry Semel, chairman and CEO of Yahoo!, was paid $120 million. Lew Frankfort, head of Coach, was paid more than $58 million. Robert Nardelli, who runs Home Depot, made $36 million. Ed Zander, Motorola's chairman and CEO, got $32 million. Meg Whitman, president and CEO of eBay, received $26 million.

Many CEOs were also paid above and beyond these salaries in stock options, which gave them an incentive to run up their companies' stock prices for their own immediate benefit at the expense of long-term corporate gains.

Among those enjoying huge paydays have been CEOs at big defense contractors. Since September 11, 2001, these CEOs—whose businesses are supported by our tax dollars—have received pay raises of 200 percent. While we're trying to figure out how we're going to pay for the war in Iraq, at least now we know where some of the money is going—and who is profiting from it.

Defense contractors aren't the only ones getting rich at the expense of working people in this country. The record gas and oil prices of the past several years—prices that have affected each and every one of us—have squeezed the middle class while making oil company executives incredibly wealthy. There is no better example than Lee Raymond, the recently retired chairman of ExxonMobil. Mr. Raymond appeared before Congress in 2005 and stated that the huge increase in oil prices was the result of supply and demand. He even told the members of Congress, "We're all in this together, all over the world."

Not exactly. Raymond isn't in it with the rest of us by any stretch of the imagination. During his thirteen-year run as chairman and CEO, Raymond's compensation worked out to be $144,573 *a day*. On top of that, his retirement package is currently the most generous in history, valued at approximately $400 million. That includes not only stock options and a pension, but personal and home security, a $1 million consulting contract, the use of a corporate jet, and many other perks. Raymond is obviously one person who gets great satisfaction—and reward—from seeing high prices at the local gas station.

The standard rationalization for these astronomical salaries by CEOs, boards of directors, and their consultants is that these CEOs are worth it because the companies they run benefit from their leadership, and bring great value to shareholders. How, then, do they explain the fact that over the past five years the CEOs of AT&T, BellSouth, Hewlett-Packard, Home Depot, Lucent, Merck, Pfizer, Safeway, Time Warner, Verizon, and Wal-Mart were paid an aggregate $865 million in compensation—while shareholders lost a total of $640 billion? Clearly, these CEOs were not being paid for delivering value to those who held stock in the companies.

In fact, CEO compensation is often directly inverse to the performance of the companies they lead. Because their compensation is not tied to how the business performs, their pay isn't a reflection of their executive ability, but an aberration. The former CEO of Time Warner, Gerry Levin, walked away with a $163 million pay package after his last year at what was then called AOL Time Warner. How much do you think he should have made that year if he *hadn't* entered into the worst corporate merger in history, one that eventually led to the write-off of nearly a hundred billion dollars?

Levin's story is not unique. Alfred Lerner, the former CEO of MBNA, made more than $194 million in 2002 ($9 million in salary, another $185.9 million in options and other compensation). Lerner died that same year, and his successor, Charles Cawley, was paid nearly $49 million. That's nearly a quarter of a billion dollars in compensation for two people. With such high-paid executives, how did the people who'd invested in MBNA fare? Return to them was *negative* 18 percent. And then there's Larry Ellison, founder and CEO of Oracle. From 2000 to 2002, Larry's personal take from the company was $781 million. But shareholder return was negative 61 percent.

Proponents also argue that there are so few qualified CEOs that corporations *have* to pay inordinately for their expertise. But how much, really, is enough? Some twenty years ago, Drexel's Fred Joseph told me that $5 million was enough. That was the same year that Fred and Drexel Burnham Lambert paid Mike Milken a $100 million bonus. By the end of the nineties, $5 million was chump change for CEOs. Most CEOs will tell you they should make whatever the market will bear. Now, no one is more pro–free enterprise than I am, yet I am absolutely unpersuaded by this argument. The "market" in this case is made up of the CEOs themselves, the boards they nominate, and the executive search and compensation firms that recruit them and negotiate their pay packages—not employees, not shareholders. Many corporate boards are comprised of close associates of the CEO. There are plenty of incestuous board relationships where executives have business ties with one another, or sit on one another's boards, approving one another's compensations. One glaring example is Home Depot, where CEO Ray Nardelli has been awarded $245 million over the past five years, even as the company's stock dropped. Mr. Nardelli, who was previously an executive at General Electric, has the good fortune to have two of his former GE associates on the Home Depot board, associates who have awarded him millions of dollars while stockholders have seen their shares slide more than 10 percent during Mr. Nardelli's tenure. No one expects Ed Zander to say to Motorola's board that he really doesn't want the $32 million in compensation he's been offered. The compensation of Zander and other CEOs is not set by the owners of the enterprise. The owners—the shareholders—have no voice in whether the board turns over a percentage of the stock in options or restricted stock to a CEO, or in how much their ownership is diluted.

Where is the incentive to constrain these levels of compensation? Where are the countervailing forces that would work to hold down pay? I can't think of one. (And as you might guess, my opinion on executive compensation means that some CEOs I've known for twenty years or so don't talk to me anymore.)

Interestingly, most of these CEOs run companies listed on the New York Stock Exchange. The NYSE is supposed to set a standard for corporate America in governance, in transparency, and in integrity, espousing and advocating the values that are critical to our financial system and investor confidence in it. So what did the New York Stock Exchange do in its capacity as a not-for-profit organization and quasi-regulatory body? It paid $140 million to its own CEO, Richard Grasso—more money than the CEOs of many for-profit financial firms made. When there was a public outcry over the sum, Grasso said he had been "blessed" by his board of directors. Blessed, indeed. Grasso's predecessors were not so blessed. They were foolish enough to regard the position as primarily one of public service.

Although CEOs should be ultimately beholden to the shareholders—the real owners of any company—some have taken steps to undermine the influence of shareholders in the hopes of eliminating interference in the way they run the businesses. This comes as investors, primarily those whose pension funds or 401(k) plans have significant stock holdings in large corporations, have begun to try to protect themselves from unrestrained greed. These investors, who collectively own billions of shares in corporate America, saw what happened at WorldCom, Adelphia, Tyco, Enron, and many other companies when senior executives abused their positions and power. They are now demanding accountability from management. They want approval over exorbitant pay packages, or over political contributions, and they are seeking to have important corporate issues determined by majority voting.

There are plenty of CEOs who don't like this level of involvement one bit. To keep these "activist" shareholders at bay, and out of the way, CEOs are looking for ways to thwart their efforts. This has taken a number of forms. Some have hired firms that provide a service called "shareholder surveillance" that identifies major stockholders, tracks their voting history, and tries to determine their future intentions. Proxy adviser Georgeson Shareholder, which offers what it calls "shareholder optimization" to its large corporate clients, says this on its Web site: "If you don't know who your shareholders are or what they want, then you won't be able to predict and influence their behaviour." Merrill Lynch has put a group in place to help clients defend against investor activists. The rationale for creating this type of consulting was spelled out in an internal memo that stated, "Activist investing and the appropriate response have become increasingly important topics for our clients and their boards. . . . It is essential that we identify and advise clients who are likely targets, prior to the announcement of the activist position."

Investor activism is raising alarms in all the usual places, including the U.S. Chamber of Commerce. As its vice president, David Chavern, told *BusinessWeek*, they view this issue as one of "activists who want to have some degree of leverage over companies for political or other goals." Read that again. The Chamber of Commerce doesn't want majority owners to have leverage? Apparently they prefer that investors just stay away and let executives do as they please.

Increasingly, many large corporations are run like fiefdoms. Some are so big they might as well be their own independent political, as well as financial, entities. In fact, of the one hundred largest economies in the world, more than half are corporations. For instance, in economic terms, Wal-Mart is bigger than Sweden, Austria, and Norway. ExxonMobil is bigger than Turkey and Denmark. General Electric is bigger than Finland, Thailand, Portugal, and Ireland. Ironically, General Motors is bigger than oil-rich Saudi Arabia.

These mammoth corporations are in most cases multinationals—businesses that produce goods everywhere and sell them everywhere. Nearly all do business in the United States, which offers them not only the richest consumer and capital market in the world, but the most hospitable. The problem is that for many multinationals based in the United States, geography now means absolutely nothing. They are incorporated here, and they reap extraordinary benefits by being headquartered here, from participating in our stock exchanges to receiving tax breaks. Unfortunately, that's where the relationship ends. When it comes to giving something back to the United States in return for those benefits, too many multinationals are myopic in the extreme.

Fifty years ago, corporate income taxes made up a third of all federal revenues; now corporations account for just an eighth. Income taxes from middle-class working families, in contrast, contribute roughly half of all tax revenue collected by the federal government. In 2004, when Congress approved billions in corporate tax cuts, a report by Citizens for Tax Justice showed that the United States's biggest and most profitable companies had been paying decreasing federal income taxes over the previous three years—despite reporting higher profits. Many of them were paying no taxes at all. The CTJ study found that the average effective tax rate for the largest

275 American corporations had dropped by a fifth over those three years, from 21.4 percent in 2001 to 17.2 percent in 2003. These 275 companies reported pretax profits from U.S. operations of almost $1.1 trillion in that three-year period, yet they paid taxes on only $557 billion. That rate is around half of the statutory 35 percent corporate tax rate that companies are obligated to pay to the U.S. government.

Not only are some corporations paying no federal income taxes at all, but others are actually *making* more money after taxes, mostly due to tax havens and additional breaks passed by the Bush administration in recent years. Twenty-eight of the 275 companies surveyed paid no tax at all from 2001 to 2003, despite having profits of nearly $45 billion in that period; more than 80 paid no income tax in at least one of those years. In 2003, 46 of the 275 companies surveyed paid no federal income tax. During that same period, though, the Commerce Department reported that pretax corporate profits rose 26 percent. U.S. multinationals are earning higher profits, but they're also finding more ways to protect that money from flowing back into our country.

Martin A. Sullivan, contributing editor for *Tax Notes* and a former Treasury Department economist, blames the corporate tax problem on the ways our laws are structured. "I think Congress and the administration have dropped the ball on enforcing and strengthening the laws," he explained. "It's not just the corporations on their own doing this, and they're not doing anything illegal. They're doing everything within the law, but they have a lot of leeway within the law right now."

Not only is the government weakening the laws to aid U.S. multinationals, they're handing out more than tax breaks. The federal government has awarded billions in government contracts to companies that shelter their profits or set up headquarters in offshore tax havens. More than half of the top one hundred contractors doing business with the government also have subsidiaries in tax-haven countries. That may explain why these corporations now pay only about 6 percent of federal revenue, the lowest level since World War II.

Congresswoman Rosa DeLauro (D-Connecticut) introduced legislation to block government contracts for U.S. companies that relocate overseas in order to avoid paying U.S. taxes. Amazingly, it failed in the House of Representatives with strong opposition in both parties. As she told me, "This is not a Democratic or a Republican issue. I think there ought to be overwhelming support for this effort. These are industries that go offshore. They set up a shell corporation in order to diminish their tax obligation to the United States. And then they have the audacity to come back and to ask for taxpayers' dollars for federal contracts. And you know what? They get them. It's about $1.4 billion in contracts. And we lose about $5 billion in revenue every single year. That's an outrage."

But it's an outrage that is unchecked. There is simply no congressional will to buy American or contract American. And because of our declining manufacturing base, it's not at all clear that the federal government could even successfully find American-based suppliers of products and services to meet its needs.

U.S. multinationals are not only paying lower taxes than ever, but are offshoring production and outsourcing jobs to cheap labor markets overseas. American corporations are incentivized not only by low-cost foreign labor, and by the absence of environmental and labor protections elsewhere, but also by the U.S. Congress, via legislation such as the American Jobs Creation Act of 2004—which, rather than specifically creating jobs, provided businesses with a preelection tax break of $145 million.

American corporations are also rolling back employee benefits, including health care and retirement plans. In fact, recent congressional legislation designed ostensibly to safeguard pension plans actually does the opposite: It will allow corporations to cut their contributions to pension funds over time. The stated purpose of the Pension Protection Act of 2005 is to protect the Pension Benefit Guaranty Corporation and avoid a bailout by taxpayers. Yet the proposal also does away with some of the reporting requirements and financial disclosures that companies have to make when paying into the PBGC. Companies will also get more time to cover their commitments. According to the government's pension agency, there are enough loopholes in the legislation to result in an underfunding of the PBGC to the tune of more than $150 billion for multiemployer plans; that figure rises to $600 billion if you include single-employer plans. The PBGC is already running a deficit of almost $30 billion from picking up the pieces of the airline industry's pension funds, and the airlines are pressing Congress for the waiving of rules that would only apply to them. The likelihood is that that number will rise astronomically. Further damage will result in more of our taxpayer money going to cover the broken pension promises of big business.

There is, of course, nothing new in the history of American business when management is forced to lay off workers. What *is* a relatively recent anomaly in our business history, however, is the idea that management should make money—and lots of it—whether they're successful or not.

When Kmart announced its bankruptcy filing in 2002, it laid off twenty-two thousand workers without giving any severance pay. At the same time, CEO Chuck Conaway—the man in charge when the company went belly up—got a $9.5 million severance package. When Polaroid went bankrupt, it laid off two thousand workers and shut down the company's employee stock ownership plan—even while company executives demanded $19 million in so-called retention bonuses.

It was in the last three decades that the traditional contract between employees and management began breaking down—and not, in my opinion, because of the influence of international competition or globalization. Rather, it was the result of two important developments that marked a sea change for American workers. The first turning point came in 1978, when a corporate finance genius named Michael Milken set up his Los Angeles office of investment bank Drexel Burnham Lambert. It was from that office that Milken started heavily promoting junk bonds as an instrument for leverage in corporate takeovers.

Milken's contribution to finance and markets will be debated for decades. But there is no arguing about the fact that the use, promotion, and marketing of junk bonds created the highest debt leverage for corporate acquisitions in American history. Milken and Drexel's deals included some of the best-known brands in America, such as Disney, Revlon, Beatrice, Union Carbide, National Can, Gulf, Fruit of the Loom, Owens-Corning, Fox, MCI, Turner Broadcasting, and dozens of others. Junk bonds and highly leveraged debt overtook cash and commercial lending.

Milken empowered financiers, entrepreneurs, and executives to do the unimaginable. With junk bonds they could raise billions of dollars and seize control of a company—even the company for which they worked—without risking a dime of their own. It didn't take traditional managers long to figure out how to play the game. They could use junk bonds to take over the companies they managed themselves through a leveraged buyout. As soon as they had ownership of the assets, they and the companies they owned—under the terms of the Milken money matrix—became buyers of junk bonds to support the ambitions of other greenmailers, takeover artists, and other managers who saw the opportunity to enrich themselves.

Junk bonds rendered any business with low profit margins and significant assets vulnerable to takeover by much smaller companies or by individuals. No longer could corporations, even those with tens of billions of dollars in assets and reasonable profits, expect to honor the traditional American contract between employer and employee. Companies that once prided themselves on retaining employees even in the worst of times could no longer afford to do so without looking over their shoulders in fear of greenmailers and takeover artists.

The second major development occurred in 1993, with the widespread issuance of stock options to management, which permitted companies to "align" management and shareholder interest. Throughout the 1990s, technology companies in particular were desperate to retain their workforces, and they offered stock options throughout their organizations. This was due in large part to the fact that professionals within the high-tech industry stayed with their companies an average of only thirteen months. Stock options put managers in the position of also being "owners" of the company. Their success was tied to that of the stock price. The dilution of a company's outstanding stock was acceptable to most shareholders—who own too little and are too passive to influence management—so long as stock prices rose. And rise they did throughout the 1990s. From 1990 to 1999, stocks propelled the Dow to a gain of 336.5 percent, the S&P rose 344.9 percent, and the NASDAQ rose an astounding 988.5 percent.

When the technology and telecommunications boom of the 1990s blew up in 2000, the traditional corporate contract between employer and employee had already been effectively torn up by both sides. The nineties had seen the creation of twenty-two million jobs, most of them high paying; the twenty-first century began with the bursting of the bubble and a recession, with more than three million manufacturing jobs lost in the first five years of this new century. The migration of our manufacturing base from the United States was already well under way, as management sought to avoid environmental and labor regulation; other jobs started being outsourced to foreign labor markets in offering plentiful, cheap labor. The workers who lost those manufacturing jobs were the first casualties of the war on the middle class, a war that in retrospect began not with a declaration or the firing of a single shot, but with the emergence of business practices and capital shifts that have proved to be the primary economic forces working against American labor.

The administrations of three presidents, two Republicans and one Democrat—and a Congress that has been predominantly Republican over the past twelve years—have underwritten this war on the middle class. Both political parties have embraced the misguided politics and faith-based economics of so-called free trade, which philosophically exculpates our elected officials from any responsibility for the declining quality of employment. They can, in fact, defend the lower standard of living their policies are creating by declaring that lower wages and benefits are actually making America more competitive in a global marketplace.

And by embracing what Daniel Patrick Moynihan once called "benign neglect," politicians of both parties can merely shrug and mindlessly maintain that our rich are getting richer, our poor are getting poorer, and our middle class is shrinking because of "market forces." God knows, we wouldn't want our policymakers to interfere with the creative destructionism of unfettered capitalism. Never mind that there is nothing free about either the trade policies or the markets that are dominated by multinational corporate interests. Political power and economic wealth are increasingly concentrated in the hands of our business and political elites, and "our government" is complicit—when not instrumental—in ensuring the outcome of what has become outright class warfare.

— Chapter 3 —

The Best Government Money Can Buy

Lobbyists for corporate America and special interest groups are the arms dealers in the war on the middle class. They broker money, influence, and information between their clients and our elected officials, all of which are used to render working men and women in this country little more than cannon fodder.

In my entire career, I've literally never heard a single congressman or senator argue that lobbyists are bad for America. Quite the contrary: Most have told me, with a straight face, that lobbyists are an essential part of our system of government, and that little could be accomplished without them. I disagree vehemently. I believe strongly that our government will never work as it should until the role of lobbying in Washington is dramatically and drastically diminished.

In 1968, there were only sixty-two lobbyists in our nation's capital. By the mid-1980s, approximately eight thousand people had registered as lobbyists or as agents representing foreign governments. Today, there are more than thirty-four thousand, and lobbyists now outnumber our congressmen, senators, and their staffs 2 to 1. From 1998 to 2004, lobbyists spent nearly $13 billion to not only influence legislation, but in many cases to write the language of the laws and regulations they sought.

Lobbying is legal, but it straddles a fine line, and too many lobbyists and elected officials cross that line. A recent example is former San Diego congressman Randall "Duke" Cunningham, who sat on the House Appropriations Committee and its Defense Subcommittee, which approves spending for defense programs. While doing so, and supposedly overseeing the needs of his constituency, Duke took $2.4 million from defense contractors. By the time investigators caught up with him, Duke had gotten a yacht, a mansion, a Rolls-Royce, and a second home out of his tenure. After pleading guilty to conspiracy to commit bribery, mail fraud, wire fraud, and tax evasion in November 2005, he was sentenced to more than eight years in prison. Assistant U.S. attorney Jason Forge said the sentence was the highest ever given to a former member of Congress.

We should all be deeply grateful to people like Forge and Mary Butler, the Justice Department's lead prosecutor in the case against superlobbyist Jack Abramoff. Butler and her investigative team had the guts to take on Abramoff, a figure who was emblematic of political corruption in Washington, and whose influence peddling and connections in the Republican Party was unrivaled on Capitol Hill. But the Justice Department nailed Abramoff. He pled guilty to tax evasion, fraud, and—this is the notable charge—conspiring to bribe public officials.

Politicians did everything they could to distance themselves from wrongdoing or the appearance of impropriety in the Abramoff case, and more than a hundred, including President Bush and Senator Hillary Clinton, washed their hands of Abramoff-related money, by either giving it back or donating it to charity. It's a nice gesture, if nothing more.

But the fact remains that Abramoff's business practices were tolerated and accepted by everyone on Capitol Hill. Not only did he defraud many of the Native American tribes he took on as clients, he spread the resulting riches around to both parties. Everyone was happy to get a piece. Abramoff even opened the upscale Signatures restaurant in Washington to attract members of Congress, many of whom ate for free, courtesy of Mr. Abramoff and his clients.

He was part of a lobbying industry that for years has lavished campaign contributions, luxurious gifts, and exotic trips abroad on our elected officials. Representatives in the House and Senate look upon those "gifts" not as bribes to do the bidding of their corporate and special interest masters, but rather as perks appropriate to their lofty positions of power. And, of course, the lobbying industry couldn't agree more.

But even in this Orwellian era, our laws still count for something, sometimes. For his backroom dealings, Abramoff gets to spend nearly six years in jail. And as part of his deal with the prosecutor, Abramoff has agreed to cooperate with the Justice Department in its investigation of lobbying fraud and other instances of bribery. That means he will have to name names. Because the investigation is still ongoing, we don't yet know who Abramoff has identified, but the speculation on Capitol Hill is that more than twenty people are in the prosecutor's sights.

In April 2006, just as the Democrats were set to use Cunningham and Abramoff as examples in their campaigns against the Republicans' "culture of corruption," the ranking Democrat on the House ethics panel was forced to temporarily resign his post. Representative Alan Mollohan from West Virginia was being investigated over possible connections between campaign contributions he had received and companies that had received business due to his membership on the House Appropriations Committee. A month later, Democratic representative William Jefferson of Louisiana was being investigated by the Department of Justice for possibly taking bribes, which led to the first time the FBI had ever raided an office on Capitol Hill. His particular situation united the Congress against the other branches of government, when members of both parties questioned the constitutionality of the raid;

they claimed the DOJ had overstepped the bounds of the separation-of-powers doctrine by conducting such a search. President Bush subsequently sealed the documents retrieved from Jefferson's office, but to many of us, it looked as if Congress was simply trying to protect its own in the midst of another scandal.

These incidents briefly incited our lawmakers to cries of shock, outrage, and righteous proclamations about the urgent need to reform ethics rules and guidelines, and curtail the corrosive influence of lobbyists. In fact, the congressional rush to "fix the system" had already been under way by the end of January 2006, when lawmakers had decried the abuses of lobbying, while at the same time promoting the virtues of the practice when done lawfully. They had promised then to "restore the bonds of trust" with voters.

So what did our reform-minded senators actually do? In March 2006, by a vote of 90 to 8, they approved a bill that would prevent registered lobbyists from bestowing free meals, sports tickets, and other gifts on elected officials. It also required disclosure of indirect lobbying, such as that done by nonregistered lobbyists. Despite promises of more disclosure, transparency, a curtailment of influence peddling, and public pronouncements that they would hold themselves to a higher standard of conduct, lawmakers couldn't quite bring themselves to approve a call for an independent investigative office to monitor ethical conduct and lobbying activities. Pitiful.

In America, politics is always about deciding who gets what. And while our elected officials in Washington proudly describe their work as doing the people's business, the reality is that most often lobbyists and our lawmakers are just giving the American people minimal attention, while corporate America and special interests and their army of lobbyists make certain that the middle class remains the least represented in our nation's capital. Our federal government has evolved to the point of doing the business of business, and frequently simply doing the bidding of big business.

When it comes to issues of real importance to the middle class—education, public safety, the environment, infrastructure, economic security, and a rising standard of living—our politicians are for the most part deaf, dumb, and blind. For instance, the people of this country are deep in a health care crisis. Health care is too expensive for many families, and more and more companies are opting to drop full coverage from the benefits they offer employees. Yet our government is giving $10 billion in subsidies and risk-sharing payments to insurance companies and health care organizations that sign on to the nation's Medicare program, which the Bush administration revamped in 2003. That money goes to the businesses that are part of the problem, not to the working men and women who need the help.

Our highways, bridges, and dams are literally crumbling. Congress passed the massive Transportation Act of 2005, which any reasonable citizen would have expected to deal with our critical infrastructure needs. The reality? The Republican-led Congress and Bush White House agreed to spend $286 billion over five years, much of which went directly to pork-barrel spending in the districts of congressmen and the states of senators that does little to meaningfully respond to the nation's need to repair and improve our national infrastructure. Instead, the legislation includes funding for 6,371 pet projects demanded by our nation's representatives, at a cost to the taxpayer of $25 billion. Prime examples of just how extensive the pork is in this bill is the inclusion of $1.2 million to install lighting at the Blue Ridge Music Center in Virginia; $2.3 million to beautify California's Ronald Reagan Freeway; $4 million for the Packard Museum in Ohio; $5.8 million for a snowmobile trail in Vermont; and $6 million to remove graffiti in New York. And Alaska, the third least populous state, managed to get the fourth highest number of "earmarks," the politically correct congressional term for pork.

Even by recent standards of sorry conduct on the part of our legislators, the transportation bill took the congressional apathy to the public interest to new heights, and the influence of special interests and the role of lobbyists to new depths. Those are murky depths, indeed.

For the past decade, the influence of lobbyists has become pervasive, and in many cases that influence is determinant of public policy. As Tom Donohue, the president of the largest business lobbying group in the country, the Chamber of Commerce, said on my show: "We're spending money so that the government doesn't put so many impediments in the way that we kill the goose that laid the golden egg."

Tom Donohue truly believes what he said, but I couldn't disagree with him more. The foundation of our prosperity is our free enterprise democracy, and when any part of our society deems itself to be preeminent in our political economy, the national interest surely suffers. But that is precisely the roll of lobbyists who represent special interests and corporate America: to put their own agendas above the public interest, to demand the defeat of laws and regulations that limit their activities, and to support those that give them advantage. With few exceptions, lobbyists work against the electorate, working men and women, middle-class taxpayers. Of course, there is no lobby for the American middle class.

Because of their ubiquity throughout Capitol Hill and most of Washington, lobbyists have become known as part of the "fourth branch of government." And even that may be an understatement of the power and influence they wield. Lobbyists have, as John Kenneth Galbraith put it, "power in the meaningful sense of the term, which is to say that they [are] able to direct the actions and command the obedience of countless other individuals." They now comprise an industry whose power exceeds, by countless multiples, the capacity of individual citizens to voice their concerns and desires. Just how powerful is lobbying? Individual firms, corporations, and national organizations spent a record $2.14 billion on lobbying members of Congress and 220 other federal agencies in 2004. That's $5.5 million a day spent to influence our elected officials and convince them that what is good for thousands of lobbyists and their clients—whether corporations, business associations, or special interests—is far more important than the needs and wants of tens of millions of citizens.

In just the past five years, the number of registered lobbyists has more than doubled (as have their fees), and there are now 4,755 such firms in Washington representing the interests of their high-paying clients, from the computer industry and oil companies to foreign governments and casinos. The pharmaceutical industry alone has two lobbyists for each and every member of Congress.

Lobbyists and special interest groups influence legislation in a number of ways. They can contribute directly to a political campaign, thereby helping a candidate get elected or reelected. They can't contribute more than a legal limit allowed to campaigns, but they can certainly pour it on when giving to political action committees, which don't have the same restrictions when it comes to accepting donations. PACs are organizations started by, or championed by, elected officials. They serve as support organizations for these politicians, raising funds for individual campaigns, creating television ads, and publicizing one side of a given issue. PACs also have fewer restrictions on where they put their money than do registered lobbyists, so the latter often channel their money into PACs to circumvent these restrictions.

One example is Tom DeLay's Texans for a Republican Majority Political Action Committee, or TRMPAC. DeLay created the PAC with the intent of getting a Republican majority elected in the Texas state legislature. It received both individual and corporate donations, and used the money for administrative expenses and to help fund Republican campaigns throughout the state. A current indictment by Austin district attorney, and Democrat, Ronnie Earle charges that

TRMPAC funneled money from corporations directly to campaigns, which is illegal in Texas. Earle also charges that TRMPAC's directors laundered money in order to hide where it was coming from and to whom it went.

The money from these sources is generally given to politicians who can have a direct bearing on legislation that's of interest to the lobbyists and their clients, such as members of Senate and House committees. For example, from 1984 to 1993, when Senator Larry Pressler of South Dakota was a member of the Commerce, Science, and Transportation Committee, special interest groups representing the telecommunications industry gave the senator a total of $110,400—the least amount of money given to any commerce committee member. But after Pressler became chairman of that committee in 1995 and began drafting a telecommunications act, special interests gave him $107,985 in that year alone—more money than the telecoms gave anyone else in the Senate.

Special interest money also pays the fees for politicians to attend industry gatherings, where they are invited to speak about pet projects and weigh in on how important the host industry is to America. Lobbyists have paid out more than $50 million to take congressmen and senators on all sorts of trips over the past five years, including shopping for our lawmakers' wives, tours of exotic locations around the world, and "fact-finding" tours nicely balanced with rounds of golf and fly-fishing. Nonprofit organizations often pay for those trips, and our legislators don't have to disclose what organization is the source of that money. Among all his other ethical and legal problems, former House majority leader Tom DeLay was brought down in part by accusations that he took such lobbyist-funded trips, including a Jack Abramoff–sponsored golf outing to Scotland. DeLay's defense? He said they were paid for, in that case, by the National Center for Public Policy Research. Not coincidentally, this think tank reportedly received millions of dollars in contributions from Jack Abramoff and his clients.

Then there are public policy institutes, called think tanks, such as the Cato Institute, the Brookings Institution, and the American Enterprise Institute. These organizations issue policy reports and provide research to politicians that can be used to influence an elected official's point of view.

All of this activity is supposed to be monitored. Elected officials are obligated to file paperwork detailing where funds come from and who paid for what in accordance with the Ethics in Government Act of 1978. But no one's checking to make sure that everything is aboveboard; the House Ethics Committee has been all but ineffectual in this regard.

Of course, a lot of lobbyist money also ends up at 1600 Pennsylvania Avenue. Between 1999 and 2005, lobbyists paid White House officials almost $2.5 million to speak at their events. Prominent names among those speakers include Sandy Berger, President Clinton's national security adviser, and Karl Rove, President Bush's deputy chief of staff and senior adviser. Some of these payments cover speaking fees, while others underwrite expenses for travel. During the Clinton years, Harvard University paid the White House $85,000 for members of Vice President Al Gore's staff to travel to speaking engagements.

The billions of dollars being spent by lobbyists and their corporate and special interest clients lubricates not only desired legislative results, but also what has become a revolving door for public officials, public servants, and lobbyists. It doesn't matter whether they are Democrats or Republicans; the odds are high that they will end up as lobbyists, one way or another. At this writing, forty pharmaceutical lobbyists, for example, are former members of Congress. Those forty former congressmen earned just over $150,000 annually in the House and Senate. As lobbyists they make a minimum of $300,000 a year. Compensation packages for those with personal political clout to go along with their access reach into the millions of dollars a year. Whatever the business interest or the special interest, there is at least one lobbyist making a lot of money to influence the outcome of legislation in Congress.

Since 1998, 273 White House staffers have registered as lobbyists. There are an estimated 2,390 former public officials working as lobbyists. And how about Capitol Hill? Some 240 congressmen became lobbyists after their faithful service to their constituents, whom they all but ignored while in office. Political appointees, agency heads, and well-placed government bureaucrats also find new careers as lobbyists. At present, half a dozen former officials of the Federal Energy Regulatory Commission are working at oil companies, or lobbying for them.

Former congressman James Greenwood of Pennsylvania currently works as the top lobbyist for the biotech industry, and heads a Washington-based trade group that represents more than one thousand companies around the world. As chairman of the House Energy and Commerce Subcommittee on Oversight and Investigations, Greenwood launched a number of investigations into consulting arrangements that many of these companies have with scientists and officials at government agencies such as the National Institutes of Health and the Food and Drug Administration. Now he's representing those same companies, and serves as president of the Biotechnology Industry Organization, whose arrangements he once investigated. (By the way, the biotech industry still has those same arrangements.)

Haley Barbour, a former chairman of the Republican National Committee, ran a top-ten lobbying firm before being elected governor of Mississippi in 2003. The years he spent from 1993 to 1996 as the head of the RNC certainly gave him access to anyone whose campaign he may have assisted during those years—and that's just about every Republican on the Hill and in the White House. It was a very lucrative arrangement for Barbour. In 2000 alone, his firm was paid nearly $11 million in fees, more than any other lobbying firm in the country.

Marc F. Racicot, a former governor of Montana, went to work on the Bush campaign in 2000, and then became chair of the Republican National Committee. He is now the top lobbyist for the American Insurance Association, making more than $1 million a year looking out for the interests of the insurance industry.

Former Democratic senator Dennis DeConcini represented Arizona from 1976 to 1994. He was involved in the savings-and-loan scandal of the late eighties and early nineties as part of the infamous Keating Five. After being cited for questionable conduct during the investigation of failed S&Ls, DeConcini served out his term and retired from public office. Interestingly, when Mr. DeConcini was elected to office by the people of Arizona, his net worth was roughly $1 million. By the time he left eighteen years later, his net worth was approximately $13 million. Today he is a partner in Parry, Romani, DeConcini & Symms, a lobbying firm, which according to its Web site "is one of the most successful and effective in the crowded field of Washington legislative advocacy."

Robert L. Livingston was a twenty-two-year member of the House of Representatives (R-Louisiana) and a former chairman of the House Appropriations Committee. In line to replace Newt Gingrich as speaker of the House, Livingston resigned in 1999 under the cloud of a sex scandal. He started his own company, the Livingston Group, which is now a top ten lobbying firm.

The revolving door between public service and lobbying seems to never stop spinning for some people. Philip Cooney was a lawyer and "Climate Team Leader" at the American Petroleum Institute, an oil industry lobbying group. He headed to the White House with the election of President Bush in 2000, and served as chief of staff at the White House Council on Environmental Quality from 2001 to 2005. Then he was accused of editing government climate reports to minimize links between emissions and global warming. And what did he do in response? He stepped right back into the revolving door, and immediately landed a job at ExxonMobil in June 2005. ExxonMobil financed highly criticized and suspect scientific work aimed at disproving any link between emissions and global warming.

In 2002, Susan B. Hirschmann, chief of staff for Tom DeLay, joined Williams & Jensen, a lobbying firm that represents a hefty number of Fortune 500 companies. When she announced she was leaving DeLay's office, the media reported a veritable feeding frenzy of lobbying firms trying to attract Ms. Hirschmann. She had so many job offers from K Street, where many have their offices, that she had to hire Bill Clinton's high-powered lawyer, Bob Barnett, to help her sort through them all.

Representative W. J. "Billy" Tauzin (R-Louisiana) served as chairman of the House committee that regulates the pharmaceutical industry, and cosponsored the 2004 overhaul of the Medicare prescription drug bill. In 2005, he took a job as CEO of the Pharmaceutical Research and Manufacturers of America, the drug industry's premier lobbying organization. This group led the fight to overhaul Medicare, so it was only fitting that they reward Tauzin with a job paying an estimated salary of $2 million a year. After all, Tauzin's bill saved the industry untold millions in costs. "It's a sad commentary on politics in Washington that a member of Congress who pushed through a major piece of legislation benefiting the drug industry gets the job leading that industry," said Public Citizen president Joan Claybrook.

Another master of the revolving door, Thomas Scully, was administrator of the Centers for Medicare & Medicaid Services (CMS) from 2001 to 2004. When he left, he joined lobbyists Alston & Bird, which had lobbied for the Medicare bill on behalf of Johnson & Johnson and the National Association for Home Care and Hospice. In a way, though, he was going back to his roots. Prior to his stint heading Medicare for the American public, he was CEO of the Federation of American Hospitals, and had been a health care lobbyist at Patton Boggs.

Former congressman Bob Walker, a Republican from Pennsylvania, and Anne Wexler, a former assistant to Jimmy Carter, joined forces to form the lobbying firm of Wexler & Walker. The firm's clients include dozens of multinational corporations. Walker argues that there is nothing wrong with the revolving door. As he said on my show, "I happen to think it's a positive thing to have members of Congress who have worked for the American people in their role as Congress to come out into the representational community and carry those same standards and those same values into the work that they do in the private sector, because I think that does assure that the public interest is protected."

Let's try that again. Walker says the public interest is protected when former congressmen and public officials carry those same standards of conduct into the lobbying industry. I don't know about you, but I'm hard-pressed to tell which has the higher set of principles, lobbyists or congressmen. So are the American people. The only public officials with a lower approval rating than the White House is the U.S. Congress.

Danielle Brian, of the Project on Government Oversight, told our show, "I really am amazed that people seem to be not at all embarrassed. And frankly, for the most part, the media sort of yawns when you point out one of these revolving-door stories, because it happens nearly every day."

There are a few restrictions that attempt to apply some safeguards to this system, but they barely slow the revolving door. Former members of Congress and senators hired by special interest groups are required to sit out for a year after they leave office—a cooling-off period—and cannot do any direct lobbying during that time. But they can still direct staff members and instruct them on whom to lobby. Not only that, but congressmen, as former members of the House, have floor privileges for life. This means they can—as lobbyists—walk onto the House floor during a vote. The average citizen is not allowed to do so. Proposed legislation, drafted only in the wake of the Abramoff scandal, may put an end this perk.

Lobbyists not only outnumber congressmen and their staffs, but spend more money than the federal government does on congressional and committee staffs. In addition to the various institutes and think tanks that are business-supported—the American Enterprise Institute, Heritage, Cato, Brookings—lobbyists generate more research and more sources for the political and legislative decisions that are made by the legislature than does Congress, which means that big business and special interests control much of the knowledge base upon which Congress usually legislates. This knowledge base, which is carefully created and crafted to serve the views and interests of their clients, is often, if not nearly always, a fundamental source for our national media and its reporting. Larry Noble of the Center for Responsive Politics, speaking on the show, said, "I think the problem with lobbying, with this much money behind lobbying, is that it may distort the field. It may give the impression that the public is in support of something that the public may not be in support of. And it really tends to drown out other voices."

Lobbyists are equipped with—or armed with—huge amounts of money, research, and favorable analysis to bolster their positions and support their views on any given piece of legislation. The Center for Public Integrity currently ranks the Chamber of Commerce as the largest and richest lobbyist in the country. Looking out for the general interests of corporate America, the chamber spent almost $205 million on lobbying our elected officials from 1998 to 2004. The next largest spender was Altria, the cigarette maker formerly known as Philip Morris, which spent $101.2 million during that same time. It was followed by General Electric, which spent $94.1 million, and the American Medical Association, which came in fourth with spending of $92.56 million.

The pharmaceutical industry has the largest number of lobbyists, employing a veritable army of 1,274, making drug companies the biggest contingent of lobbyists. In the 2004 elections, the drug industry gave some $17 million to federal candidates, including $1 million to President Bush and $500,000 to Senator John Kerry. There were eighteen members of Congress who each received more than $100,000.

The Business Roundtable, a coalition representing most of the Fortune 200 corporations, has spent $80 million lobbying for free trade since 1998. The organization gave $58 million in campaign contributions in 2000 during the fight to normalize trade relations with China. The ten politicians who received the most money from the roundtable each voted for the motion in favor of China. Not surprisingly, nine of the top ten politicians who received money from labor unions—which were against normalizing trade—voted against the motion. The exception? Representative Martin Frost (D-Texas), who was in the top ten in both categories, getting money from the roundtable and labor. Obviously, he could only vote once, so he cast his vote against labor. The move to normalize trade relations passed, 237 to 197. Today we have a trade deficit of over $100 billion with China.

With the U.S. trade deficit at an all-time high, jobs being moved to cheap foreign labor markets, and production that was once part of the American manufacturing base being shipped overseas, it shouldn't come as a surprise that lobbyists for other countries and foreign businesses ranked third out of all special interest groups influencing our senators and congressmen. Working on behalf of those foreign interests, Washington lobbyists have spent $624 million since 1998 to shape American public policy. The United Kingdom alone spent more money lobbying the U.S. government than did thirty-five of the individual U.S. states. Trade and defense topped the list of issues discussed on behalf of the UK. The payoff for all these efforts? Well, $5.5 billion in defense contracts awarded to foreign companies all over the world were "no bid," meaning American companies were not even in the running. In fact, UK-based Rolls-Royce had to compete for only 14 percent of the contracts it received from the U.S. Department of Defense.

The China National Offshore Oil Corporation (CNOOC), the Chinese oil giant controlled by the communist-run government, recently tried to take over the American oil company Unocal. When our legislators began to question the wisdom of selling an American energy asset to a communist government, the Chinese were indignant. Not only did they warn lawmakers not to interfere with the deal, they hired lobbyists to argue their case on Capitol Hill. As we reported on the show, top-tier lobbying firm Akin Gump contacted federal officials—all the way up to the Oval Office—250 times in nine days, all on behalf of a communist government that was utterly shocked by the sudden resistance on the part of our lawmakers to turning over a key energy asset to a foreign government. China also hired Patton Boggs, perhaps K Street's best known lobbying firm.

China has spent almost $20 million since 1997 lobbying our lawmakers directly. Of course, this figure doesn't take into account the vastly larger sums of money spent by American companies who lobby on behalf of China. According to Michael Wessel of the U.S.-China Commission, American companies who lobby for China are in effect making an investment in low wages, unfair labor conditions, and a lack of democracy. And as he told us on the show, "They're able to get others to spend money on their own behalf, which is about as good as it gets in the political system." The communist Chinese investment in political influence on Capitol Hill has proven to be a very good expenditure. As Wessel says, "They were able to get by without any real action on currency. They continue to flood our market with their products. Our trade deficit is up once again, and jobs keep flowing over to China."

But the costs incurred in this arrangement include more than deficits. Representative Rahm Emanuel (D-Illinois) said on our broadcast that foreign lobbying is "costing America in its technology, it's costing America in its jobs, and most importantly, it's costing America in its public policy. Is this the best way we should operate?" Emmanuel's question was obviously rhetorical. And the answer is clear to the millions and millions of hardworking men and women in this country who haven't witnessed Congress represent their interest in years.

Big Oil is another industry that has seen fit to keep lobbyists well paid. In the past seven years, oil companies and their representational organization have donated almost $70 million to various political campaigns. For every campaign dollar it spends, the oil industry spends six dollars or more on lobbying. From 1998 to 2003, it spent more than $381 million lobbying the government, approximately $80 million a year. When the Senate Energy and Commerce committees decided to hold joint hearings on rising energy prices in the fall of 2005, they called upon the executives of Big Oil to testify. At the outset of the hearings, though, the senators did not find it necessary to insist, as is customary, that the Big Oil executives appearing before them raise their right hands and testify under oath. There could hardly be a more symbolic testament to the power of Big Oil on Capitol Hill.

And what about the energy bill passed by Congress last year and signed by the president? Nothing symbolic about the effect of that legislation: The benefits to Big Oil can be measured in the billions of dollars. Congress gave Big Oil a combined $12 billion in taxpayer subsidies at a time when the major oil companies are making record profits. Two billion dollars of that subsidy, over the next decade, is earmarked for deep-water drilling in the Gulf of Mexico. And President Bush and the Congress also granted an additional $7 billion worth of "royalty relief" between 2006 and 2011 to the same oil companies that are expected to take some $65 billion worth of oil and natural gas from federal lands. Royalty relief reduced the royalties that oil companies had to pay the U.S. government for the rights to drill in the Gulf of Mexico, providing them with an incentive to develop U.S. production. This came from rules passed in 1996, a time when oil prices were low—and the rules haven't been updated since, even as oil hovers near $70 per barrel, and ExxonMobil just reported the highest profits in the history of American business. As the global prices for crude oil skyrocket, and gasoline prices in this country head toward $4 a gallon, American drivers are helpless and the budgets of working families are swamped.

At a time when wages are stagnating and our middle class is being forced to compete with the lowest-cost labor in the world, what does President Bush want to do—aided and abetted by Congress? He wants to support illegal immigration. The guest-worker program proposed by President Bush was supported by pro-amnesty organizations like the National Council of La Raza and LULAC, the League of United Latin American Citizens. While these groups claim to be fighting for the rights of illegal immigrants in the name of humanitarianism, they are in fact funded by major corporations that want continued access to cheap labor. These include Levi Strauss, Home Depot, Wal-Mart, and many others. Other groups lobbying for amnesty include the Mexican American Legal Defense and Educational Fund (MALDEF), the Mexican-American Political Association, the Ford Foundation (which sponsors and funds many of these groups), and the ACLU.

Port and border security is an issue of great concern to the American people, and the administration's seeming indifference to it is especially disturbing. The Dubai Ports World deal to take over the operation of six major U.S. ports is a perfect example. We made a point of reporting on our broadcast on an agreement that most of the country didn't even know about. The *Wall Street Journal* summed it up this way:

> On Monday, Feb. 13, as Americans were fixated on media accounts of Vice President Dick Cheney's weekend hunting accident, CNN commentator Lou Dobbs weighed in on a different story. In a "special report" on his evening program, he asserted that "a country with ties to the Sept. 11 terrorists could soon be running significant operations at some of our most important and largest seaports with a full blessing of the Bush White House.

When I reported on this arrangement with Dubai Ports World—a company owned and operated by the United Arab Emirates—my audience was shocked that such a deal could possibly be allowed to happen. Far from being just another close ally, as President Bush claimed, the UAE has a history of links to terrorism. It was one of the only countries in the world to recognize the Taliban government when it took control of Afghanistan. Concerned Americans were outraged that such an arrangement could be made in secret only a few years after the September 11 attacks.

At first, the president dismissed such concerns. But lawmakers such as Maine senator Susan Collins, who had previously introduced legislation for better port security, and New York representative Peter King soon voiced their objections to the deal. It became apparent as our show looked deeper into the deal that it was about more than just doing business with a trusted ally and matters of port security. It was also about the lobbying efforts intended to make sure the deal went through. DP World wanted those ports badly, and the company was putting pressure on Washington via lobbyist and former Minnesota congressman Vin Weber, who worked hard to get Senator Bill Frist and other people on Capitol Hill to ignore the outcry. (Weber's lobbying firm is paid $65,000 a month to represent the interests of the UAE in America.)

We even felt the pressure on the show. DP World wanted the story to go away and actively tried to make us stop reporting it. The company refused to grant CNN interviews from Washington or London, and refused to allow CNN to videotape its operations in the United Arab Emirates and Hong Kong if the resulting video was going to be shown on my broadcast. Additionally, Mark Dennis, a spokesman for the public relations firm that represented DP World, declared, "CNN won't shut up Lou Dobbs."

There was more. Istithmar, another UAE-backed company, chose this period in which to purchase $2 billion worth of shares in CNN's parent company, Time Warner—giving it an ownership stake of nearly 2.5 percent. It also hired one of Carl Icahn's companies as a consultant—just as Icahn was ramping up his plan to break Time Warner up.

At one point I was invited to speak at the commencement ceremony at American University in Dubai—for a fee of $160,000. I turned them down.

We ran fifteen segments on the DP World deal, and the mail we received from viewers expressed nothing less than incredulity and anger. Eventually, lawmakers could no longer ignore the American people, who forced the president to defend the deal almost every day. With enough citizens raising a ruckus about the issue, the president had to back down. The deal was squashed, but the brazenness of it remains: putting our country's security at risk in the name of business as usual on Capitol Hill.

It's worth noting that the CNOOC and DP World fiascoes have failed to resonate with this administration. In May 2006, after both deals had been scuttled, U.S. Deputy Treasury Secretary Robert Kimmitt claimed that new proposals in Congress to require automatic investigations of certain foreign acquisitions of U.S. companies could overwhelm the governmental review process. Kimmitt stated that, in particular, a Senate proposal requiring investigation of companies deemed part of our national critical infrastructure would have added fifteen cases to his workload. So instead of asking for more resources to ensure that the proper review process is in place, Kimmitt would prefer that the proposed legislation be killed and these acquisitions should just be approved without oversight. This is how the current administration chooses to deal with matters affecting critical infrastructure and security.

It appears that our elected officials are ready and willing to give foreign interests all the assistance they need to do business in this country, regardless of the consequences. In fact, former congressman Weber's role in the DP World story brings up a disconcerting fact: Those who've spent time on Capitol Hill are very heavily recruited to represent foreign interests. Trade officials, as you might imagine, are especially attractive. There are no exact numbers for this type of lobbying today, but a Center for Public Integrity study conducted back in 1990 found that 47 percent of former trade officials were representing foreign governments and foreign companies. Now the reason this number hasn't been updated is that Congress has changed some of the rules for reporting, so it's difficult to track which officials end up where. Fifteen years ago almost half of all former trade officials had been hired to represent overseas companies, associations, and foreign governments. That overwhelming number was of course embarrassing to Washington, and when Washington is embarrassed, the rules change—in this case, not for the good, or for the public's right to know. The Lobbying Disclosure Act of 1995 allowed many representatives of foreign interests to register as lobbyists instead of with the attorney general, which had overseen the business of "foreign agents" and required public disclosure of financial and business information.

It's easier to track those higher-level American trade officials who go to work for other countries. A former deputy assistant U.S. trade representative, Amy Jackson, was hired by the international lobbying firm Crowell & Moring. As a top U.S. government employee, Jackson's primary duty had been to oversee U.S. trade relations with Korea. As a Crowell & Moring lobbyist, her main job now is helping the Korea International Trade Association, representing eighty-one thousand Korean businesses.

Neither Crowell & Moring nor Amy Jackson has broken any law or violated any rules on lobbying. But the awkward symmetry of her responsibilities as a public servant and her new duties as a lobbyist is quite a bit more than ironic. I'm sure most Americans would join me in thanking Amy Jackson for her service to our country, just as I'm sure most Koreans are grateful to her for her current service to their country.

In the end, is it worth it for these entities, whether businesses or foreign governments, to be spending millions of dollars on hoped-for favors? Consider one of the biggest business debacles of all time, Enron. Over the course of the decade before its collapse, Enron and its 2,832 subsidiaries paid out $5.9 million in political contributions, $1.1 million of which was PAC-driven. The vast majority of that total was spent after 1996. Was it a good investment for Enron? Certainly. Those dollars—which are insignificant given its size at its collapse—kept the company in business. It enabled Enron to make a lot of money, and bought them a lot of friends in places where it needed them.

That investment chilled regulatory fervor as well, as Enron led the charge for energy deregulation in the 1990s. Thus, when the time came for hearings, representatives appeared before a very friendly—one might say "predisposed"—congressional committee, and a friendly White House. People forget that this didn't happen after George W. Bush got into office. It was happening in 1996, when Bill Clinton was running for a second term.

The result of a great deal of lobbying is the passing of legislation—and the granting of favors—that are a direct affront to the people of this nation. For example, identity theft and credit card fraud are the most recent scourges of our increasingly digital world, crimes that directly affect individuals. Large financial institutions, including Visa and Citibank, have already had the names of millions and millions of customers stolen from their computers and facilities. To make these companies work harder to protect your data, thirty-two states are considering security-breach notification laws. Similarly, legislation proposed in Washington would fine a company one thousand dollars for every piece of data that it loses. But lobbyists are already working against the passage of these laws, arguing that they would be too burdensome for the banks and credit card concerns. Wouldn't we all be better off if they were putting as much effort into securing our information as they are into securing lobbyists? Of course, if you don't trust them to keep your personal information safe, you can buy identity theft insurance. Incidentally, some of the very financial institutions that have lost customer information are now also offering identity theft insurance, including Citibank and Bank of America.

Under pressure from lobbyists, Congress turned its back on its core constituency by passing the revised bankruptcy law. Our representatives demonstrated yet again that they align themselves not with the voters, but with special interest groups and lobbyists. In this case, the law—which restricts the ability of middle-class, working Americans to seek financial protection via bankruptcy filings—was virtually handcrafted by lobbyists who are working for the sole benefit of the credit card companies.

Credit companies have been extremely successful in our country, and over the past decade they've seen healthy increases in profits. However, bankruptcy filings by individuals have always stuck in their craw. That's understandable, because they are unable to collect unpaid debts from those who have sought bankruptcy protection. What's inexcusable is that, in order to recover a bigger chunk of that debt, the credit card companies turned to Congress for assistance, portraying bankrupt individuals as lazy scofflaws who routinely thumbed their noses at their creditors.

Plenty of people do find themselves in bankruptcy through irresponsible behavior, and if it was this population that constituted the vast majority of bankruptcies, I wouldn't object to tougher laws. But the reality of the situation is far different. For starters, personal bankruptcy filings actually fell in 2004, so the situation was hardly as dire as portrayed by the lobbyists. And, as a recent Harvard University study showed, nearly 50 percent of bankruptcy filings in the United States are the result of illness and the enormous bills associated with treatment. (This despite the fact that the majority of filers had insurance coverage—which apparently wasn't quite good enough. Of course, even minimal health insurance coverage is getting harder and harder to come by.)

So bankruptcies tend to be filed by hardworking people who have fallen on tough times. The new bill doesn't take that factor into account; it just makes sure that the interests of big companies who have well-placed and highly paid lobbyists are satisfied. In the process, the last safety net protecting the middle class from financial disaster has been yanked away.

How does Congress justify this new law? By claiming that it forces people to be more fiscally responsible and to pay off their debts. That claim would hold a lot more weight if it hadn't come from a body that has managed to run up $412 billion worth of deficit, the biggest in this country's history.

There are hundreds of thousands, if not millions, of personal stories that are emblematic of how our government has not only turned its back on working people in this country, but how it has acted to make their lives more difficult. In particular, this e-mail I received from John Washington of Southfield, Michigan, gives voice to the frustration and confusion that Americans feel when they find themselves victimized by the behavior of our elected officials.

Lou:

Another comment from the "forgotten" minority . . . an African American who votes, worked for 38 years at one job, is still married to the same woman, and tried to follow all the rules. My wife never worked, I am retired now and in bankruptcy, and the IRS is chasing me. Why is it that my country is overrun with people who are illegally in this country, don't pay taxes, and get all the benefits people like me are being refused? Why is it that a "proud" employer from Georgia says he wants "more illegal aliens" on national TV, and he's not in jail? And the IRS is chasing ME?

There's much more proof of Congress's lack of interest in our financial well-being, as if you or I actually needed it. The House of Representatives voted to permanently repeal the estate tax for the wealthy, eliminating what is called the "death tax" on estates worth more than $1 million. Guess what? That affects barely 2 percent of the American population. Proponents of the bill claim that the estate tax doesn't bring in much to the federal coffers, perhaps a mere $40 billion. My thinking, however, is that if you add $40 billion here and $40 billion there, it all adds up pretty quickly. By eliminating the tax, the House is essentially forgoing revenue equal to a tenth of the deficit. That's a lot of money, especially when you start asking where the funds to make up for that shortfall will come from. And the obvious answer is from increased taxation on the middle class. Either that, or Congress will continue to pretend that the deficit doesn't exist. Both are bad choices. Interestingly, funding for the lobbying effort to overturn the estate tax came in part from rich families running the corporations that produce Mars candies and Gallo wines. Now that they're not paying their fair share, you will be paying more than yours. You can thank their lobbyists, and their deep pockets, for that.

Big business has been masterful in cloaking its lobbying efforts in disarming and even deceitful language and nomenclature. The National Wetlands Coalition was formed in 1989 when President George H. W. Bush declared that there would be no net loss of wetlands in the United States as a result of development. The coalition created a duck and water logo, and anyone unaware of its membership could have been forgiven for believing it was an environmental group committed to the public policy of preserving our national treasures. They would, of course, be wrong. The National Wetlands Coalition's sponsors included ExxonMobil, Shell, the National Association of Home Builders, and the International Council of Shopping Centers. Its purpose was to lobby Congress for increased use of wetlands, to drill in wetlands, and to build housing developments and shopping centers on wetlands.

Another organization whose name evokes a "green response" and bills itself as an "environmental resource" is the National Council for Air and Stream Improvement. In fact, it is funded by forest product companies. Similarly, the Foundation for Clean Air Progress was formed in 1995 and is funded by industry groups like the American Trucking Association, the American Petroleum Institute, and the Chemical Manufacturers Association.

The Americans for Balanced Energy Choices (ABEC) is "a nonprofit, non-partisan citizen group that advocates for energy policies that balance meeting America's growing demand for electricity with the need to protect the environment." It is funded in part by coal producers, railroads, and coal-using electric utilities such as Burlington Northern Santa Fe Railway and the Southern Company, all of which are committed to the increased use of coal for this country's electrical power.

There is a group called the Alliance for Worker Retirement Security that thinks it's a very good idea to privatize Social Security, that is, to put those funds under the control of Wall Street. The group is backed by companies like Charles Schwab and Wachovia. Why? Because Wall Street firms stand to gain close to $1 trillion in fees if the government privatizes Social Security. Of course they're pushing for privatization—it's worth spending thousands of dollars when many times more that is waiting to be picked up.

But my personal favorite is the American Council on Science and Health, whose research and conclusions are often used not only by Congress as part of their ready-made knowledge base, but also by the national media. The American Council on Science and Health is, as its Web site states, "a consumer education consortium concerned with issues related to food, nutrition, chemicals, pharmaceuticals, lifestyle, the environment and health. ACSH is an independent, non-profit, tax-exempt organization." That's about as pure as it gets. What it doesn't declare is that it is trying to influence politicians and the American public about issues that are favorable to its supporters. These include Anheuser-Busch. And Coors. And the Wine Growers of California. And Seagrams. And Amoco, the American Meat Institute, Burger King, Coca-Cola, Dow Chemical, Frito-Lay, Kraft General Foods, Merck, and the Sugar Association, to name a few.

If you were to read in a newspaper that Anheuser Busch had data suggesting alcohol consumption was actually very good for your health, you'd be skeptical . . . considering the source. But if you were to read that a study by the American Council on Science and Health reported that alcohol was good for your health, you might be more inclined to believe it, especially if it was widely reported in the media, as the data from such organizations often are. And here's exactly what the American Council on Science and Health reported:

> Among middle-aged and elderly people, moderate drinkers have lower mortality rates than do abstainers. . . . The potential health benefits of moderate drinking in middle-aged and elderly people can be achieved at consumption levels as low as one half of one standard drink per day. . . . It is possible that moderate drinking by young people might reduce their risk of heart disease in later life.

These are only some of the groups and organizations whose sole purpose is to influence Congress and the public. Over the past decade, I can think of only one example of big business losing a single battle in Congress, and that was the passage of the Sarbanes-Oxley Act in 2002, at the height of the worst corporate corruption scandals in U.S. history. That legislation requires corporate officers to certify that their financial statements and public reportings are accurate, and is intended to create a greater transparency for public investors. Not surprisingly, corporate America has unleashed a powerful lobbying effort that is now under way on Capitol Hill to overturn or weaken the law.

— Chapter 4 —

The Politics of Deceit

I can't take seriously anyone who takes either the Republican Party or Democratic Party seriously—in part because neither party takes you and me seriously; in part, because both are bought and paid for by corporate America and special interests. And neither party gives a damn about the middle class.

The Republican Party doesn't embrace the conservative ideology it's alleged to, and the Democratic Party doesn't embrace its supposed liberal ideology. In both Democratic and Republican administrations, Congress has passed and sustained billions of dollars in royalty payments and subsidies to big oil companies, passed a consumer-crippling bankruptcy law, embraced the death of the estate tax, approved every free trade deal brought to a vote, and supported illegal immigration, and, despite global terrorist threats, open borders. Quite a record.

Both parties typically put forward candidates for Congress or president who personify the least objectionable, lowest common denominators of candidates who are mere shadows and echoes of the historical principles that originally guided each party. Although we remain a nation divided along partisan lines, we are primarily a nation confounded by uninspiring candidates whose chief attributes are generally breathtaking mediocrity. Let's be honest. In 2004 a country of three hundred million people was forced to choose between two white guys from families of privilege and wealth, both of whom attended Yale, and were members of the Skull & Bones Society. The Yale thing shouldn't be an automatic disqualification to be president, but it is worthwhile to note that throughout almost all of the last two troubled decades, a Yalie has been in the Oval Office: President Bush, President Clinton, and President Bush. Please, let's let up on the Yale thing—I, for one, don't think it's working. How about somebody from a Midwestern state school who has actually worked for a living in his or her life, and whose intellect, character, and leadership would lift the nation with a clear vision of our future and a commitment to the common good and our national interest? Just a thought.

Republicans and Democrats have brought us, with the sometimes conscious complicity of the national media, to the point where there is rarely a national debate on great issues. In 2004, John Kerry and George Bush met in face-to-face debates three times, yet neither candidate ever mentioned the total indebtedness of the United States; discussed the economic, social, or environmental impact of illegal immigration; or acknowledged the stunning dropout rates of high school students all across the country. But nearly every voter was informed of John Kerry's Swift Boat service in Vietnam and George Bush's undocumented National Guard service in Alabama. The campaign organizations of both Kerry and Bush got away with it.

In 2004, more Americans went to the polls than in any election since 1968. Nearly seventeen million more voted for president in 2004 than in 2000, perhaps spurred on by the determination that the Supreme Court wouldn't decide in a second consecutive election who would be our president. It was the largest increase in voter turnout from one election to the next since 1952. And despite that improvement, just about four in every ten eligible voters still chose noninvolvement over participation.

The optimists among us would say that our low voter turnout means that so many people think we're already so well represented that their vote is unnecessary. A skeptic, and I am certainly one, believes that low voter turnout partly reflects disgust and disdain for the candidates offered and the lack of real choice between our two major parties.

President Bush exulted in his 2004 victory, and quickly declared that he had earned "political capital" that he would spend on reforming Social Security and education, and on improving our intelligence capabilities. His second-term agenda has turned out to be a political disaster. President Bush's approval ratings plummeted from a high of 57 percent right after the 2004 election to lows as of this writing matched only by three other presidents: Carter, Nixon, and George H. W. Bush. Political analysts and strategists attributed the president's plunge in the polls to an anxious public that grows more impatient each day with the conduct of the war in Iraq. As I write this in 2006, more than twenty-five hundred of our troops have been killed since the war began, and more than seventeen thousand wounded. And the rate of American casualties in Iraq has been increasing, not slowing. Four hundred billion dollars has been spent in Iraq, with only the barest of tangible results for the Iraqi people.

But I believe that our unpopular president's decline in the polls more accurately reflects a rejection of his style of governing, and of nearly every aspect and element of his administration. The Bush administration has not even been able to successfully claim credit for an economy that is now growing robustly and that has the lowest historical unemployment rates in five years. That's the case because the American public intuitively understands that an economy stimulated by record federal budget deficits and a housing boom, if not a bubble, should be growing strongly. But the president apparently does not share public anxiety over skyrocketing energy and health care costs, higher interest rates, lower real wages, and job insecurity. After all, President Bush is a victim of his own identity and transparent cronyism. He's a former oil man at a time of record oil profits and obscene pay packages for oil executives. He's the "CEO president" at a time when CEOs are offshoring production, outsourcing jobs, and blaming workers for their own failures of leadership, and at a time when some of them are on trial or in prison for outright corruption. And no president in my memory has been a less gifted communicator.

That the Bush administration is out of touch is no secret to the working men and women of this country. Robert Fiorella, a viewer from Maryland, sent me the following e-mail, which captures the sentiment I've heard from thousands of viewers:

> *Lou:*
> *I keep hearing pundits trying to explain why the economy is good, yet Bush's poll numbers on the economy are low. People like me (middle income) see an economy that is not in a situation of massive unemployment or skyrocketing inflation; that's good. Yet personally I have not benefited at all from six years of Republican control. My wages have gone down, I lost my pension, my utility bills have followed gas prices into the stratosphere, my property taxes have risen to make up for federal and state shortfalls. I still have a job . . . but get less out of it. I can still pay my bills . . . but barely. I can still drive my car . . . but it hurts more. In short, we see top executives make obscene incomes while asking workers to tighten expenses and "do more with less" by working longer hours, having less co-workers and bearing more of the costs associated with the job. Bush has kept the economic indices looking good but people like me feel that we are the backs upon which these numbers are built, and see little of the rewards that the wealthy are enjoying. Yes I give the national economy*

high marks, but President Bush and the Republicans have certainly NOT *improved my personal situation.*

President Bush has failed to articulate a vision of America's future even after winning two elections. His administration has no visible substantive strategy to contend with geopolitical and economic threats that are rising around the globe. Leftist movements are gaining in Mexico and throughout Latin America. Communist China is asserting its influence in the Western Hemisphere, building relationships with Venezuela's Hugo Chavez, Bolivia's Evo Morales, and of course, Cuba's Fidel Castro. The U.S. government has had only one tepid response; that is, to continue its campaign for hemispheric free trade. The Bush administration has been altogether unsuccessful in advancing the United States's relationship with Russia, and has no European alliance to call upon to deal with the threat of Iran and Syria. Iran continues to pursue its nuclear weapons program, and both Iran and Syria continue their support of the Iraqi insurgency.

The Republicans have controlled the presidency and Congress for almost six years and, in my opinion, have squandered their power and opportunity at nearly every turn—and have failed miserably in their responsibilities to the nation. And what of the loyal opposition? The Democratic Party, as President Bush has correctly asserted, has been bereft of ideas. In two successive presidential elections, Vice President Al Gore and Senator John Kerry pursued what they and their advisers believed were safe courses of drawing dull distinctions between themselves and President Bush. And like Bush, neither Gore nor Kerry possessed the courage to convey a vision of our future that would compel or excite American voters.

In Congress, Democrats have conducted themselves as if a Senate or House seat were a mere sinecure until the next election. Obviously, the Republican leadership in both the Senate and the House controls its respective agendas. But Democrats have been all too willing to go along with Republicans in abandoning their oversight responsibilities, and to serve as the junior partner in pork-barrel politics.

Senate minority leader Harry Reid and House minority leader Nancy Pelosi and their fellow Democrats have leaped on the failures and distortions of intelligence that led us into the Iraq war. But only within the last year have they begun to seriously, but inconsistently, criticize the conduct of the war. When Congressman John Murtha (D-Pennsylvania), a decorated Marine Corps veteran, stood up on the floor of the House of Representatives to call for an orderly withdrawal of our troops from Iraq, the Senate and House Democratic leadership was silent. So were his fellow Democrats in the rank and file. And there is still no concrete Democratic proposal for either victory or withdrawal from Iraq, still no demand for an accounting of the Pentagon's general staff, for what has now been a three-year failure to defeat the insurgency.

Democrats seized upon the Bush administration's failure to respond to the Hurricane Katrina disaster, but during the special committee hearing on September 27, 2005, they chose to not even show up. The Bankruptcy Abuse Prevention and Consumer Protection Act of 2005, which is arguably one of the pieces of legislation most injurious to middle-class families in the past ten years, was supported by seventy-three Democrats in the House and eighteen in the Senate.

In the wake of Tom DeLay's K Street Project—created to force lobbying firms to hire Republicans—and the widening Abramoff lobbying scandal, Democrats are trying to brand the Republican dominance of Washington as a "culture of corruption." But it was little more than fifteen years ago that the Democrats created their own culture of corruption under the direction of Tony Coelho, a man who helped usher in the culture of money-based politics. The California congressman and majority whip was an exceptional fund-raiser and chairman of the Democratic Congressional Campaign Committee, yet he was forced to resign from office in 1989 during a scandal involving improper contributions and the misuse of funds.

The American people think even less of Congress than they do of the president: A recent Gallup poll gives Congress an approval rating of only 23 percent. Unlike President Bush, whose precipitous decline in popularity is relatively recent, Congress has been out of favor with the American people for years. Congressional approval ratings were 35 percent in March 1997, and have only rarely reached a rating of more than 50 percent in the years since.

But those public opinion polls don't mean much at election time. In 2004, 401 members of the House of Representatives went to the voters seeking reelection. All but five got voted back in—we returned 396 of these people to their jobs. Over in the Senate, 25 of 26 senators got their jobs back during the same election. In all, voters reelected an incredible 99 percent of incumbents to their offices in 2004. No matter how much citizens say they want to "throw the bums out," they apparently want to hang on to their own particular bum. According to Richard Niemi, professor of political science at the University of Rochester, incumbents remain in office more often than not because they have the advantage of established avenues for fund-raising, access to journalists, the ability to bring home pork, and the public's conviction that a representative with seniority is better able to bring home that pork. He also states that gerrymandering, the redistricting that parties in power regularly engage in, is a "significant factor, and is of some importance" in the high election rate of incumbents.

Not only are our representatives entrenched, they are well compensated. While the average income for a family of four is just over $60,000, our congressmen and senators are paid $168,500 per year. The speaker of the House gets $212,100, and the majority and minority leaders in both chambers make $183,500. Of course, because our representatives set their own compensation levels, they see to it that they receive a substantially better deal than those available in the private sector.

But that's only the base of a pyramid of perks, thanks to the largess of the American taxpayer. In addition to their salaries, our servants on Capitol Hill have pension plans that would make even some CEOs envious. Congressmen are eligible for a pension at age sixty-two, as long as they have completed at least five years of service. Fifty-year-olds receive a pension if they have completed twenty years of service, and those of any age completing twenty-five years of service receive pensions. Pension amounts are determined by the number of years in office and an average taken from the highest three years of salary.

Representatives get annual staff allowances for hiring up to eighteen permanent and four nonpermanent aides. These staffers can be divided up between the members' Washington and home offices. In addition, up to seventy-five thousand dollars of funds for the staff can be transferred to the representative's expense account for use in other categories, such as for computers and office services.

Senators get a bit more largess, and the size of their personal staff allowances varies according to the size of their states. They can hire as many aides as they want to within that allowance. Depending on how they parse out the salaries, the number of aides can run anywhere from twenty-six to sixty. In addition to their personal staffs, senators and representatives receive additional staff support from the committees on which they serve.

Congressmen get an additional allowance for domestic travel, stationery, newsletters, overseas postage, telephone and telegraph service (how recently do you think the latter has been used?), and other incidental expenses incurred in Washington or at home. Of course, you don't hear about all that. Usually the only perk discussed is the franking privilege, which lets Congress mail letters to its constituents for free, and that hardly raises any eyebrows.

Elected officials give themselves the best deals, and that applies from the day they take office to long after they've taken their leave. In addition to the pension plan described above, retired lawmakers receive a generous 401(k)-type savings plan, plus Social Security, giving them three sources of retirement income. Meanwhile, most corporations have done away with pension plans, leaving 87 percent of all American private sector workers with only Social Security and any 401(k) savings.

All of these approved perks are underwritten by your taxes. They don't include benefits that come from someplace other than taxpayer dollars. There are rules for just how much lobbyists and other special interest groups can give our congressmen and senators, as set forth in the 1989 Ethics Reform Act. Here are a few examples of the burdensome constraints under which they operate:

- Special interest–paid foreign travel is limited to seven consecutive days, not counting the days spent traveling. This applies to both chambers.
- Special interest–paid domestic travel is limited to four consecutive days for the House, including the days spent traveling, and three consecutive days for the Senate (not counting travel time).
- For each trip, one relative may accept special interest–paid travel expenses. The ethics committee can grant an extension in certain circumstances.

After reading this, you may be thinking of a career in public service. And why not? Congress has been in session only an average of 153 days over each of the past six years. (And did I mention how well those lobbyists would take care of you? Of course, that's not a guaranteed perk, because the American people someday soon may actually demand reform. All right, fairly soon.)

But before you decide on that career, you should decide how you fit into our current House and Senate. If you happen to be a teacher, a small business owner, a carpenter or a plumber, electrician, factory worker, technician, white-collar worker, or manager, Congress may not be the place for you. Our representative bodies in the legislative branch aren't particularly representative of our society.

More than half of the members of the U.S. Senate in the 109th Congress (58), and more than a third of those in the House of Representatives (163), are lawyers. How typical of the population as a whole is the makeup of Congress? While one out of every three hundred people has a law degree, on Capitol Hill one in three does. It's somewhat ironic that one of the country's least respected vocations has the largest representation in one of our least respected institutions—namely, the U.S. Congress.

There are a handful of other professions represented by a single individual, but all of these are dwarfed by the presence of the legal profession. At least one florist, one librarian, one steelworker, one carpenter, one taxicab driver, a paper-mill worker, and a hotel bellhop did make it to Congress. So did one commercial airline pilot, one television reporter (no comment), an astronaut, and a geologist. Four ministers, two physicists, two chemists, two veterinarians, three dentists, three nurses, and nine medical doctors are also serving in Congress. Again, as a group it is not exactly representative of American society.

How about racial, ethnic, and religious diversity in Congress? The House of Representatives is more representative, with forty-two blacks, twenty-four Hispanics, four Asians, one Asian Indian, and one Native American. Over in the Senate—not so diverse: one black, two Hispanics, and two Asian Americans. As for religion, if you want to serve in Congress, it's good to be Roman Catholic, the largest single religious denomination in both the House and the Senate.

It's very likely that Congress looks and acts nothing like the community in which you live, which reinforces the real problem: Our elected officials most likely wouldn't recognize you or your community, its concerns, problems, and values, and its needs and desires.

— *Chapter 5* —

He Says, She Says

Our working men and women of the middle class and their families are also victimized by a national media that too often runs in packs, adopts prevailing wisdom, and genuflects to the prevailing orthodoxies of political and economic thought. And they do so while hiding behind assertions of objectivity and neutrality. But I'm not neutral or objective about the well-being of this country and our people. If you watch my nightly broadcast, you know where I stand on nearly every major issue facing this country. I believe that middle-class working men and women are the foundation of America. I sincerely believe that public education is the great equalizer in our society, or should be. I strongly oppose illegal immigration. I hate political correctness and all those who would try to control thought by controlling language. I believe we're waging a war against radical Islamists, not a nameless war on terror. I believe that corporate America and special interests have absolute dominance in our political system. In my opinion, free trade is faith-based economics: By removing barriers to trade, the economies of the world would ultimately specialize in producing a particular range of products and services, and thus come to enjoy a so-called competitive advantage. I believe that free trade as defined and promoted by the Clinton and Bush administrations, and by both Republicans and Democrats, is destroying America's manufacturing base and middle-class jobs, and is bankrupting the nation. I believe the Bush administration's conduct during the war in Iraq has been disastrous, and that the general staff in the Pentagon has failed our brave young men and women fighting the insurgency. I believe that there is absolutely no excuse for the Bush administration's failure to secure our borders and ports. And I'm critical of Congress for its failure to provide oversight and leadership as a co-equal branch of government.

Some politicians in both parties, more than a few columnists, and many special interest groups have attacked me personally for expressing those positions on the air each night. They've called me all sorts of names; not quite everything from A to Z, but their dictionaries are well worn from finding phrases like "blithering idiot" to "xenophobe." As my former boss and good friend Ted Turner has said to me over the years, "Every dog has its fleas."

Especially frustrating to most of my critics has been my refusal to adopt a partisan view or to drink the Kool-Aid of any popular orthodoxy. Each time I take a position on the air, you can be assured that I've come to it after long and careful research reporting on the issues, and that whether you agree with me or not, I am absolutely 100 percent sincere in my view. I don't shade anything for partisan reasons, and I don't posit anything out of fear of offending any political party, big business, big government, or constituencies of any kind.

My colleagues and I take seriously our obligation to report on the independent, nonpartisan reality that makes up all of our lives in this country. I look at what's going on with what can be called an American perspective, which is certainly not shaped by partisan politics, or ideological commitment, or religious fervor. From that perspective, the national interest is paramount, and the well-being of our fellow Americans is the first duty of all of us as citizens, no matter what we do for a living—even if we happen to be journalists.

Each night, my audience expects me to deliver the news that is most important to them and the lives they are leading. They expect analysis of the news and issues that are dominating our society. They expect debate, and they expect me to take a position. That's what I've done, and will continue to do. And ours is the only broadcast on CNN in which that happens. When *USA Today* asked CNN president Jon Klein about my journalistic approach, he said, "Lou has zero tolerance for B.S." Jon's right, and my audience knows it, my guests know it, and so do all my colleagues and those we cover with our reporting.

I believe that every journalist and every media outlet in this country has an obligation to the truth. That includes finding it and reporting it. The truth should not be tilted toward any ideology, or nuanced by spin or partisan politics. It should stand on its own merits, regardless of who's doing the reporting.

Our democracy has as one of its most important tenets the guarantee of a free press. As Thomas Jefferson wrote:

> The basis of our government being the opinion of the people, the very first object should be to keep that right; and were it left to me to decide whether we should have a government without newspapers, or newspapers without a government, I should not hesitate a moment to prefer the latter.

The founders of this nation determined that the public interest was to be served by a press that would pursue and report the truth, and would also serve as a means by which citizens could make their own voices heard.

The way that news is reported today belies this ideal. What has happened is nothing less than a shift of emphasis in journalism. The national media has turned away from the hard work and expense of fact-finding and investigation to the reporting of what is easy and convenient. And yes, cheaper. All too frequently, what is easy and convenient is what is coming out of the mouths of politicians and business executives—many of whom are leading the war on the middle class. By relying on political pronouncements, press releases, and self-serving research, along with utilizing the he says, she says method of reporting, the media has become complicit in the war on the working men and women of this country. Where once the media could be counted on to aggressively uncover the truth and present the facts, it now serves all too frequently as an unobstructed conduit of the agenda of this country's elites into the lives of the American middle class. Those in power want to convey a message, and the media delivers it.

Because of the standards to which I hold this craft, and of my belief in what journalism can and should accomplish, I find its current role in the assault on the middle class to be especially disconcerting. If there is any place where the injurious policies of this administration and the disdainful behavior of many CEOs should be on full view every single day, it is on the front pages of newspapers and in the lead stories of news broadcasts. Instead, the media chooses to highlight stories featuring runaway brides and misbehaving celebrities.

This type of reporting is hardly the hallmark of a responsible free press, which has the power to bring about substantial change at every level of society. Instead, the press in this country has become primarily just another means to attract advertisers and deliver better returns to corporate parents. The idea of investigation and analysis is giving way to feeding the bottom line. And the media, rather than doggedly attempting to get at the truth, is stepping aside and repackaging the two sides of every argument, arguments that are often little more than the party lines of two opposing agendas. The truth is never identified. The common good and the public interest is not served.

Instead of getting the truth, we've come to accept he says, she says as an actual form of journalism in this country, in part because it's become so pervasive in all forms of media. Not only do our national news outlets use opposing political viewpoints in lieu of thorough investigation and analysis, but this form of he says, she says reporting has become the foundation of an entirely separate form of so-called news and current events shows. Partisan hosts are pitted against one another and argue over issues using nothing more than their political affiliation as the basis for their diatribes. They take a stand, Republican or Democrat, conservative or liberal, and they stick to it without regard for the facts. These *Crossfire*-style shows have nothing to do with real news or journalism—in fact, many of the hosts and guests have been political party operatives at some point in their careers. They are interested in pushing an agenda, and their shows are little more than theater.

Why don't I practice he says, she says journalism as most other news organizations do? Because I think it's a cop-out. For many news organizations it's a cop-out necessitated by budget constraints. Rather than asking their journalists to dig through their facts, analyze the issues, and reach for the truth, it's much less expensive to simply quote a Republican and a Democrat and satisfy an editor that the reporting is balanced. It's also a lot safer for everyone involved. Never mind that the readers, listeners, and audiences of such reporting are left no closer to the truth.

In fact, lies and misdirection often go unchecked or unquestioned. It was Ray McGovern, a former CIA analyst, who ultimately confronted Donald Rumsfeld for lying about the war in Iraq. During a speech by the secretary of defense at the Southern Center for International Studies in May 2006, McGovern stood up and asked, "Why did you lie to get us into a war that was not necessary?" When the secretary denied having done that, McGovern deftly trapped Mr. Rumsfeld with his own words. The inconsistencies should have been pointed out long ago by the press corps. Instead, a retired government employee did it of his own volition.

The entire media has a responsibility to report the truth, which requires doing research and getting facts straight. It does not, however, mean that journalists should all speak with the same voice and take a homogeneous approach to reporting the news. While my approach and my voice may be unique, my voice is only one of thousands in broadcasting today. And the diversity of those voices is critically important to the ideals of free speech, to the public's right to know, and to providing critical, independent scrutiny of our government and public institutions. The constitutionally protected tradition of a free press in this country means that readers, viewers, listeners, and users determine which voices will be heard by how many people. The people decide. I think that's exactly how most Americans like it.

These voices now have more outlets and forums than ever. As the Internet grows to maturity, some of the biggest brands in American journalism are also some of the biggest brands on the Web: the *New York Times,* the *Washington Post,* CBS, and CNN. But the Web has also birthed new brands and voices that are important to millions of Americans: the *Drudge Report;* TheSmokingGun.com; aggregators of news like Yahoo!, AOL, and Google; and hundreds of blogs that are contributing to the vitality and substance of our marketplace of new ideas and voices.

When we started CNN almost a quarter century ago, ABC, CBS, and NBC were the only national television news outlets. And while the broadcast networks dominated the news with their half-hour broadcast each night, they were essentially independent businesses. NBC was owned by RCA, which made it a subsidiary of a major corporation—but only a small part of it. Over the past quarter century, even as we hurtled toward the so-called 500-channel television set, broadcasting became even bigger. Capital Cities and ABC merged in 1985. Then came the merger of GE and RCA that same year. The Disney acquisition of Cap Cities occurred a decade later, as did the purchase of CBS by Westinghouse. And four years after that, Viacom bought CBS; the AOL deal for Time Warner occurred the following year.

Over the past decade, broadcast news became synonymous with big business. The cable news networks—CNN, Fox News Channel, and MSNBC—are all subsidiaries of major corporations. In fact, nearly all of the biggest brands in mainstream media journalism are owned by just eight companies. These are the eight, along with their most notable media holdings:

Viacom and CBS

While these became two separate companies as of December 31, 2005, Sumner Redstone is chairman of both and has a 71 percent controlling interest in each.

Viacom: MTV Networks (MTV, VH1, Nickelodeon, Nick at Nite, Comedy Central, CMT: Country Music Television, Spike TV, TV Land, and many other networks around the world), BET, Paramount Pictures, Paramount Home Entertainment and Famous Music, DreamWorks SKG

CBS: CBS Television Network, CW, CBS Radio, Viacom Outdoor, Viacom Television Stations Group, Paramount Television, King World, Simon & Schuster, Showtime, and Paramount Parks

Disney

ABC, ESPN (partial), A&E (partial), The History Channel (partial), E! Entertainment Network (partial), Disney Channel, Soapnet, E! Entertainment (partial), Lifetime (partial), Touchstone Pictures, Hollywood Pictures, Miramax Film Corp., theme parks, resorts, ten Buena Vista television stations, sixty-plus radio stations, Broadway theater productions, Pixar

General Electric

NBC, MSNBC and CNBC, Telemundo, USA Network, Bravo, Sci-Fi Channel, equity investments in A&E, The History Channel, and Sundance channel, nonvoting interest in Paxson Communications (sixty-three television stations), twenty-nine Vivendi Universal owned-and-operated TV stations

Time Warner

CNN, TNT and TBS, HBO, AOL, New Line Cinema, Castle Rock Entertainment, Time Warner Telecom, Time Warner Cable, Cartoon Network, Warner Bros. Entertainment, DC Comics, Hanna-Barbera, CW (partial), the Atlanta Braves. Approximately 130 magazines, including *People, Sports Illustrated, InStyle, Southern Living, Time, Entertainment Weekly, Fortune, Real Simple, What's on TV,* and *Cooking Light*

NewsCorp

Fox TV (News, Sports, Kids, FX), HarperCollins (book publisher), *TV Guide* (partial), DirecTV (partial), 20th Century Fox (movies), the *New York Post,* Fox Broadcasting (two hundred TV affiliates), STAR, the *Weekly Standard,* thirty-five TV stations, National Rugby League

Gannett

USA Today, ninety-one daily newspapers, twenty-one TV stations, roughly three hundred nondaily publications

Washington Post Corp.

Newsweek, the *Washington Post,* six TV stations, Cable One, military and community newspapers, Kaplan Professional (educational and career services), the *Herald, Slate*

New York Times Corp.

The *New York Times,* the *Boston Globe,* the *International Herald Tribune* (partner), sixteen additional newspapers, eight TV stations, two radio stations, more than forty Web sites, the Boston Red Sox (partial), the Discovery Times Channel (partial), 80 percent of New England Sports Network

These eight corporations dominate American mainstream media, especially television. And our culture is dominated by television: Eighty-six percent of people get their news from TV, more than four out of five. Media research shows that the average American spends more time watching television than doing anything else except sleeping and working.

The number of people who get most of their news from television makes me more than a little nervous, even though I'm a television journalist, in part because all television news has turned to the he says, she says brand of journalism. Broadcast news has homogenized its coverage to the point that the evening newscasts—aside from their anchors—have become almost indistinguishable. The executive producers at the networks don't hold daily conference calls with one another to discuss their leads, but they might as well.

Part of the problem is that none of us, whether in cable news or broadcast, can escape the New York and Washington, D.C., axis. ABC, CBS, NBC, CNN, and Fox all broadcast primarily from these two cities. New York is the media and financial capital of the country; D.C. is the political capital. That leaves us about 250 million people across the rest of the country to account for, and to. We call it "national news," but we might just as well call it New York and Washington News.

What is the impact of television news that is primarily domiciled in the axis of power in America? For one, we've occasionally become captives of those we cover, the business and political elite of the country. All of the news networks not only have studios in New York and Washington, but concentrate most of their correspondents in those two cities. Seventy percent of network news anchors and correspondents are based in New York and Washington. The five leading news networks (ABC, NBC, CBS, CNN, Fox) allocate their correspondents among the following cities: New York City, 73; Washington, D.C., 72; Los Angeles, 21; Atlanta, 19; Chicago, 11; Miami, 5; Boston, 4; Denver, 3; Dallas, 3; San Francisco, 2.

I often wonder what the impact would be on the values and perspectives of the national media if each network was headquartered in a different midwestern state, and our leading national newspapers and magazines were also headquartered in different places around the country, with the only rule being, no headquarters on the left or right coast. My guess is the national media would be a lot more national, and certainly less homogeneous in the values and views that shape our daily coverage. And it might be less liberal.

Most national media organizations have fought against the liberal label for decades, while their editors, reporters, and anchors claim objectivity. But the liberal bias of the media is real. As Walter Cronkite once put it, "Everybody knows that there's a liberal, that there's a heavy liberal persuasion among correspondents. . . . Anybody who has to live with the people, who covers police stations, covers county courts, brought up that way, has to have a degree of humanity that people who do not have that exposure don't have, and some people interpret that to be liberal. It's not a liberal, it's humanitarian, and that's a vastly different thing."

Now, I greatly admire Walter, but I truly doubt that there's any confusion on the part of journalists or the audience between what is humanitarian and what is liberal. In 1996, the same year that Walter was trying to rationalize liberalism in the media, the American Society of Newspaper Editors (ASNE) surveyed 1,037 reporters at 61 newspapers. It asked them, "What is your political leaning?" Sixty-one percent said they were liberal/Democrat, or leaning that way. Only 15 percent said they were conservative/Republican, or leaning that way.

A 1996 Roper Poll covering the 1992 elections surveyed 139 Washington bureau chiefs and correspondents. It found that 89 percent of these reporters had voted for Bill Clinton, while only 7 percent had voted for George H. W. Bush. In the general populace, by contrast, the vote was 43 percent for Mr. Clinton and 38 percent for Mr. Bush. The American public voted for Mr. Clinton by a margin of less than 4 to 3, while journalists supported him by a margin of 13 to 1.

Going back further, all the way to 1985, the *Los Angeles Times* surveyed 2,700 journalists at 621 newspapers. The survey was comprised of sixteen questions addressing national interests as they pertained to foreign affairs, economic concerns, and social issues. In fact, the survey was similar to one the *Times* had used in assessing the mood of the general public. When the answers from the journalists were tallied, the responses to fifteen of the sixteen questions demonstrated a bias that was qualitatively more liberal than that of the general population. For example, liberals in the media outnumbered conservatives in the media by a margin of more than 3 to 1. Yet less than one fourth of the public identified itself as liberal during this time. In the same survey, journalists admitted to voting 2 to 1 for Walter Mondale over Ronald Reagan—completely out of proportion to the landslide Reagan won by.

Personally, I'm not alarmed by the news media's liberal bias. I'm far more concerned by the denial that it exists. I encourage everyone in our newsroom at *Lou Dobbs Tonight* to freely and fully express their political views—their bias, if you will. I prefer a newsroom whose journalists are energetic and engaged with one another in discussions of the day's news and issues, and who have to support their political points of view and biases with the facts. While such open discussion of politics, and even of religion, makes some of our younger journalists uncomfortable initially, they quickly find greater respect for the facts and the truth, and a diminished commitment to ideology and partisanship. The result is that our newsroom has far more independent thinking and honest discussion.

I have always put my own biases front and center. My audience knows I've been a lifelong Republican and, through the magic of television, that I'm an aging, overweight white guy who just happens to care more about them and their lives than about being invited to the White House or playing golf with CEOs and celebrities.

I've often wondered why those critics of my particular brand of journalism aren't more forthcoming about their own political views. By doing so they could give their audience—whether electronic or print—a far better understanding of any potential bias or lack of "objectivity," whether due to their economic and financial interests, or their political and religious beliefs. My bio reveals not only which organizations I belong to and the fact that I was a liberal Republican, but also my principal financial investments. How far would my colleagues in the craft like to go? National newspapers and networks might consider identifying writers and reporters and news anchors by political affiliation. We do it all the time in print and on television, putting a little R, D, or I after names of elected officials. It might be fun to see bylines in the *New York Times, New York Post,* or CBS and CNN and every other news organization including that R, D, or I next to the names of their journalists. Just an idea.

But given the current state of journalism, what does the audience think of the news media? A February 2006 CBS/*New York Times* poll showed that only 15 percent of those surveyed had a great deal of faith that the media was reporting the news fully, accurately, and fairly. Forty-eight percent thought the media got a fair amount of it right. But 36 percent said that it didn't get very much right, if anything at all. That's an embarrassing indictment, when you consider that in 1974, a Gallup poll found that 21 percent of respondents thought the media got a great deal of it right, and only 29 percent said they had little or no confidence in the media.

I don't blame anyone for lacking faith in the media's ability to get it right. When the National Hurricane Center released its prediction for the 2006 hurricane season—which was eagerly anticipated, given the devastation wrought by hurricanes in 2005—the media couldn't even report that without bewildering the public. Reuters featured the story under the headline "U.S. Expects Busy Hurricane Season," while AP titled its story "Hurricane Center Predicts Calmer Season." Side by side, those headlines appeared to contradict each other. Which was accurate? In actuality, the National Hurricane Center predicted substantial hurricane activity in 2006—more than the norm but less than the previous year. Given that fact, neither quite got it right. And confusing the audience is not the way to earn journalistic credibility.

I not only take the criticism of my colleagues in journalism—whether working journalists, academicians, or media critics and monitors—but I also welcome it, even when I think it's ill founded. Such examination is healthy for all of us, and ultimately makes all of us who practice this craft better at what we do. Of course, broadcast journalism is as varied and diverse as each individual and his or her unique experience, talent, knowledge, and skill. The standard of the craft as it should be is the energetic gathering of facts and the objective reporting of the news, without fear or favor. But it is naive of anyone to believe that personal beliefs and biases aren't insinuated in some way, slight or significant, into the reporting of news.

The very act of deciding what constitutes news is not only a professional judgment, but one based on an individual editor's knowledge, experience, and perception of society and the audience for that news. I often wonder, however, what knowledge and experience some of the editors in our national media use. The choice to regularly eliminate the word "illegal" from the debate on immigration reform is a particularly glaring example. The issue at hand does not concern immigrants who are here legally, although you'd never know it from most of the headlines. Those same news outlets cover President Vicente Fox of Mexico whenever he chastises U.S. treatment of illegal immigrants. Yet few of them look at Mexico's own immigration issues. The U.S. media doesn't do investigative reports about the fact that Central American immigrants who find their way to Mexico are often the victims of rape, robbery, and even murder by border authorities. They don't report that only fifteen thousand people have been given legal immigrant status in Mexico in the last five years; that the country detains nearly a quarter of a million illegals every year; and that illegal immigration into Mexico is a felony punishable by two years in prison. Somehow, none of this information accompanies President Fox's highly publicized rants. The decision to omit these facts is made regularly by news editors across the United States.

I made the decision years ago that our broadcast, for which I have editorial responsibility, would recognize our audience as intelligent, engaged, knowledgeable citizens, and that we would present the news of the day and the issues we cover straightforwardly. In other words, we make every effort on my broadcast to treat our audience as equals, and to never dumb down the news.

My everyday editorial decisions are based on presenting facts that are essential to the news. For example, we report every night on the number of deaths in Iraq, an important measure of America's progress, or lack thereof, in the war. However, nationally there have been more broadcast news stories about the disappearance of Natalee Holloway than there have been about how many soldiers we've lost and how many have been injured in the Iraqi war. I also report on the trade and budget deficits, two numbers that hang ominously over this country yet receive short shrift from both the government and the media. Broadcast news outlets devote more time every year to reporting movie box-office grosses than they do our national debt.

This is another indication of the media's failure to do the hard work when it comes to reporting. According to Professor Barbie Zelizer, the Raymond Williams Professor of Communication at the University of Pennsylvania's Annenberg School of Communication, "The tendency for broadcast media is to often go with the story with a face and with a story that seems to have an end. Often journalists will lean toward a story with a proven template that captures the fears, interests, and agenda of the American people. The Natalee Holloway story was visually simple, easily understandable, and an already understood story. And that's easier than going after the more nuanced and complex stories."

In other words, viewers are typically presented with stories that are expected to wrap quickly or have a whiff of celebrity, instead of with the dogged pursuit of the facts or investigative reporting on stories that have a protracted life span.

While media critics say that TV panders to an audience with no attention span, our viewers have tuned in night after night to get updates not only on the daily news, but on stories we've covered month after month. I've been called "relentless" by critics and supporters alike for our ongoing coverage of issues that matter to people in this country, be it illegal immigration, outsourcing of American jobs, our soaring national deficits, or our elected officials' increasing lack of interest in the people who voted them into office. "Relentless" isn't a term typically associated with broadcast news, but I'm proud that we stay committed to stories for as long as they remain important to the interests of this nation. Obviously, our audience shares that commitment.

I don't think celebrity, fame, or people's personal lives should drive the news. I have also made a commitment to not intrude on anyone's personal life, and we only report on personal matters if they become critical elements of a news story. For example, we did not report on Bill Clinton's involvement with Monica Lewinsky until it became a factor in legal proceedings. Prior to that I truly felt that the relationship was a private matter. News should be based on facts, not titillation or voyeurism.

While my editorial decisions, and those of many others, shape our nightly broadcast, the very fact that we are a one-hour television news program necessarily limits the amount of time we can devote to each subject. My producers and I have never gone through a news day in which we could turn to one another and say there was no news, nothing to report today, or that we would have to "fill" some part of the broadcast because there was nothing of interest or import to our audience. In point of fact, we could easily do a two-hour show every evening. I cannot imagine how the executives of NBC, ABC, and CBS justify giving their news departments only a half hour. And while my colleagues on *Lou Dobbs Tonight* are among the most talented in television news, our time budget forces us to be disciplined, and to focus on that which matters most to the audience.

I've actually been accused of covering free trade, outsourcing of American jobs, illegal immigration, and border and port security for the purpose of driving our ratings higher. Imagine that. If these issues are such ratings drivers, you have to wonder why every other broadcast hasn't followed our example. If we really wanted to drive ratings, we would be taking the path of most other news programs and dedicating our airtime to the Natalee Holloway story, the Duke lacrosse alleged rape case, car chases, celebrity interviews, and the escapades of popular entertainers. We don't do that, I'm proud to say. Instead, my colleagues and I dare to be dull. Our audience expects to be taken seriously, and we take them seriously.

There is a nonpartisan reality in every story, and it is our obligation to report that reality. It doesn't matter if the viewer is a Democrat or a Republican. I'm interested in the nonpartisan reality that exists for 98 percent of the population of this country, a country that is first and foremost American. Being a Republican or Democrat is of ancillary importance.

The truth stands by itself. The idea that fair and balanced is a substitute for truth and fact is mindless nonsense that has captured too much of the national media. There seem to be only two sides, both political, to every story. Does that mean that if we had three major political parties there would be three sides to the truth? If we had four parties, would there be four sides?

— *Chapter 6* —

The Exorbitant Cost of Free Trade

Few terms have as benign and noble a connotation as "free trade." But free trade as it's been practiced by the U.S. government over the past several decades is neither noble nor benign—unless you happen to be one of America's principal trading partners, such as China, Japan, Germany, Canada, or Mexico. For America itself, the cost of so-called free trade has been exorbitant and destructive. Millions of manufacturing jobs have been destroyed, our manufacturing base has been drastically diminished, and we are on an uncertain path to becoming a debtor nation in perpetuity.

For the past several years on our broadcast we've devoted immense resources and airtime to reporting on the reality of what the Bush administration, and before it the Clinton administration, calls free trade. Today the United States faces a trade deficit that is approaching $1 trillion a year. We've run up a total trade debt nearing $5 trillion, after posting trade deficits for thirty consecutive years. I quoted Albert Einstein in my previous book, *Exporting America,* on the failure of our policy makers and political leaders to take note of these less than trivial results of so-called free trade. Einstein said, "Insanity: doing the same thing over and over again and expecting different results." Free trade, as the Bush administration promotes it in its policies, and as American business practices it, is nothing less than insane.

In his 2006 State of the Union speech, President Bush warned that America is addicted to foreign oil. And we are. But because of our free trade policies, we have an even greater dependency: We are addicted to foreign goods. Our dependence on products manufactured in other nations is two and half times greater than our dependence on foreign oil. The Economic Policy Institute estimates that 99 percent of our trade deficit is a result of our need to buy goods and products that are no longer manufactured in the United States. So we import. And we're importing not only foreign goods and services, but also the money with which to buy those imports.

We are borrowing almost $3 billion each and every day to pay for the goods and services we import. The result is that the only nation in the world that can claim to be a true superpower is being bankrupted by a nearly $9 trillion national debt and an almost $5 trillion trade debt. And we can thank not only the administrations of Bill Clinton and George Bush, but the Republicans and Democrats in Congress who have ceded their constitutional responsibility to formulate trade agreements by granting the president so-called fast-track authority, which gives him absolute control over the negotiations of these pacts—and relegates Congress to a straight up-and-down vote on them. The results have been unambiguously devastating. Our free trade agreements over the past fifteen years have been so one-sided and so unfair to American workers that you would be forgiven for believing that the U.S. trade representatives simply forgot to show up for the negotiations. Incredibly, these agreements are the perfect expression of the desired policies of President Bush and President Clinton. Both leaders believed free trade to mean unrestricted access to the world's richest consumer market without reciprocal concessions by our trading partners, giving American companies access to their markets.

The Bush administration's free trade policies are killing our manufacturing industry. Our policy makers have cut tariffs and allowed China and other low-cost producers to flood our stores with goods made by workers usually earning less than a dollar an hour. Those imported products are not attractive because they are better or of a higher quality, but because they are less expensive. American industry cannot compete against the cheapest manufacturing environments in the world. And that is precisely the intent of those so-called free trade policies: to force middle-class working men and women to compete directly with global workers making literally pennies per hour.

For a while, the big lie of free trade was persuasive. Over the course of the past decade, President Bush and his economic advisers and their supporters initially claimed that because America is a knowledge-based economy, we needn't worry about the loss of more than three million manufacturing jobs since 2000. They claimed that since we are also a technology economy, Americans should accordingly leave the manufacturing of basic goods and products to those economies unable to compete with our vast global lead in technology. By 2005, the Bush administration free traders, and supporters in both parties, were claiming that our rising trade deficit was really the fault of an uneducated, uninspired American labor force. It's been quite a rationalization, but the facts are clear to all who will acknowledge them: thirty years of bad policies causing record and rising trade deficits and mounting trade debt.

There are very few industries in which America can now claim to be the world leader. Not automobiles, an industry once dominated by the United States. There are only two U.S.-owned car companies remaining, even though politicians and even journalists still talk about the "Big Three" in Detroit. It's really the "Big Two," and they're getting a lot smaller. General Motors now proudly claims it can survive if it can hang on to 25 percent of the American car market, while Toyota is expected to sell more cars worldwide than GM by the end of this year. What about the popular claim that we're a technology economy? Afraid not. China now sells more high tech to the world than we do—more computers, more consumer electronics, more of just about everything it manufactures.

While we can still claim to be number one in a number of exports, the problem is that they're not the sort of exports you would expect from a superpower economy. For example, we ship more than $10.5 billion worth of waste and scrap out of the United States every year. We're number one in waste and scrap. A good portion of that leading export goes to China, as do some of our agricultural products. In fact, our leading exports to China are waste, scrap, soybeans, and semiconductors—and the semiconductors get packaged into goods that are sold right back to us.

We are still the world's leading exporter of agricultural products, such as soybeans, corn, cotton, and wheat. But we may soon lose that global title. In fact, the United States is on track for the first time in half a century to import more food than it exports. It is likely that in the next two years that we will not only be dependent on the rest of the world for our automobiles, computers, consumer electronics, and clothing, but also for our food.

President Bush's shortsighted policy of free trade at any cost is imperiling not only our economy but our claim to being the world's only superpower. Having the world's most powerful military is the foundation of our claim to superpower status, as is, of course, our wealth. We are still the world's biggest consumer economy, but we have also become the world's biggest debtor. And that debt will only rise while the administration's so-called free trade policies continue to export our capital and wealth to foreign companies and governments.

The direct cost of globalization as structured by our current free trade policies is straightforward: We have exchanged self-sufficiency for dependency. As Tom Nassif, president and CEO of Western Growers, told me, "From our industry's point of view, just like energy supply and our military sufficiency, a secure domestic food supply is a national security imperative. We can't let happen to our food supply what we've let happen to our energy supply."

There is no reciprocity in our trade relationships. The United States encounters trade barriers and high tariffs put in place by our trading partners while we reduce our tariffs and restrictions. In 1951, the average U.S. trade tariff on imported goods was approximately 15 percent. By 1979 it had sunk to 5.7 percent. Today our industrial tariff on foreign goods is just under 3 percent.

The imbalance is glaringly evident in the global automotive market, which China is just now entering. When Chinese-made automobiles, the Geely and the Cherry, begin coming to this country next year they will face a 2.5 percent tariff. Ford and General Motors will face a 25 percent tariff should they muster the courage to even export to China.

Our trade relationship with China in general is particularly troubling. The U.S. trade deficit with China last year hit $202 billion, up some $40 billion from the previous year. And despite the posturing of President Bush, then treasury secretary John Snow, and Commerce Secretary Carlos Gutierrez, the imbalance is not likely to be righted in the near future. Calling our trade with China "free" is a sad joke played by the Bush administration and other faith-based free traders who ignore its realities. The fact is that Chinese ships carry millions of containers filled with Chinese-manufactured goods to what are often Chinese-owned and -operated terminals in American ports. And, as we reported on our show, less than a quarter return to China with American-produced goods.

It's obvious the Chinese are overtaking the United States in manufacturing. But we now have a trade deficit with China in information and communication technologies, threatening U.S. leadership. That gap doubled in just the past three years: a deficit of $14.6 billion of 2002 became last year a deficit of $50.8 billion.

Alan Tonelson, the author of *Race to the Bottom,* told our show that "China is still very much a student in technology policy, but it's learning very quickly, in large part because it's got the world's best teachers, that is to say, U.S. multinational companies in technology areas. They have been transferring much of their very best and most militarily relevant technology not only to Chinese factories, but to Chinese laboratories."

Not only are U.S. multinationals transferring our knowledge base and production capacity to communist China, but despite protestations by President Hu Jintao, and contrary to what he said when he met with President Bush in April 2006, China continues to steal technology and products that it can't develop itself. As much as 95 percent of the U.S. software and entertainment products—including CDs and DVDs—used in China are pirated. In all, the Chinese stole an estimated $2.3 billion worth of goods from copyrighted industries in 2005.

The same week that President Hu met with President Bush, he also met with Bill Gates. As a matter of fact, he met with Bill Gates and the head of Boeing and other business leaders for a state dinner. President Hu announced in Seattle (where he spent two days of his four-day visit to the United States) that communist China was buying $15 billion worth of Boeing aircraft, and would spend $400 million to install Microsoft's operating system software on computers manufactured in China, rather than continue the practice of permitting pirated operating systems. It's a beginning, but it is only that, and is in perfect keeping with the Chinese practice of granular gradualism in addressing the trade imbalance with the United States.

The Bush administration has spent four years trying to convince the Chinese to unpeg their currency from the dollar. In the summer of 2005, Treasury Secretary John Snow was at last able to announce that the Chinese had agreed to a 2 percent adjustment in the value of the yuan to the dollar. There is no more blatant statement of our dependency, and of the incompetence of the Bush administration in trade policy, than the United States's inability to influence a change in China's currency practices and gain American access to the Chinese market. The slavish attitude of our policy makers and business leaders toward China would make you think they held office and headquartered their businesses in a banana republic rather than in the United States. For the privilege of doing business in communist China, American companies have aided and abetted the communist regime. And without apology.

I'm frequently asked why we refer to China as communist China on our broadcast. The answer is simple: China is the world's largest communist country. Its government is communist. President Hu and Premier Wen Jiaboa are not elected officials. China is not a democracy; it is a communist state. The real question is, why do other news organizations and our political leaders ignore that reality? Perhaps the juxtaposition of free trade and communism makes them uncomfortable. It should.

U.S. technology giants Microsoft, Yahoo!, Cisco Systems, and Google have capitulated to demands by the Chinese government that they censor their content in order to gain a foothold there. This prompted Congress to convene a caucus on global human rights in February 2006 to query these four companies on their rationale for doing business with a country the State Department deems repressive of human rights. All of them denied that it was "business as usual," but admitted that doing as the communist Chinese government asked was the cost of establishing themselves there. Google, in particular, well known in America as being a source for almost any information on the Web, made headlines by agreeing to restrict what Chinese citizens could search for, see, and find on the Chinese version of the Internet. "Don't Be Evil" is Google's corporate motto. If restricting individual freedom and abandoning freedom of speech for access to China's millions of nascent Internet users isn't evil, I don't know what is. What is good for Google is certainly not good for America.

A report by the OpenNet Initiative reached this sad conclusion:

"China operates the most extensive, technologically sophisticated and broad-reaching system of Internet filtering in the world." But one of the most publicized arguments for granting China permanent normal trade relations in 2002 was the promise of the Internet. As Bill Clinton said, "We know how much the Internet has changed America. And we are already an open society. Imagine how much it could change China." Executives of Microsoft, Yahoo!, Cisco Systems, and Google have put the lie to that promise.

Free-trade-at-any-cost advocates choose not only to ignore our record high and accelerating trade deficits, and the crushing costs of our ever mounting multitrillion-dollar trade debt, but they even go so far as to declare failure to be success. I'm one of those who in 1993 hoped that the North American Free Trade Agreement would be a success. I believed that with appropriate worker and environmental protections, NAFTA could work, and that if we in the United States were to enrich anyone in the world, we should enrich our neighbors. Among those opposing NAFTA were Ross Perot, Congressman Richard Gephardt, and Senator Byron Dorgan, who believed, correctly as it turned out, that NAFTA would "suck away" American manufacturing, capital, and jobs.

I was wrong; Perot, Gephardt, Dorgan, and everyone else who opposed NAFTA were right. In part, NAFTA failed because the Clinton administration failed to secure binding side agreements with then Mexican president Salinas to create labor, workplace, and environmental protections. But failure was substantially assured because the concept of NAFTA did not sufficiently take into account the difference in living standards between Mexico, the United States, and Canada.

NAFTA proponents claimed that American and Canadian business investment in Mexico would relatively quickly raise the standard of living there; that Mexican workers would see an increase in their wages, which would then stem what was becoming a rising tide of Mexican illegal immigration to El Norte. They also claimed that NAFTA would create 170,000 U.S. jobs annually. Instead, as many as a million jobs were lost as a direct result of NAFTA. The U.S. trade deficit with Mexico is nine times as large today as when NAFTA was signed.

Instead of rising, Mexican manufacturing wages actually fell 25 percent by 1998. More than half of the Mexican people now live in poverty. And the result is that NAFTA has spurred, rather than stemmed, illegal migration to the United States. More than half of the illegal immigrants now living in this country have crossed our southern border in the last decade. As Nobel Prize–winning economist Joseph Stiglitz said on the show, "It's turned out that in NAFTA, there were a lot of things that we didn't know then, that weren't talked about. The investment agreement, for instance, which has been bad for the environment. Chapter 11—Mexico has not gotten the benefits, because Mexico hasn't been doing a lot of the investments."

In my opinion, Stiglitz was being kind. We did know and many of us assumed there would be side-letter agreements that would ensure worker and environmental protection. Despite early assurance that these agreements would be forthcoming, Mexican president Carlos Salinas de Gortari simply overwhelmed U.S. negotiators. Bill Clinton, craving the political opportunity to be a part of history, wasn't about to risk the treaty.

NAFTA has thrown North American trade completely way out of balance. NAFTA proponents and free-trade-at-any-cost advocates point to the doubling of U.S. exports to Mexico and Canada over the past decade. But during that period our *imports* from these countries have tripled, and the U.S. trade deficit with Mexico and Canada combined is almost $127 billion as of 2005. We buy almost everything that Canada exports; 85 percent of their exports come to the United States.

Despite the clear concrete evidence to the contrary, President Bush and his administration claim that NAFTA is a success and, moreover, should be the model for a free trade of the Americas agreement, which would include every country in this hemisphere. But even the president's own party is awakening to a clearly nonpartisan independent reality: Free trade as an ideal, and America's free-trade-at-any-cost policies of the past thirty years, are disastrous and unsustainable.

The results can be seen across our nation. Our broadcast featured the story of Apricot, Inc., a textile maker in Hertford, North Carolina, that felt the negative effects of NAFTA. A longtime family business run by Carl Terranova and his wife, Cathy, the company had monthly revenues of more than $1 million making shirts, flags, and other textile products. As Carl told us, "You'd have people making four hundred to five hundred a week. And they were making money, I was making money, so we were all happy."

NAFTA changed everything. As we reported, thirty days after NAFTA took effect, Apricot saw its business drop sharply because of the competition from cheaper products, to less than $1 million a *year*. The Terranovas hung on for the better part of a decade, diversifying into athletic jerseys and chefs' uniforms. But by the beginning of 2006, they couldn't compete anymore. They made the difficult decision to shut down their business, which had been run by the family for three generations. The toughest part came when they had to let their employees go. As Carl told us, "It's terrible, telling everyone they have no more . . . they don't have a job anymore. Not that the people weren't aware or couldn't intuit it, but rather having to say good-bye to everyone, you feel as if you failed, you know, not only on a financial level, but on a personal level. It's very difficult."

Carl has made plans to become a general contractor now that his company is gone, but he had valid concerns about his employees' futures. Many of them were in their forties and fifties, and the textile business—from cutting to sewing—was the only business they'd ever known. But North Carolina, which once boasted 265,000 textile jobs, has lost more than 65 percent of them since NAFTA passed. That doesn't bode well for those looking to find new positions in the textile business.

Despite the obvious failures of NAFTA, the Bush administration pushed ahead with plans to enter another poorly-thought-out free trade agreement. Flush with political capital from his reelection, President Bush managed to win congressional approval of the Central American Free Trade Agreement (CAFTA) with Costa Rica, El Salvador, Guatemala, Honduras, Nicaragua, and the Dominican Republic. But it was a close vote, and the president had to use up a lot of that political capital. In fact, Congress passed CAFTA in the middle of the night, because it could not begin to defend the economics of the plan. CAFTA is clearly an outsourcing and offshoring agreement, not a trade agreement, despite its title. The economics are so bad that the president and his supporters finally tried to sell it as a security guarantee. The best the administration could do was position it as promoting democracy, peace, and prosperity in Central America and the Dominican Republic. Representative Jim Kolbe (R-Arizona) told me, "I think it's a national security issue, and this is a very important national security vote. . . . The last thing in the world we need right now, with Castro and President Chavez in Venezuela, is to turn those [CAFTA] countries into battlegrounds for Chavez and Castro." And Scott McClellan, then the White House press secretary, added, "It helps to strengthen democracy in our own hemisphere. This goes right to our own national security. This is an agreement that will help extend peace and prosperity throughout the Western Hemisphere. While we're working to advance freedom abroad, we also need to be looking in our own hemisphere, and make sure that we're supporting the democratic efforts that continue to advance in our own hemisphere."

Still, few were buying. Congressman Charlie Rangel (D-New York) told it like it was: "They brought this bill to the floor, and they didn't even have enough Republicans to pass it. What it was is a lot of arm twisting, a lot of promising, a lot of pork, and Condoleezza Rice visited me and said the communists were coming, that if we didn't have this done for them to go into effect January 1, that the Sandinistas were going to take over the area."

As Congressman Sherrod Brown (D-Ohio) explained on our show, "The whole point is, it's an outsourcing agreement. In Guatemala and Nicaragua, the average wage is less than three thousand dollars a year. We're not going to sell products to them. They can't buy cars made in Ohio, or software from Seattle, or prime beef from Nebraska, or textiles and apparel from North Carolina. But they are places where American companies will move. We'll lose American jobs, and exploit workers in Guatemala. These trade agreements aren't working for Americans or for the countries who are our trading partners."

Brown is right. The five countries of Central America and the Dominican Republic amount to an economy the size of New Haven, Connecticut, some $85 billion. They can't buy much. In point of fact, the International Monetary Fund is supporting three of those countries, either directly or indirectly, with loans.

That there were no benefits to CAFTA was evident in the fact that a midnight vote with plenty of arm twisting had to occur. But the Bush administration needed a win on free trade for its business allies, and it got one. Two weeks before the vote was taken, Congressman Robin Hayes from North Carolina declared, "Every time I drive through Kannapolis, and I see those empty plants, I know there is no way I could vote for CAFTA." Reassuring, strong words from an elected official. Especially since Congressman Hayes changed his mind, and under cover of darkness voted yes on CAFTA.

One of the reasons the administration has wanted to keep CAFTA out of the harsh light of scrutiny is the dark little secret buried in the fine print of the agreement. Once CAFTA is in full force, the sovereignty of the United States is diminished. Within the CAFTA agreement are one thousand pages of international law, which become the highest law of the land, determining rules from health care to zoning to immigration. Lori Wallach of Public Citizen's Global Trade Watch told our broadcast, "Any violation of one thousand pages of international law imposed on us is taken to an international tribunal, not U.S. courts, where if the U.S. does not conform its law, we face perpetual trade sanctions. It's a huge attack on our sovereignty and our democracy."

For example, as we reported on the show, if your community passed a law to limit urban sprawl, it could be challenged under CAFTA by a foreign investor who wants to build in your town. States with "buy American" laws that give preference to local companies might be ordered to reverse those laws under CAFTA. And here's one that fuels the fires of illegal immigration: Any company wishing to come to the United States either to start a business or to complete a contract can bring their employees in from the country of origin. This is allowed under CAFTA even if our visa quota is full.

CAFTA, now officially called DR-CAFTA, was supposed to go into effect on January 1, 2006. It didn't, and there's hope it might not ever. Not because the president and the U.S. Congress awakened suddenly and put the national interest above partisan politics and the interest of corporate America, but rather because some of the CAFTA members have determined that like NAFTA it might not work. Not a single country among the Dominican Republic and the five Central American nations complied with the deadline of the agreement. Costa Rica's legislature hasn't even approved the pact—and they may never do so.

Like the proposed CAFTA provisions, our membership in the World Trade Organization allows that organization to rule not only on our trade practices, but also on our democratic process and sovereignty. For example, under WTO rules, the United States is required to offer sixty-five thousand H-1B work visas each year. If for any reason we don't, other countries can demand international arbitration, and the United States can be penalized and fined for not allowing enough foreign workers into the country. This would seem to usurp Congress's power over immigration policy.

Our own multinational corporations have begun turning to the WTO to get U.S. law changed. The WTO is currently assisting Wal-Mart in taking on state policies, by helping the world's biggest retailer get concessions opposed by local governments. Wal-Mart has been lobbying the WTO to get the federal government to remove limits on the size, height, and number of stores that can be established in the United States. This would make it easier for the retailer to move into smaller communities over the objections of its residents. In effect, since it has lost out against local laws, Wal-Mart wants the WTO to force the United States to allow the retailer to do as it wants. The organization Public Citizen warns that American towns, cities, and states could find zoning laws challenged in international trade court. And if our 1994 WTO general agreement on trade and services is changed, it could be harder for cities and towns to limit hours of operations and restrict the growth of huge retail stores. As California state senator Liz Figueroa said, "Why even have a city council, why even have state governments, if WTO agreements are superseding our judgment?"

Clearly our trade agreements aren't working to the direct benefit of the middle class. And how are the Bush administration's free trade policies working for America around the world?

- American automobile exports are laughable given our trade agreements. For instance, in 2005, America imported 700,000 cars from South Korea. American car companies sold a grand total of 3,900—*three thousand nine hundred*—cars in Korea. That's because Korea limits the number of cars that it will allow into its country.
- The Bush administration proposed a rule change that would allow foreign airlines to control U.S. air carriers. Europeans demanded that provision as part of world trade negotiations to open

up greater access by U.S. carriers in Europe. As we reported on the show, granting foreign control of our airlines was a condition for granting equivalent access by the E.U. But the Department of Transportation wanted to change the rules and allow foreign control, despite the fact that foreign carriers do not allow U.S. airlines to control them. It's no surprise that the airline industry was lobbying in support of these changes.

The Bush administration's Department of Transportation and its negotiators were in absolute support of this idiocy. They were obviously unconcerned about our national security, the need to have our troops transported by U.S. air carriers whenever they are deployed, and the assault on the working men and women in this country. The good news is that the House aviation subcommittee, chaired by Representative John Mica of Florida, told the Bush administration to go to hell on this one.

- The Commerce Department accepted a NAFTA panel ruling that would virtually eliminate tariffs on more than $7.4 billion worth of Canadian lumber imports. As Commerce Secretary Carlos Gutierrez said, "We have serious concerns about the panel's decision. However, consistent with our NAFTA obligations, we have complied with the panel's instructions." It's been a bitter battle, first led by former Canadian prime minister Paul Martin, who was seeking to show his constituents that he could get tough with the United States. The White House rolled over, giving our timber industry a good reason to be upset and angry about how this was handled.

The United States argued that, to counter the fact that Canada subsidizes its industry, we collected duties of roughly 16 percent on the lumber that comes into the country from there. Our neighbors to the north balked, argued that this was a violation of NAFTA, and demanded a $5 billion refund—and they got most of it. Canada is clearly unimpressed by the fact that the United States is its leading customer; that it enjoys a $75 million trade surplus with the

United States; and most amazingly, that the World Trade Organization actually supports the U.S. position.

The cost of free trade is truly exorbitant. The United States is losing not only production, capital, and jobs, but our sovereignty, the ability to determine our destiny as a nation. We've permitted our elected officials and corporate America to put our destiny in the hands of international bureaucracies and U.S. multinationals. As Senator Byron Dorgan (D-North Carolina) told me, "This is about the corporate agenda in America. Big corporations, more powerful than ever. They want to access cheap labor overseas; they want to sell the product back in this country, [and] run their earnings through the Cayman Islands to stop paying taxes. And who are the victims here?"

I believe all Americans are the victims, but unquestionably our working middle-class men and women are the most severely affected. As Mark Weisbrot of the Center for Economic Policy and Research told *BusinessWeek,*

> We have had a 30-year period in which the real median wage has grown 9%, while productivity is up 80%. Almost none of that improvement has gone to the majority of the labor force. If you have competition with people who are paid very low wages and have no right to organize unions, you will have downward pressure on prices. The downward pressure on wages is really hurting most employees in this country more than the cheaper consumer goods are helping them.

— *Chapter 7* —

Exporting America

Competition is the hallmark of a free enterprise economy. For the past thirty years, however, corporate America has been doing everything it can to cut competition, with major corporations merging and consolidating at every opportunity. But our corporate leaders do continue to embrace competition in one single market: the labor market. And through offshoring of production and services, the outsourcing of jobs to cheap foreign labor markets, and their support of illegal immigration, they have put the American worker into direct competition with the cheapest labor in every corner of the world.

We first started reporting on the outsourcing of American jobs to cheap foreign labor markets in 2002. And as often happens, we were responding to our viewers, who were telling us in increasing numbers that they had lost their jobs to workers in India, Romania, China, the Philippines, or some other cheap labor market. As the stories of jobs lost mounted, it became clear that we were witnessing the onset of a new business practice. Outsourcing was becoming epidemic, and we titled our reporting on the phenomenon "Exporting America." That also became the title of a book I wrote two years later in an effort to bring what I considered an assault on working men and women to the attention of the public and our elected officials.

Now, two years after that book appeared, outsourcing continues apace and is an established practice among thousands of businesses, rampant throughout the technology and financial services industry, and growing. As I reported in 2004, the University of California–Berkeley estimated that as many as fourteen million American jobs are now at risk of being outsourced. Consulting firm A. T. Kearney estimated that a half million of those jobs would come from the financial services industry alone.

I concluded at that time the assault on our middle-class workers would continue unless corporate America found a conscience or, failing that discovery, unless Congress took action to curtail it. Neither has occurred, and the result has been as I predicted: Millions of our fellow citizens have lost their jobs, and their new jobs usually pay less than the ones lost to outsourcing.

Corporate leaders defend the outsourcing of American jobs by claiming that they are only interested in increasing the competitiveness of their businesses, improving efficiency, and raising productivity. That isn't even clever obfuscation of their true motivation and purpose. Competitiveness, productivity, and efficiency are nothing more than code words for "cheaper labor." And in finding that cheaper labor all over the world, they have effectively put the great American middle class into direct competition with workers earning pennies an hour or a few dollars a day.

When George Bush and corporate America say that the United States can compete globally so long as there is a level playing field, they obviously mean to cut the American standard of living down to the level of the third world.

And how are American workers doing? On a superficial level, pretty well. We have a 4.7 percent unemployment rate, and our economy is growing on average by 3 percent a year. But a closer examination of economic statistics, or a discussion with your neighbors or coworkers, or a stop at your local gas station quickly reveals a troubling reality. Whether because of stagnant real earnings, higher mortgages, higher gasoline and heating oil prices, the rising cost of health care, or the cost of sending a kid to college, working men and women in every part of the country are getting hammered. And getting hammered during what is, by nearly every conventional standard, a period of prosperity. But how prosperous a nation are we when working Americans aren't being allowed to share equally in what we glibly call "prosperity"?

Corporate America is likewise doing great, by the standard metrics of business and economics. Corporate taxes are at the lowest level in almost a hundred years. Corporate profits have risen more than 20 percent in 2005–2006, and those profits account for the largest share of national income in forty years. Corporate America is enjoying the best of times.

But what about the employees who make it all possible? While corporate profits increased in the past year, real wages have actually declined. While productivity is skyrocketing, the share of national income going to workers has fallen to the lowest level in forty years. At the same time, corporate America is cutting benefits and pensions. If this is Adam Smith's invisible hand at work, it's balled up in a fist and striking the solar plexus of the middle class. And outsourcing is playing a part in the decline of both pay and opportunity for American labor.

Some business leaders and politicians defend both outsourcing and illegal immigration by claiming that America has an insufficient number of workers—an inadequate labor force. But if that were the case, real wages would be rising, not declining, and benefits and pensions would at least be stable, if not growing.

In 2004, Gregory Mankiw, then chairman of the President's Council of Economic Advisers, stated, "Outsourcing is just a new way of doing international trade. We are very used to goods being produced abroad and being shipped here on ships or planes. What we're not used to is services being produced abroad and being sent here over the Internet or telephone wires. . . . I think outsourcing is a growing phenomenon, but it's something that we should realize is probably a plus for the economy in the long run."

Notice how Professor Mankiw left out an important element of what constitutes outsourcing in his statement, "What we're not used to is services being produced abroad and being sent here over the Internet or telephone wires." What we're not used to, in fact, is corporate America packing up jobs in this country and shipping them abroad to produce goods and services that are then exported back into the U.S. market.

Mercifully, Mankiw is back at Harvard teaching undergraduates that flipping burgers at McDonald's is part of the manufacturing process. But his endorsement of outsourcing still resonates throughout corporate America. It is the rationalization used by CEOs of multinationals who have continued to prove that they don't care what happens to the working men and women of this country. Hundreds if not thousands of big American companies are ignoring the needs and interests of their employees and the communities in which they are based by outsourcing work to the citizens and communities of other nations. As Ramalinga Raju, CEO of Satyam Computer Services, said on the show, "Market forces today are operating in such a manner that it is blurring boundaries between countries, and in fact, blurring boundaries between companies as well." Raju has every reason and motivation to embrace outsourcing and the blurring of boundaries, because he, his business, and his country benefit immensely from them.

These multinationals, and the management consultants and lobbyists in their pay, have convinced our lawmakers in both parties and the Bush administration that outsourcing is good for America. Both the Commerce Department and the Labor Department are complicit in the outsourcing outrage. Instead of using their resources and researchers to carefully examine the impacts of outsourcing, they are refusing to gather any data or information. Our federal government has not only not analyzed the economic impacts of outsourcing, but has steadfastly refused to even investigate how many American jobs have been lost to cheap overseas labor.

In their free trade fervor, Republicans and Democrats alike, most economists, certainly corporate leaders, and business columnists assure us that the loss of millions of jobs to other countries is the inevitable result of a modern global economy. The result, they promise us, will be a higher standard of living for everyone in America—and especially for the rest of the planet. Of course, those assurances are largely based on the research and financial influence of business-bought think tanks, management consultants, and economists serving their corporate masters.

Despite their claims, the United States has already lost millions of manufacturing jobs. Many more will be lost in the next few years, even if by some miracle we could quickly alter our current business practices and trade policy. An estimate by Forrester Research states that $136 billion in wages will be taken from the United States and transferred to lower-wage countries by 2015. This includes approximately 550 of the 700 service-job categories in the United States. These aren't just manufacturing jobs—we're also talking about 3.3 million white-collar service jobs. The sector leading the way will be the information technology industry. Yes, you remember correctly: The free trade at any price enthusiasts once promised us that all those millions of people who lost their positions in manufacturing would find even better ones in the tech industry. But today no one is saying which industry will be the source of replacements for those jobs lost to outsourcing.

However, we are now being told that the following jobs will have the greatest demand for workers in the next decade:

1. Waiters and waitresses
2. Janitors and cleaners

3. Food preparation
4. Nursing aides, orderlies, and attendants
5. Cashiers
6. Customer-service representatives
7. Retail salespersons
8. Registered nurses
9. General and operational managers
10. Postsecondary teachers

Only three of these positions require a college degree; the rest rely on on-the-job training. Obviously, the advantage of some of them is that at least they can't be outsourced.

Corporate outsourcing of middle-class jobs to cheap overseas labor markets is inconsistent with a corporation's responsibility to its stakeholders. A company's stakeholders are comprised of more than just senior management, investors, and their financial interests. They include the employees of the company and the community and nation in which it is headquartered and operates. In short, everyone and every entity that has a vested interest in how the company performs, and that in some way contributes to that performance, is a stakeholder. All stakeholders should benefit from the operations of the business, not just a select few, and the business must make a commitment to all of them.

American companies, including U.S. multinationals, are corporate citizens. And like any citizen, a corporation not only enjoys that nation's rights and privileges, but has a responsibility to it, as well. The outsourcing of American jobs to cheap foreign workers not only damages the employee stakeholders, but the community stakeholders as well. With the loss of jobs, employees are often forced to leave the community, diminishing the local economy and cutting the tax base that supports public education and infrastructure. And the public interest costs of outsourcing are worsening, not abating:

• In the final days of 2005, three of our nation's largest corporations announced plans to expand their pace of investment in, and outsourcing to, India and the Far East. This news came at the same time as our nation's once proud auto giants geared up to cut thousands and thousands of jobs, and to close factories. Intel announced an expansion of nearly $300 million in Malaysia, along with plans to invest $1 billion in India. JPMorganChase said it would hire forty-five hundred new employees, all of them in India, to perform back-office support work. As we reported on the broadcast, Morgan spokesman Michael Golden explained, "We have found high-quality, low-cost staff in India, and we want to continue investing in the country." Then there's Microsoft. Bill Gates said that Microsoft would invest more than $1.5 million in India over the next four years, a move that would nearly double Microsoft's workforce there. As Gates said, "Microsoft will be able to build great products, because of the work done by our employees here in India, and the work that we give to our partners here in India. This is the country where the percentage increase in our employment is going to be absolutely the highest, going from, I mentioned going from about four thousand to about seven thousand over the next three to four years. And that's literally hiring as fast as reasonably we can do it." Unfortunately, he's not hiring in the United States as fast as he can reasonably do it.

• The two remaining American car companies, General Motors and Ford, are both closing U.S. plants, laying off their American workers, outsourcing jobs, and offshoring production as fast as they can. Ford has plans to layoff some thirty thousand workers over the next several years, reducing its workforce by 25 percent. General Motors is asking workers to consider an "early buyout" retirement program that would allow it to eliminate thirty thousand employees from its payroll and close nine factories by 2008. Ironically, foreign car makers have built more new plants in the United States, and hired more American workers, than General Motors and Ford combined. GM and Ford executives have seemingly tried to convince everyone who would listen that their lost market share is based on the costs and performance of their employees. But to my mind, it is the management of both companies that bears the responsibility for the failure of their companies to succeed in the world's richest auto market. GM and Ford have fallen behind because of terrible design, a lack of innovation, their refusal to go to the highest-quality production methods and techniques, and their refusal to embrace, across their entire product lines, the same quality assurance demanded by the leaders of the Japanese car companies. Certainly GM and Ford have a competitive disadvantage in their overwhelming legacy costs, and the burden of their union contracts over the past two decades, but nonetheless their greatest failing has been pitiful leadership.

General Motors loses $1,100 on every car it produces in the United States largely because of high wages and extraordinarily generous pensions and benefits. To scale back those losses, CEO Rick Wagoner has embarked on a crusade to cut the number of GM jobs in the United States and to minimize health care benefits for those lucky enough to keep their jobs. He's planning cuts of some thirty thousand positions. Guess where those jobs are going? Well, GM is investing in its China plants, because while the average auto industry worker in this country is paid roughly $54 per hour, a Chinese one makes about $5.50 per hour. Yet at the same time that GM and Ford claim they have to send production overseas in order to make a profit, foreign carmakers continue to invest in the United States, and to claim a rising share of the American market—by far, the richest auto market in the world.

General Motors's stock actually rose slightly recently as business columnists and pundits asked whether the company would go bankrupt. Why did it rise? Because General Motors announced it was confident it would be able to maintain 20 percent of the U.S. market. GM and Ford have about 41 percent of the U.S. market share, while German-owned DaimlerChrysler has 14 percent, and Toyota, Honda, and Nissan together have almost 30 percent. As speculation continues about whether General Motors and Ford will eventually go bankrupt, Toyota is about to overtake the number-one position in car sales worldwide.

• We reported on the show that 374,000 textile workers in the United States have lost their jobs since 2001, many of them replicated in China, which now produces most of the world's clothing. Why has that business gone overseas? Not because U.S. textile and apparel workers were making outrageously high salaries (usually between eight and thirteen dollars an hour), but because U.S. trade negotiators opened the American market to foreign manufacturers, primarily those based in China. Textile and apparel workers there are paid between thirty-five cents and eighty cents per hour. Ninety-six percent of our clothing is now imported.

• The U.S. airline industry has been accused of putting its cost-cutting efforts ahead of concern for safety, by sending American jobs to cheap foreign labor markets as it outsources mechanical work. The increased use of overseas maintenance contractors is one of the reasons Northwest Airlines mechanics walked off the job in 2005. Following an industry trend, Northwest has increasingly been servicing its planes in Singapore and Hong Kong, where labor costs are significantly lower than in the United States. Foreign repair shops have to be certified by the Federal Aviation Administration, but the mechanics of those shops do not have to comply with U.S. drug testing rules or criminal background checks rules.

This is a major safety concern, according to the mechanics union. I think Steve Macfarlane, of the Aircraft Mechanics Fraternal Association, put it in just the right context when he told us: "All of us fly on our own airplanes, our families do, our friends do. When you outsource an airplane, these people have no real connection to the aircraft."

A Department of Transportation Office of the Inspector General status report found that the FAA has "not responded to the shift in the source of air carriers' maintenance and continues to concentrate its inspection resources on maintenance performed at carriers' in-house maintenance facilities." Former National Transportation Safety Board chairman Jim Hall believes this lack of oversight of outside contractors is troubling. As Hall said on a broadcast, "At the same time we see the increase in outsourcing, we're seeing a decrease in the number of FAA inspectors that are assigned these responsibilities. So, I think, as the inspector general pointed out, it is an area that Congress needs to be paying attention to." Congress isn't, and neither is the Federal Aviation Administration.

To add insult to grievous injury, Northwest plans to eliminate eight hundred of its American flight attendants and replace them on international flights with foreign attendants who make as little at $250 per month. The company claims it can save more than $20 million a year by getting rid of American workers. This comes after Northwest's employees were hit with pay reductions: Pilots took a 24 percent cut; flight attendants, 21 percent; and ground workers, 19 percent. Not affected by these substantial decreases is Northwest CEO Doug Steenland. His compensation package is nearly $4.5 million, with a guaranteed annual retirement pension of nearly $1 million.

This is nothing short of outrageous. Northwest received $250 billion in federal taxpayer money to bail it out. It then decided to hire overseas workers to staff its planes and perform maintenance work. It also used that money—our tax payments, and those of its workers—to buy Airbus airplanes from Europe. It could have purchased Boeing airplanes, but it chose not to use our money to buy American. And this airline has the temerity to want to destroy twenty-five hundred American jobs?

Northwest's treatment of its employees is just one example of a nasty trend in the airline industry—an industry that on the whole received billions in taxpayer relief after September 11, 2001. It seems that no one who works for an airline is safe—except senior executives. In December 2005, pilots for UPS fought to stop the company from outsourcing work to pilots from cheap foreign labor markets. Six times a week a China Airlines 747 arrives in Nashville carrying cargo as part of the UPS supply chain, according to the Independent Pilots Association, which represents twenty-seven hundred UPS pilots. Union leaders protested that work should be done by their pilots, but UPS countered that the union had nothing to complain about, that U.S. pilots were well paid.

Economists say the UPS negotiations highlight the larger issue of globalization. They point out that job security, not salary, is the sticking point for many American workers, regardless of income bracket. According to Ross Eisenberry of the Economic Policy Institute, "There are millions of American jobs at risk, and people with a college education who have been insulated from this in the past are increasingly going to be faced with the same kind of threats that blue-collar workers have faced."

- The Department of Homeland Security awarded a multimillion-dollar contract to U.S.-based VF Solutions to produce uniforms for U.S. border patrol officers. That company, in turn, subcontracted the work out to Mexico. The result? The people who are guarding our border against illegal aliens are wearing uniforms made in the country they're watching. But the terms of the contract with VF allow the work to be done in Mexico as a cost-saving measure.

This is an embarrassment, but the situation transcends that. It becomes a security issue. As T. J. Bonner, president of the National Border Patrol Council, told the show, "It causes us great concern from a security and officer safety, and public safety standpoint. Someone could come across the border masquerading as a border patrol agent. We rely on the identification patches on there to distinguish between the good guys and the bad guys."

With border patrol uniforms made in Mexico, what other brilliant cost-saving scheme can we expect from the Bureau of Customs and Border Protection? Outsourcing of border patrol jobs?

• Ten of China's top forty exporters are U.S.-based companies, like Motorola. Our multinationals are making products in China, and then selling them back to us here. Why? Because the average manufacturing wage in China is $0.57 per hour, while the average in America is $16.68. These products aren't built in China for the Chinese to buy; the majority of the Chinese people can't afford them.

• The production of Hollywood films and television shows is frequently exported to Canada. The Canadian government is increasing subsidies that give Canadian production companies an advantage over American companies. These subsidies cut production labor costs by as much as 40 percent. Hollywood labor unions say this practice has wiped out more than twenty thousand American jobs and is a $10 billion a year drain on the U.S. economy.

• Wachovia, the fourth-largest bank in the United States, announced plans to outsource jobs. The company is set to eliminate back-office and data-processing work in this country and pay an Indian concern, Genpact, to hire workers in India to do those jobs. This is part of a corporate plan to eliminate some four thousand U.S. jobs over the next two years. Not only is Wachovia unapologetic about the quickening pace of sending work overseas, it appears downright giddy over the prospects. Wachovia's director of corporate development said, "We believe that establishing a presence in India with Genpact will improve productivity for our company and enable us to explore overseas growth opportunity."

Wachovia's chairman, Ken Thompson, has become a veritable outsourcing cheerleader: "We are buying products manufactured in low-wage countries. That's good for consumers in the United States. It creates job loss in the United States, but to try to staunch that, in my view, would be like putting your thumb in a dike to hold back the Atlantic Ocean."

On the air, I wondered what Ken Thompson would think about

the idea of bringing Filipino, Indian, and Chinese banks into American markets to see if the consumers who are now using Wachovia would prefer the lower-cost approach that those institutions might make possible. Using his logic, it would be good for the economy: more money for the consumer, more competition, greater productivity for everybody.

Need more proof that executives are increasingly decimating their workforce as they unfairly reward themselves? Here's a quote from Robert "Steve" Miller, chairman and CEO of Delphi, made as his company was heading into bankruptcy: "We are in a market for human capital, supply and demand. If you pay too much for a particular class of employees, you go broke. . . . There is a market for manufacturing labor, and we are paying triple for that labor. And there is a market for executives, and we are underpaying for it, and we are at risk of losing our management." After hearing this, I asked Steve Miller to join me on the broadcast to discuss his ideas. He chose not to. As I pointed out on the show, Miller made these profound statements about Delphi's American workers after he'd been on the job for only three months. I'd like to know how he made such determinations in just ninety days. If his intention was to blame workers for the problems that Delphi has faced over the course of a decade, that strikes me as an example of poor, and simpleminded, management.

J. T. Battenberg, the former Delphi CEO who drove the company into bankruptcy, told me that outsourcing, including building production in China, were going to be his next big strategy for Delphi. That was about a year and a half before he took the company into bankruptcy. Despite rushing into cheap foreign labor markets, Delphi's business model failed. Again, if we were to follow Delphi's lead, we should urge the company to look to the Chinese for its own CEOs, not a quick-fix executive who does a two-year tenure at various turnaround opportunities.

While Delphi is one of the most egregious examples, there are thousands of smaller cases of outsourcing that go unnoticed or unreported, yet they have the same devastating affect on American workers. Barbara Ebsch of Dayton, Ohio, is married to a union president and wrote me the following to bring attention to what outsourcing was doing in just one small factory.

> *Lou:*
> *My husband is the President of the Local 1666 International Brotherhood of Boilermakers. He is currently employed, at least for the short term, at Harris Thomas Industries Dayton Ohio. You see, his company is one of the many that is being affected by manufacturing outsourcing and business being sent overseas. This company has been in business for 82 years. With this plant closing at least 130 employees will lose their jobs and source of survival. His concern is not only himself, but with the employees who have worked every day for the last 30+ years who will lose their income, insurance, and some even their homes. My husband tried to get the local community coverage this story deserves and get this reported on the news and through the newspaper, but it only received a small one time statement. I realize this company is not a Delphi or GM, but it has at least 130 real life people that need their income and health insurance. These hard working employees took major concessions (at least 23 percent) in salary, vacation pay and holiday pay three years ago to try and save the company, but still the inevitable happened.*

Barbara's story is not unusual. Small factories all over the country are shutting down their domestic operations. Manufacturing companies have been especially hard hit by the exporting of American jobs, as the manufacturing sector was the first to take advantage of offshoring production. The result was that factories opened up overseas, and factories were shut down here. Manufacturing was followed to cheap foreign labor markets by call-center work, such as customer support. (Call centers are the facilities that handle operations for telephone-based services, including toll-free airline reservations and computer help desks.) India, with its huge number of educated English speakers, attracted scores of call centers. After all, no one sees you when you're on the phone, and few people ask where they're calling. (Indian companies were especially prescient in giving employees American nicknames and teaching them regional U.S. accents.) It wasn't long before back-office accounting and software programming were outsourced in the same manner.

Today the exporting of jobs goes far deeper than that. Professions that require higher skill sets, such as architecture, business management, law, and medicine, are already outsourcing jobs to other countries. As Daniel Pink, the author of *A Whole New Mind,* put it on the show, "You have to be able to do something that people overseas can't do cheaper, and that computers and software can't do faster. And increasingly, if you're an accountant, you face competition from a chartered accountant in India who makes five hundred a month."

Outsourcing as we've come to know it is a fairly recent practice. The word has been used for quite some time to describe the subcontracting of data-processing services or centralized corporate functions. It came about when companies that were straining to keep up with technological advances outsourced the management and maintenance of their computer systems to companies that could handle and support the technology.

Outsourcing was different than offshoring, which involved American companies producing goods and building factories in countries such as Taiwan and Korea. Many of those factories were built to extend the company's capacity as their businesses—especially in the high-tech industry—ramped up. Some of these factories were set up to create goods that would be sold in local markets: Production from a factory in Taiwan, for instance, would be distributed throughout Asia. Products made in Asia were sold in Asia. In most cases, the primary manufacturing facilities, and those building products for the American market, were still located in the United States.

Sending American experts to oversee these facilities led to a transfer of the expertise from U.S. shores to the Pacific Rim. American companies came to the conclusion that the workers in overseas factories were as good as those in stateside factories. From a big business standpoint, however, they were much more valuable. They worked for pennies on the dollar. They toiled in countries where factory safety and health regulations were essentially nonexistent, eliminating the need for expensive employee protection systems. And those countries had what can charitably be called relaxed attitudes toward environmental pollution. This last fact was especially appealing to companies that used or produced toxic chemicals in their manufacturing processes. Finally, these countries, which were almost inevitably in the third world, were willing to provide monetary incentives to almost any American company that promised to show up.

With the arrival of the Internet and the fear of Y2K, jobs in the white-collar sector likewise headed overseas. During the scare over the Y2K bug, organizations all over the world rushed to have their code upgraded or checked so that their computers wouldn't fail in the millennium. Y2K compliance threatened to overwhelm nearly every organization that depended on computers. To handle this monumental task, cheap yet skilled programmers in Bangalore offered their services to U.S. companies. Software to be checked was sent to them via the Internet and dedicated networks. The nearly instantaneous transfer of files removed the remaining barriers to doing business in real time with anyone else anywhere on the planet. It became easier to have someone review a document halfway around the world by e-mailing it than it was to walk down the hall to another person in the same office.

Plus, when goods are manufactured in outsourcing arrangements, they still have to be transported back to the United States, which takes weeks and even months. For white-collar work, getting information back via the Internet happens literally in the blink of an eye. When services are completed by the Indian workers—when an analysis is complete or a medical review written up—they're ready to ship it back to corporate America with the press of a button.

Adding to the attractiveness of a site like Bangalore is its location on the other side of the world, where its twelve-hour-long workday coincides with America's nighttime hours. Indian programmers could have their work ready for U.S. companies when they opened for business.

In the aftermath of Y2K, companies including Wipro, Infosys, and Tata began selling the capabilities of their Indian employees to U.S. companies. These employees spoke English, knew their way around computers, and worked for a tenth of the pay that American programmers were getting. From the perspective of management, there was no difference between an American worker telecommuting from his home and an Indian worker telecommuting from the other side of the globe. Except that the Indian worker was much cheaper and looked better on a profit-and-loss statement.

Corporate America immediately embraced the idea, and soon repetitive and time-consuming functions like payroll and back-office accounting were being sent overseas via high-speed telecommunications lines. Thousands of American companies now outsource their business processes and technology maintenance needs to Bangalore—a city that today has more than 150,000 programmers, nearly double the number found in Silicon Valley. These American companies are helping to create a new and prosperous middle class—in India. Salaries for programmers there average about twenty thousand, which would be just about poverty level for a family of four in the United States.

Asian countries are not the only recipients of American jobs. Research firm Datamonitor estimates call-center workstations in Central America and Latin America will double to more than 730,000 in the next two years. Costa Rica has added almost 25,000 jobs from American companies in the past two years. Nicaragua is hoping to set up 4,000 new call-center jobs over the next few years. Argentina will add 7,000 outsourced positions by 2008.

Outsourcing has made for a regrettable reversal of fortune. During the twentieth century, the United States benefited from the legal (note the word is "legal," not "illegal") migration to this country by millions of Europeans and Asians after the world wars. Some of the best minds and talents in those countries—in both the sciences and the arts—came to America then to escape their daunting postwar economies. England and Germany had to effectively cede domination in science and technology to America; Britain never quite recovered, and a post–cold war unified Germany is still figuring how to deal with it. Half a century later, it is the United States that is sending its expertise and white-collar jobs out of the country.

Business groups claiming that outsourcing is good for the U.S. economy have simply gotten it wrong. They claim that jobs lost to exportation are simply transfered to new and emerging industries—that the displaced worker ends up in a new and equivalent job. As an example, the Information Technology Association of America (ITAA), which represents many of the high-tech firms that have been at the forefront of sending jobs overseas, published a report in March 2004 that, as their press release says, "conclusively demonstrates that worldwide sourcing of computer software and services increases the number of U.S. jobs [and] improves real wages for American workers." The fundamental argument here appears to be that the more jobs we send away, the better off we all are.

The fact of the matter is that the high-paying jobs lost during the last recession are being replaced by work in lower-paying industries. It doesn't matter if you're a software programmer, a lawyer, or a medical technician—if your job gets outsourced, chances are that your next job will not pay as well as the one you've lost.

While the economic downsides alone are tremendous, there are additional disadvantages that are potentially catastrophic to each of us. Large corporations, including HMOs, insurance companies, banks, and credit card companies, are processing your personal medical and financial data in other countries, many of which don't have regulations against sharing and using that information. At least in the United States there are laws to protect such data—but U.S. law doesn't apply if the records are sent overseas.

Identity theft has become one of the recent pitfalls of outsourcing. In June 2005, the British tabloid the *Sun* reported that an Indian worker sold an undercover reporter the bank details of one thousand Britons—addresses, passwords, phone numbers, credit card numbers, and more—all for about five thousand dollars. He was employed at one of the call centers in India where dozens of American companies have been outsourcing work. Outsourcing industry insiders said they were perplexed at how anyone could have smuggled out so much data from an information-technology company. Yet in April 2005, employees of another Indian call center were arrested for allegedly obtaining passwords and transferring $350,000 from the accounts of four U.S. Citibank customers. Industry groups in India say identity theft can occur anywhere, but they concede the country has to do more to deter thieves.

U.S. taxpayers expressed their outrage when it was revealed that hundreds of thousands of tax returns were shipped overseas for preparation by various accounting firms, raising serious concerns about taxpayer privacy. After months of complaints, the IRS finally proposed regulations requiring taxpayer consent before their tax information is sent overseas.

The potential threat to privacy doesn't seem to be giving big business any reason to pause. In fact, those businesses that haven't started outsourcing yet are being encouraged to jump into the water to take advantage of cheap and unregulated labor. Boosterism for outsourcing comes from consulting firms such as McKinsey, Accenture, and Booz Allen. These companies make their money by providing counsel in matters ranging from business strategy to management compensation. They are paid for their advice, and their advice is to get rid of American workers.

I invited Diana Farrell, the director of the McKinsey Global Institute, to talk about this on the show. She cited a McKinsey study that claimed that outsourcing was good for just about everyone, and said, "The basic finding of our study is that the process of offshoring, which has gotten a lot of publicity of late, is yet another example of the integration of the developed and developing worlds into one more richer global economy, and that this represents a win-win situation for both sides." I asked her if McKinsey also recommended exporting legal work and software programming. She replied, "Let me just say that we work with executives to improve the performance. And to the extent that that involves making decisions that would help save money for the company, we will help accomplish that."

Our politicians, too, are out of touch. The top Democrat sitting on the Senate Finance Committee, Senator Max Baucus of Montana, said the shipment of American jobs to cheap foreign labor markets is here to stay, and the American people will just have to learn to live with it. In an interview with the Associated Press in India, Baucus said, "The world is flat, and we must work harder to better retrain our people. Offshoring is a fact of globalization. Opportunities for U.S. companies come from everywhere, including India." Perhaps not surprisingly, Baucus made those comments while he was visiting Bangalore—for five days—on his way home from a visit to another cheap foreign labor market, communist China. Perhaps in the future, Senator Max Baucus should limit his pandering to his constituents in Montana, instead of to the citizens of India.

Senator John Kerry attempted to take on outsourcing during his

2004 presidential campaign, but even he ultimately retreated from the issue. He initially singled out "Benedict Arnold" CEOs in comments like this: "Unlike the Bush administration, I want to repeal every tax break and loophole that rewards any Benedict Arnold CEO or corporation for shipping American jobs overseas." But in an interview with the *Wall Street Journal,* Kerry backpedaled quickly, saying, "The Benedict Arnold line applied, you know, I called a couple of times to overzealous speechwriters, and said, 'Look, that's not what I'm saying.' Benedict Arnold does not refer to somebody who in the normal course of business is going to go overseas and take jobs overseas. That happens. I support that. I understand that. I was referring to the people who take advantage of non-economic transactions purely for tax purposes—sham transactions—and give up American citizenship. That's a Benedict Arnold." There was no mention of the evils of outsourcing, and no mention of the fact that Kerry himself had been associated with Boston Capital & Technology, a company that helped American companies outsource jobs to China. He also didn't mention that he had received campaign contributions from companies that actively champion outsourcing.

Despite the reluctance of many elected officials to fight outsourcing, evidence is building against its so-called benefits, evidence that shows that sending American jobs to cheap foreign labor markets may not be exactly what American corporate managers had originally bargained for. DiamondCluster International found that 51 percent of executives responding to a survey had had to terminate agreements early due to poor-quality offshore services, or cost savings that just weren't what managers had hoped for. Deloitte & Touche, meanwhile, reported that "while 30 percent of the participants have encountered normal outsourcing growing pains, 70 percent have had significant negative experiences and are outsourcing with increasing caution and in a conservative manner."

Dun & Bradstreet added even more documentation with a 2000 survey indicating that 20 percent of outsourcing relationships failed in the first two years, and 50 percent within five years. Despite this independent confirmation of outsourcing's failure to deliver, this information has not been stopping anyone, including Deloitte. Deloitte is still outsourcing itself—its accountants—to India, where it is adding more than four thousand people to serve its U.S. clients.

As I said earlier, there is a virtual conspiracy of silence regarding the truth about outsourcing. Its value has been so overstated that the Bush administration had to resort to doctoring a major report that was critical of the exportation of American jobs before the last presidential election. As we reported on the show, a Commerce Department report on outsourcing was delayed for four months while it was rewritten to better fit the administration's official stand. This twelve-page report cost more than three hundred thousand dollars to produce, and was delivered to Congress more than a year late. Its release came only after a Freedom of Information Act filing by a magazine called *Manufacturing and Technology News* and under pressure from the House Science Committee, which had funded the study.

More disturbing than its cost and its delay is that the report presented to Congress was not the report that the analysts had written. In the rewritten version, Congress was told that it is "not possible to determine whether the shift of U.S. work to non-U.S. locations resulted in job losses for U.S. workers." Yet at a presentation in December 2005, the report's authors stated that there is a "surplus of low-cost, technically-skilled labor in other countries," and that there is "growing pressure in corporate America to offshore IT work."

Representative David Wu, who is on the committee that commissioned the report, issued a statement saying that the document did not address its congressional mandate, and expressing his concern that it had been substantially changed. The committee's ranking member, Congressman Bart Gordon from Tennessee, dismissed it as "a scrubbed-down, whitewashed report." The Commerce Department denied that it had been changed or was biased, and announced that it was in the middle of a second study on offshoring. This report is on a two-year time frame, and will cost us $2 million.

A key report about an issue critical to millions of Americans was changed by our own government, doctored without explanation or apology. The government in point of fact lied to us, and again failed the working men and women of this country. As in any conflict, truth is one of the casualties in this war on our middle class.

— Chapter 8 —

Broken Borders

The United States has more than 7,500 miles of border: 5,525 miles to the north, and 1,989 to the south. Each year an estimated twenty thousand illegal aliens cross our border with Canada. Each year as many as three million illegal aliens cross our border with Mexico.

Nearly ten thousand people enter this country illegally every single day. And the number has been rising ever since President Bush started talking about his guest-worker amnesty plans and our Congress took up the issue of so-called immigration reform. Illegal aliens cross our borders not only with impunity, but with confidence that they will not be caught by our undermanned and ill-equipped border patrol, that they will be welcomed by friends and family, and often that they will have a job waiting for them. At the southern border they are aided in their incursions by Mexican smugglers and, once inside our borders, by ethnocentric activist organizations and church and community groups. Even if caught, illegal aliens know that the worst that will happen is that they will either be released into our society with a promise to appear at a later court date, or deported back to their country of origin. In either eventuality, they have either succeeded in entering our country illegally or are free to try again.

Against what has become an invasion of illegal aliens, we've placed roughly ten thousand border agents on our southern border. Because of the overwhelming numbers of attempts and the lack of facilities in which to detain even those who are caught, the border patrol has adopted a catch-and-release policy that all but ensures that illegal aliens will manage to enter our country. Border patrol agents use a rough calculation to determine how many illegal aliens do succeed in reaching the United States. Last year, they foiled 1.2 million attempts on the southern border. Extrapolating from that figure, more than 60 percent of illegal aliens were still successful in achieving what the Mexican government calls their "migration" to El Norte.

While no one—not the border patrol, not the immigration and customs enforcement agencies, not the FBI or the Department of Homeland Security, not the Congress or the president—knows precisely how many illegal aliens are now living in this country, the estimates range from eleven million all the way up to twenty million.

But we do know that the government of Mexico encourages its poorest citizens to cross our border, to live and work in the United States. We do know that those people are sending more than $20 billion in remittances back to Mexico each year. And those remittances from Mexican citizens living in the United States are by some reports the single largest source of revenue for the nation of Mexico, well ahead of even their second largest source, which is the export of oil. No wonder that President Vicente Fox and the government of Mexico not only do nothing to prevent Mexican citizens from illegally crossing our borders, but in fact promote it.

Most of the illegal aliens from Mexico don't require much encouragement. Mexico itself has a population of more than one hundred million people, and a poverty rate of about 50 percent, despite an abundance of natural resources, an influx of investment capital, (primarily from the United States), and an annual trade surplus with the United States alone of more than $50 billion. The United States is often depicted in our national media as a magnet for the impoverished and uneducated, who make up about 70 percent of all illegal aliens, but the truth is much more complex than that: The United States has in effect become Mexico's political and social safety valve.

Mexicans seeking to enter the United States are fleeing poverty, joblessness, and government corruption at both the provincial and national levels. In rural areas, only 58 percent of Mexican citizens have access to drinking water, while only 26 percent have access to sanitation services. American employers of illegal aliens exploit them, sometimes mercilessly, but even then, the Mexican citizen working here is earning a fortune in relative terms compared to what would be possible in Mexico.

As bad as the living conditions in Mexico are, they're even worse in Central American countries like Guatemala and El Salvador, and in South American countries like Bolivia. Seventy-five percent of Guatemalans live below the poverty line, as do half the people in Nicaragua, nearly 35 percent of El Salvadorans and 64 percent of the population of Bolivia. The poverty that is pervasive throughout much of Central and South America is held up by open borders and illegal immigration advocates as the humanitarian reason to permit illegal immigration to continue to go unchecked. If impoverishment is indeed a justification for allowing illegal immigration, then why are we not opening U.S. borders and ports to the more than five billion people in the world who live in poverty equal to—and in most cases, greater than—that found in Mexico? That truth inconveniences the ethnocentric open borders and illegal immigration activists, who happen to be almost universally Hispanic and Latino. Of course, the land bridge between South and Central

America and the United States offers American employers of illegal aliens an irresistible and convenient labor force, a convenience of proximity that is only enhanced by our porous southern border.

This country faces an extraordinary immigration crisis, in part because of those broken borders. The Bush administration, with the acquiescence of both Republicans and Democrats in Congress, has chosen not to enforce our immigration laws, or do anything significant to secure our borders—even with the threat of attack by radical Islamists.

The result of our government's paltry solutions is that there are now more illegal immigrants in this country than there are legal immigrants. The government's own estimates of an illegal immigrant population of eight to twelve million includes six million unauthorized workers, representing nearly 5 percent of our total workforce—at a time when we have 5 percent unemployment among actual citizens. These people pay no taxes, yet they are given jobs and provided free schooling, and now our government wants to offer them benefits that are not given to many middle-class taxpayers, such as amnesty on taxes owed and protection from prosecution.

America has become a nation of broken borders. People enter our country seemingly at will, without regard for our laws. They threaten our safety and security, they use our resources, and they take our jobs. The direct net cost of illegal immigration to our economy, including social services, is now roughly $45 billion annually, according to the Federation for American Immigration Reform. Illegal immigration depresses wages, leads to job losses, and drains the U.S. economy of public funds for social services and education.

Note that we are talking about *illegal* immigration. This is far different than legal immigration, and the distinction needs to be made—apparently over and over again. Legal immigration is vitally important to our country and its future. Every year, more than a million people from other countries come to work in the

United States, bringing valuable expertise and skills to our nation. And each of them does so with the written approval of our government. Others come seeking a better life, a new life, or a different way of life. They, too, are given permission. In point of fact, the United States has the most generous immigration policy in the world, and grants citizenship to more immigrants than any other developed country. Of the million people earning legal status in 2004, more than 400,000 were relatives of U.S. citizens, 50,000 obtained a green card through a lottery system meant to keep immigration diverse, and at least 71,000 found refuge fleeing persecution. Citizens of Mexico obtain the largest number of green cards every year—more than applicants from India, the Philippines, and China combined.

But hundreds of thousands of people continue to enter the United States without permission, without approval, and without our consent. They come nonetheless, skirting our laws and flouting our rules. When people are entering our country illegally—meaning against the law—then we need to put a stop to it.

A key reason that millions of illegal aliens are here is that there are plenty of employers willing to break our immigration laws. These employers don't face a labor shortage—they want the cheapest labor possible. Hiring these illegals cuts into the wages of American workers. A National Academy of Sciences study found that more than 40 percent of the wage losses of low-skilled workers was due to competition from immigrant workers. Other research from the early 1990s found that more than seven hundred thousand low-skill U.S. workers were jobless because of illegal immigration. This is a problem that the Bush administration chooses to overlook because it considers these low-wage workers a desirable part of our economy.

In that light, groups such as the conservative think tank the Cato Institute have proposed the legalization of illegal Mexican migration. Not surprisingly, the National Restaurant Association and the U.S.

Chamber of Commerce are among the groups supporting this plan. These organizations say they believe that the number of Americans willing to take the low-skilled jobs now done by illegal aliens is shrinking. This argument is flawed, and does not acknowledge the fact that pay for jobs that go to illegals would have to be raised to make them attractive to American workers. Americans should be paid nothing less than a fair wage regardless of the type of work.

Over a two-month period in the spring of 2006, illegal aliens and their supporters called for demonstrations and boycotts around the nation. Their intent was to derail immigration reform by showing just how important immigrants are to the economic underpinnings of the United States. They chose May 1 to try, as some organizers explained, to shut down many of our nation's cities. The selection of May 1 was intentional—it is the worldwide day of commemorative demonstrations honoring workers by various socialist, communist, and even anarchist organizations. The organizers called the economic boycott "A Day Without Immigrants." Not illegal immigrants, mind you, but immigrants.

Hundreds of thousands of immigrants, both legal and illegal, demonstrated in big cities across the United States. Many businesses planned for the demonstrations and closed for the day, including large meat-packing plants that typically hire immigrants. Outside of minor disruptions, the nation's economy did not, in fact, buckle or crumble. Perhaps the most obvious effect the demonstrations had was to cloak the debate on immigration reform in the guise of an attack on all immigrants, as opposed to an issue about controlling illegal immigration. That was exactly the intent of many of the radical organizers, including groups like ANSWER and Latino Movement USA.

In fact, it struck me many times throughout the day how well the organizers had been able to skirt the issue, and how complicit the national media was in supporting them. *USA Today* headlined its reporting of the demonstrations "On Immigration's Front

Lines." The *New York Times* titled its story "With Calls for Boycott by Immigrants, Employers Gird for Unknown." The *Washington Post* and the *Los Angeles Times* both called their coverage "The Immigration Debate," while CNN and Fox News had banners announcing "A Day Without Immigrants." MSNBC chose to run with "Immigrant Anger." These major news outlets obviously didn't want to disturb their viewers and readers with the fact that the demonstrations and boycott were about illegal immigration and amnesty for illegal aliens.

I spent the day on various radio and television shows pointing out that immigration reform isn't aimed at people who are here legally. It is about securing our porous borders, dealing with illegal immigration, and enforcing our laws. On Larry King's show that night, I joined New Mexico governor Bill Richardson, Senate majority leader Bill Frist, California congresswoman Dana Rohrbacher, and Janet Murguia of the National Council of La Raza to discuss the boycott and the underlying issues. To my surprise, both Senator Frist and Governor Richardson—both of whom are fully supportive of the president's amnesty program—stated that they were in complete agreement with the assertion that immigration reform had to begin with border control. As Senator Frist said, "We're going to have comprehensive reform come out of the United States Senate, and we're going to address what Lou has put forward on tightening the border. . . . And I agree enforcement has to be first and foremost. . . . And I also think the criticism is correct that we have failed miserably. Our borders are porous." Governor Richardson added that we need to "dramatically tighten border security, more Border Patrol agents, more equipment, dramatically more detection efforts. Secondly, you have got to penalize employers that knowingly hire illegal workers, and we're not doing it, the laws being enforced."

Although these elected officials agree that our border security is abysmal, and the enforcement of our immigration laws weak, Congress cannot commit itself to legislation that addresses the seriousness of the issue. The failures of the various immigration proposals—Cornyn-Kyl, Hagel-Martinez, Sensenbrenner, and others—to achieve any sort of consensus in the legislature is disturbing. Not that any one of these proposals would solve all the problems (some would actually exacerbate them), but Congress has done just about everything rather than face the issue head-on.

On May 25, the U.S. Senate voted for what it called a comprehensive immigration reform bill, a bill that would give amnesty to millions of illegal aliens. The vote was sixty-two in favor, thirty-six against. It was a major victory for corporate America and special interests, as well as a major defeat for middle-class Americans who now face a new onslaught of cheap imported labor. The legislation is flawed in so many ways that it is utterly breathtaking. The Senate laid bare its motivation and its disregard for border security by adopting an absurd provision that requires consultation with the government of Mexico before the U.S. government can build a security fence on our southern border. If there is any doubt whatsoever about who's in charge of U.S. immigration policy, and now border security, it should be dispelled.

The Senate passed this so-called immigration reform bill without addressing the legislation's massive impact on our legal system or on the agencies responsible for enforcing that legislation should it become law. It ignored the huge economic and financial cost to taxpayers, which could amount to as much as $54 billion over the next ten years. While just an estimate, that figure is still many times more than the cost of the House immigration bill, which focuses primarily on border security.

It is the men and women of the middle class who pay the price, not only as taxpayers but as working people. Some estimates put the overall wages lost by U.S. workers due to high immigration levels at $200 billion annually. The excessive immigration of low-skilled workers in particular is a drag on our economy. Over the past ten years, more than two million low-skilled American workers have been displaced from their jobs. And each 10 percent increase in the immigrant workforce decreases U.S. wages by 3.5 percent. Under our current immigration policies, immigrants to the United States can utilize expensive social services while offering little more in return than unskilled labor. Providing services to immigrants during the mid-1990s, for instance, cost tax-paying Californians $1,200 a year per household. States spend more than $7 billion each year on K–12 education for illegal aliens, and hundreds of millions more in treating illegal aliens in border-state hospitals.

Why is this allowed to happen? Why are so many illegal aliens allowed to stay here, and why are politicians refusing to enforce immigration laws? And why do politicians offer these people access to medical care and education, and even offer to give them citizenship once they've snuck into our country?

The answer is simple: It's what big business wants.

Big business not only favors illegal immigration, but thrives on it. Large corporations, especially agriculture companies, utilize illegal aliens in their fields and in their factories. They do it for the simple reasons that these people will not only work for less than a fair wage but won't demand any benefits. For corporate America, they offer a convenient way to cut expenses and improve the bottom line. It's an even cheaper method than outsourcing; with illegal immigration, the inexpensive workers come to *them.*

Here is where immigration strikes right to the heart of the middle class. Corporate America and our elected officials claim that illegal immigrants do the jobs Americans won't do. They imply that work in agriculture or construction is beneath Americans, who are assuredly entitled to do more valuable forms of work. This is complete nonsense. The issue isn't about the jobs Americans won't do; it's about jobs that companies and businesses and employers won't pay for. And that is a critical difference.

Show me those Americans who won't work on farms for decent pay. Show me those Americans who won't do landscaping or construction if you pay them what their effort is worth. It's tough work, and it's worth far more than the seven dollars or twelve dollars per hour that illegal immigrants get. Increase that pay, and include the necessary benefits, and you'll have no trouble finding Americans ready to take such jobs.

On the other hand, show me companies paying fair wages for those jobs. There are precious few. Most have dropped wages and working conditions to levels that are unacceptable to the citizens of this country. Corporations claim that they can't pay more for this kind of labor because it would make goods too expensive for Americans to buy. That's not true. For example, according to one study we reported on, farm wages could go up by as much as 40 percent, and it would add less than ten dollars a year to the average family food bill for fruits and vegetables. On the other hand, this increase in wages would, at the very least, finally put worker pay above the poverty level.

The litany of offenses that our government and big business has committed in turning a blind eye toward—perhaps "embracing" is a more accurate term—illegal immigration would be almost laughable if they didn't have such dire consequences for our economy and our national security. I'll list some of them here. I think they speak for themselves.

- Two states, Arizona and New Mexico, declared states of emergency in 2005 as their borders were overrun by illegal aliens. Yet during his 2006 State of the Union speech, President Bush said only this on the subject: "Our nation needs orderly and secure borders. To meet this goal, we must have stronger immigration enforcement and border protection. And we must have a rational, humane guest worker program that rejects amnesty, allows temporary jobs for people who seek them legally, and reduces smuggling and crime at the border." That's a whole forty-one seconds devoted to our nation's border security crisis out of an hourlong speech.

• One month after his statement that "our nation needs orderly and secure borders," President Bush adamantly defended a deal that would allow six of our key seaports to be operated by Dubai Ports World, a company owned by the government of Dubai, one of the United Arab Emirates states. The UAE's record on terrorism is appalling, and it has direct ties to some of the people responsible for the 9/11 terrorist attacks. The UAE was also one of only three countries to recognize the government set up by the Taliban in Afghanistan. Senator Susan Collins (R-Maine), the chairwoman of the Senate Government Affairs and Homeland Security Committee, pointed out, "Although the UAE is an ally in the war on terrorism, the country has historically been used as a base of terrorist operations and financing." Still, the president insisted that there was no problem with the UAE maintaining our ports in New York, New Jersey, Philadelphia, Baltimore, Miami, and New Orleans, claiming the UAE has been a good friend and ally. This is a clear-cut national security issue, but it was presented as if it was merely a matter of international commerce. Thus it was part of business as usual: more of the best government foreign money can buy.

• As we reported on our broadcast, only 5 percent of all the cargo containers that come into this country's ports are inspected. These containers are shipped from all over the world, yet virtually all of them are passing though our borders without the briefest glance or assurance that their cargo is what it claims to be—and not carrying something dangerous or potentially deadly.

• The border patrol arrested 1.17 million people trying to cross the border illegally in 2005. Many of those arrested are freed shortly after their detainment rather than being held, as they once were, in jails to await deportation or processing. Instead, they are simply handed a notice to appear in court, and released into the country. As you'd probably expect, somewhere between 70 and 90 percent never show up for their court date. Even Immigration and Customs Enforcement, the largest investigative arm of the Department of Homeland Security, admits that nearly half a million people have been arrested and released, and have failed to appear in court.

Local law enforcement and border patrol agents explain that the issue is one of resources, that federal agencies have limited funds for detention and deportation. Instead, they have shifted their focus to apprehending illegal aliens who have committed or are wanted for crimes. Yet eighty-five thousand of those released into the United States are known criminals.

Steven Camarota, director of research at the Center for Immigration Studies, blames the lack of enforcement on political issues rather than on practical ones. As he says, "The problem with immigration has always been the same: It's very heavily penetrated by very powerful interest groups, and that makes it very hard to enforce the law. The ethnic advocacy groups provide the moral outrage and racial politics, while the business community provides the political influence, the big guns, and the big money to prevent law enforcement."

- The Farmworker Association of Florida and the Coalition of Florida Farmworker Organizations are suing FEMA on behalf of illegal aliens. The groups say the federal government was wrong to deny housing and other aid to illegal aliens who were displaced by Hurricanes Katrina and Rita in 2005. In fact, the federal government gave emergency assistance, food, water, shelters or hotel rooms, and even cash to those who needed it in the wake of the hurricanes regardless of their status as either legal resident or illegal alien. At least half of all farmworkers in Florida are illegal aliens, and they provide cheap labor. The two Florida plaintiffs, which represent three hundred thousand of the state's farmworkers, maintain that illegal workers have a right to FEMA trailers because they are crucial to the Florida agricultural industry. Obviously, the workers' employers, the farmers and growers, are committing crimes by hiring them. And because they're here illegally, the farmers are not providing for them, but instead are trying to push the expense of taking care of their cheap labor force onto American taxpayers.

- Homeland security officials have all but conceded that they have lost the war to control our nation's border with Mexico. The rate of violence there increased by 100 percent between 2004 and 2005. In the fiscal year that ended in September 2005, there were roughly eight hundred attacks on the border patrol.
- The Dallas school district has so many illegal alien students who don't speak English that it is considering hiring illegal alien teachers to solve its shortage of bilingual faculty. Dallas public education officials say they need seven hundred bilingual teachers, and they want to fill those jobs by hiring illegal aliens. That's against federal law, and is punishable by six months in jail and fines of three thousand dollars per employee. The school district claims it can't find enough qualified American citizens to take those low-paying teaching jobs. It's interesting to note that the Dallas school district isn't considering offering higher pay. The average teacher in the Dallas school district earns forty-eight thousand dollars a year. The average Dallas high school football coach's annual salary is seventy thousand dollars.
- Illegal immigrants are not the only people taking advantage of our insecure borders. United States Customs and Border Protection says that over the past decade, there have been as many as 231 border incursions by people who appear to be Mexican government or military personnel. Mexico claims its soldiers are ordered to keep at least three miles from the U.S. border, yet law enforcement officials near El Paso, Texas, say they are certain the Mexican military has tried to cross the U.S. border and smuggle drugs into this country. One incident occurred in Hudspeth County, Texas, about fifty miles east of El Paso on the Rio Grande, where three SUVs and one Mexican military Humvee crossed the Rio Grande. The SUVs then drove about twelve miles into the United States

before sheriff's deputies and highway patrol officers caught up with them. After an armed standoff with nearly thirty sheriff's deputies and border patrol agents, two of the SUVs returned to the Mexican side of the river. A third SUV was recovered by U.S. deputies with more than fourteen hundred pounds of marijuana inside.

Mexico denies that armed members of its military have been crossing into the United States. The Mexican ambassador to the United States, Carlos De Icaza, shrugged off the controversy by saying, "We have a long, long border. And sometimes American soldiers or Mexican soldiers just cross a little because the demarcation may not be clear or whatever. But this incident does not involve Mexican military personnel." As we reported on our broadcast, Juan Carlos Foncerrada Berumen, consul general of Mexico said, "We totally reject any kind of assumption that pertain to involve the Mexican army in these incidents." He then went on to tell the Associated Press that U.S. troops "disguised as Mexican soldiers with Humvees might have been protecting the drug smugglers." The White House had no response.

The president of the National Border Patrol Council, T. J. Bonner, says that this was not the first time such a confrontation had happened along the Mexican border. "When you have people who are dressed in military uniforms, driving military Humvees, carrying military weapons, I would say that in all likelihood these are people who are in the military. Mexico has not been candid with us and forthright in their assessment of some of these incidents. So it falls upon us to protect our sovereignty." This is a violation of U.S. sovereignty, no matter who these people are, or what they're wearing.

• President Bush's $2.8 trillion 2007 budget calls for a significant increase of $1.5 billion in funding for border security. At first glance, the proposal seems to be tough on illegal immigration and border security, and includes $500 million for fifteen hundred more border patrol agents, $400 million for more detention space, and $100 million for new border security technology.

Yet the White House also proposes to eliminate about $400 million in federal payments to help cover the costs of jailing criminal illegal aliens. California alone spends nearly double that amount each year. The budget calls for completing a small portion of border fencing near San Diego, but ignores the seven hundred miles of additional barriers already approved by the House. A closer look at the budget also reveals that the president wants nearly $250 billion to implement his proposed temporary worker program. Though he denies that the program represents amnesty for illegal aliens, that's exactly what it does. By the way, a *Time* magazine poll in early 2006 showed that nearly two thirds of those surveyed disapproved of the president's handling of immigration. He's obviously not interested in the will of the people when it comes to immigration reform.

• An Arizona-based group funded and run mostly by churches is literally mapping the route for illegal aliens to make their way into the United States. The organization, Humane Borders, is distributing high-resolution maps to potential migrants in Mexico, showing how to safely cross the border illegally. The maps help aliens locate water stations, border patrol rescue beacons, roads, and railroad tracks, and they show how far aliens can expect to walk in one, two, or three days. The maps also indicate where other illegal aliens have died trying to cross the Arizona desert, and contain warnings to potential border crossers saying, "Don't go. There's not enough water, and it's not worth it." Initially the Mexican government's human rights arm agreed to print and distribute the maps in Mexico, although it has since backed off that promise.

According to Reverend Robin Hoover, the president of Humane Borders, "Our experience is that many, many of the migrants do not understand what they're about to experience when they cross the border. We believe that the most basic level of ethics is informed consent." Of course, there was no mention of the informed consent of U.S. immigration authorities. And it's telling that Humane Borders announced its plan not in the United States, but in Mexico City.

• Illegal aliens in San Antonio, Texas, have been dodging immigration officials for years with the help of a Spanish-language radio station, KROM, which is owned by Univision. The station runs a recurring segment during which listeners call in and report where they have seen so-called *limones verdes*—green limes—the code name for immigration agents who wear olive green uniforms and drive around in green vehicles.

• When Hurricane Mitch struck Honduras and Nicaragua in 1998, President Bill Clinton allowed some 150,000 people from those countries to stay in the United States for eighteen months without risk of deportation, by granting them temporary protected status. Eight years and five extensions later, a majority of those refugees remain. Seventy thousand Hondurans and 3,600 Nicaraguans are still here, with the right to work. Five years after two earthquakes devastated El Salvador, there are 222,000 Salvadorans who are in the United States, working temporarily. Even if their status expires, there's little chance they will be deported, since Immigration and Customs Enforcement's stated focus is national security and violent criminals.

The fact that these predecessors to President Bush's planned "guest worker program" can't handle an existing situation raises questions about just how feasible any future one will be. My guess is that it won't work, and I'm not alone in that assessment. In fact, during his Senate confirmation process, the new director of the U.S. Citizenship and Immigration Services, Emilio Gonzalez, said, "I don't think the systems—in fact, I know the systems that exist right now wouldn't be able to handle it."

• We reported that, in 2005, some twenty-four hundred cars were driven across the border illegally into Yuma County, Arizona. Half of those resulted in law enforcement pursuits. More than one hundred officers were assaulted. Yuma's sheriff estimates 75 percent of the crime in Yuma is related to illegal immigration.

- In January 2006, the United States shut down the largest border tunnel ever discovered on the U.S.–Mexican border, a passage linking Otay Mesa, California, with an industrial neighborhood near the airport in Tijuana, Mexico. This tunnel is almost a half mile in length, seventy-five feet deep, has electricity and a ventilation system, and is lined with concrete. Inside, officials found an estimated two tons of marijuana. Police were first tipped off to its existence in 2004, and finally found it after a two-year search, using ground-penetrating radar. Since September 2001, law enforcement officials have discovered some twenty-one tunnels beneath the Arizona and California borders with Mexico. Officials are not ruling out the possibility that the Otay Mesa tunnel may have—surprise—also been used to smuggle illegal aliens into the United States.
- California has an absurd state education policy that rewards illegal alien students while effectively penalizing middle-class American citizens from outside the state. Out-of-state students who attend California colleges pay about seventeen thousand dollars a year more in tuition than in-state students. Incredibly, illegal aliens pay the cheaper in-state tuition rate. Activists have filed a class-action lawsuit on behalf of sixty thousand out-of-state students who are forced to pay higher tuition in California, arguing that the state has been violating a federal law since it began giving illegal aliens reduced tuition in 2002. The University of California says it believes in-state tuition for illegal aliens is consistent with federal law. Many immigration reform advocates believe that the policy, legal or not, is wrong. They contend that offering illegal aliens in-state tuition benefits denied to out-of-state students functions as an open invitation for illegal aliens to simply break the law. When California lawmakers first tried to approve reduced tuition for illegal aliens, the law was vetoed by then governor Gray Davis. It eventually passed

without his signature. California is one of nine states that offer discounted tuition to illegal aliens, and a similar lawsuit has also been filed in Kansas.

Meanwhile, Congress is thinking about cutting back student loans to the tune of $14 billion. These loans are one of the primary sources of financing for middle-class and working-class kids in this country who want a college education. One of the points to note is that by giving tuition benefits to illegal aliens, the states are taking more funding away from citizen students.

• The nation's top law enforcement official, Attorney General Alberto Gonzales, who refuses to enforce immigration laws, wrote a memo blasting immigration judges for being too tough on illegal aliens. The memo condemns the conduct of some of them as "intemperate or even abusive," and was issued after several appellate judges reviewing the immigration courts' work criticized the handling of cases. Immigration judges responded by pointing to the increase in illegal aliens crossing into the United States and the corresponding spike in their caseloads. The nation's 215 immigration judges handled 254,000 cases and other matters in 2000. In 2005, that number was up 27 percent, to 350,000 cases. Plus, immigration judges act as their own bailiff and court reporter, don't have their own law clerks, and work with outdated equipment. They are among the most overworked judges in the country. For the attorney general to focus on this particular issue while allowing his Justice Department to completely ignore the enforcement of immigration law sends a loud, clear statement about its sorry state.

• In Burbank, California, residents were outraged over a day laborer site at a new Home Depot. These sites provide a fixed location for illegal immigrants who are looking for work—and an easy way for employers to find them. The city forced Home Depot to build the center and to pay ninety-four thousand dollars a year to operate it. Neighboring Glendale also required Home Depot to pay for a day laborer center, and Los Angeles is considering a law requiring all home improvement stores to open them. Area residents said it was outrageous that Burbank's city officials and Home Depot executives were making it easier for illegal alien day workers to break the law. As we reported on the show, the number of illegals in front of the centers in southern California has doubled in the last three years. Home Depot transferred ownership of the center to the city, and its management to Catholic Charities, one of the largest groups advocating against tighter control of illegal immigration. It also supports expanded rights for illegal aliens.

• Illegal aliens being paid substandard wages and off the books creates a massive underground economy that drags down wages for millions of working Americans, while cheating American taxpayers. They're gardeners and nannies, and construction, restaurant, and garment workers, usually getting paid under the table in cash. A new study by the Milken Institute found that at least 15 percent of all jobs in Los Angeles County are part of this undocumented economy, and that more than half of them are filled by illegal aliens. The result is the loss of more than $2 billion a year in Social Security, Medicare, workers' compensation, and other taxes in Los Angeles alone. The study found that the underground jobs drive down wages for aboveboard workers by about 10 percent.

• Mexico's president Vicente Fox has blasted the plan to build a seven-hundred-mile fence along the U.S.–Mexico border, which he charges would violate the rights of illegal aliens. He was indignant at the idea that a fence was needed to keep illegal aliens from entering the United States, describing it as "disgraceful and shameful." Fox has long called for the easing of U.S. immigration laws. Rough estimates suggest that as much as 10 percent of the population of Mexico has entered the United States illegally. Fox is exporting his poverty and importing a substantial portion of his economy thanks to the millions of Mexicans living in the United States who send billions of dollars back to Mexico every year.

Fox has hired the Dallas-based public relations firm Allyn & Company to improve Mexico's image with the American people. The company worked on Fox's 2000 election campaign, and has boasted that they're the Texans who made Fox president. The Mexican government hired the agency again to stir up opposition to the recent immigration reform bill. Radio ads have also aired throughout Mexico, urging workers injured on the job in the United States to sue their employers. The country is lobbying religious, business, and community leaders in the United States, an effort that is likely just the beginning of an expensive battle that could dwarf national election campaigns. Mexico has effectively used U.S. public relations expertise before, notably in the early 1990s when it was promoting the passage of NAFTA, the very agreement that has helped create the illegal immigration crisis now facing the United States.

When the Senate Judiciary Committee approved illegal immigration legislation in late March 2006—with provisions for a so-called guest worker program for illegal aliens residing in this country—Fox took credit, explaining that the bill resulted from five years of work that began with his inauguration as Mexico's president in 2000. He said it was one step closer to Mexico's goal of "legalization for everyone" who works in the United States. According to Fox, "They're working with dignity, with productivity. They're doing fine in contributing to the United States economy. The least they deserve is to be recognized as legal in their work, and recognize their human and labor rights."

Mexican media commentators went even further, interpreting the lack of strong immigration reform as a payback for Mexico's defeat in the Mexican-American War of 1848. During the huge demonstrations against immigration reform held in Los Angeles in March, Alberto Tinoco of the Televisa television network said, "With all due respect to Uncle Sam, this shows Los Angeles has never stopped being ours."

- Senators John Cornyn (R-Texas) and Jon Kyl (R-Arizona) sponsored the Comprehensive Enforcement and Immigration Reform

Act of 2005 to address issues of border security. These two men are well aware of the extent of the problem; their states account for approximately 85 percent of our country's southern border. Cornyn is also the chairman of the Immigration, Border Security, and Citizenship subcommittee, while Kyl is the chairman of the Terrorism, Technology, and Homeland Security subcommittee. The two senators put together what I considered the strongest, albeit imperfect, solution to immigration reform. Their plan calls for the addition of 10,000 border patrol agents and 1,250 new customs and border protection officers; authorizes $5 billion over five years for surveillance technology and checkpoints; and requires all illegal immigrants currently in the United States to depart, and then to reapply for entrance through proper legal channels.

Representative James Sensenbrenner, Jr. (R-Wisconsin), sponsored his own bill in 2005 to amend the Immigration and Nationality Act to strengthen enforcement of the immigration laws, and to enhance border security. This bill, which passed in the House, would provide more manpower and resources for the border patrol and other immigration authorities, and would increase penalties for smuggling illegal aliens, repeated illegal entries, and crimes committed by illegal aliens. And it would require all employers to verify the legal status of their workers. Not surprisingly, a coalition of business, labor, and religious groups announced their opposition to the bill, which many consider the toughest border security measure ever to pass Congress. Two major labor unions, the U.S. Chamber of Commerce, the Conference of Catholic Bishops, and the American Jewish Committee all came out in support of amnesty for illegal aliens, and for the passage of the president's illegal alien guest worker program. This coalition vowed to do everything it could to defeat the House border security legislation and to support a weaker bill, including guest worker provisions, that is soon to be debated in the Senate.

Thomas Donohue, president of the U.S. Chamber of Commerce,

said of the Sensenbrenner bill on our show: "It is an unworkable enforcement bill that fails to recognize the contributions of immigrants and our growing need for them in the future."

Mark Franken, of the U.S. Conference of Catholic Bishops, concurred: "For those who are here in an unauthorized status, a number—eleven million—and they have been contributing members of our society. Give them an opportunity to earn the right to remain." The Catholic Church fears that if this bill passes, priests could be prosecuted for aiding illegal aliens, among other things. It is calling upon its members to do all they can to defeat the border security legislation.

Terry O'Sullivan, head of the Laborers International Union of North America: "It is not honest or fair to simply ignore or disrespect the eleven million undocumented workers who are already here."

• Among the top priorities of the U.S. Chamber of Commerce is fighting any legislation that would crack down on illegal immigration and the businesses that hire illegal aliens. The border security bill, which passed last year in the House of Representatives, also increases the penalties for hiring them. Tom Donohue calls the curbs "unreasonable and unfair," and said, "some provisions could potentially turn businesspeople into criminals and workers into felons." As far as I'm concerned, those who hire illegal aliens already are criminals, and the businesses that knowingly hire them should be punished. The chamber's position is self-serving in the extreme—it's concerned with what its CEO membership wants. I would be willing to bet that if illegal CEOs started immigrating into this country, our borders would be shut tighter than a locked door inside of a week.

We've had problems trying to implement immigration reform for decades, in large part because we try to solve the problem after the immigrants are already here, instead of taking proactive steps to secure our borders. In 1986, President Reagan signed a controversial bill granting amnesty to millions of illegal aliens. He was widely criticized for rewarding illegal behavior and virtually ignoring those who had been waiting for legal entry into the United States. The chief Senate sponsor of the bill, Alan Simpson from Wyoming, admitted at the time that the legislation's prospective effects were unclear. Nonetheless, Congress granted amnesty to illegal aliens then, despite warnings that it would only encourage more illegal immigration.

The former senator and all the rest of us now know what the legislation's effects actually were: We still haven't been able to secure our borders. In 1986, there were four million illegal aliens living in this country. Now, two decades later, there are an estimated twenty million illegal aliens here. Even a liberal like Senator Ted Kennedy has admitted that the original plan didn't work, and he acknowledges, "In the 1980s, the rate of illegal immigration was forty thousand people a year. Today it's half a million." And that's a conservative estimate.

Unbelievably, some members of Congress want to solve our current problem by simply making illegal aliens legal. This kind of mindlessness is breathtaking. The White House, meanwhile, is interested in offering many of these illegal aliens amnesty in the form of a guest worker program. Washington doesn't understand that even if it provides amnesty for eleven to twenty million illegal aliens, there's not a single plan in place that would prevent another eleven to twenty million illegal aliens from entering the country.

The illegal immigration bill that came out of the Senate Judiciary Committee is a product of business as usual in Washington. It is driven by a pro-amnesty lobby that has its roots in both political parties; in corporate America; and in American labor, religious, and of course media groups. Those fighting immigration reform are groups like the National Council of La Raza and LULAC, the League of United Latin American Citizens. What's not readily apparent is that they're being supported financially by companies including Wal-Mart, Levi Strauss, and Home Depot, as well as interested groups like the Nike Foundation, and even the AFL-CIO. That unions support illegal amnesty perhaps shouldn't come as a surprise. The United Food and Commercial Workers International Union put it most succinctly when they announced, "We don't care about green cards. We care about union cards." Self-interest doesn't get any plainer than that.

I'm not aware of a single guest worker program that's ever worked in this country. I don't know why we're even talking about guest workers when we have documents like the L1 Visa, which employers can apply for legally. Using it, they could bring in the labor they need, and by the way, be responsible for those workers. They would pay taxes, and have those employees pay taxes, as opposed to keeping that cash off the books. In point of fact, that would get rid of this shroud of nonsense and obfuscation surrounding the issue of border security. But corporate America is so hell-bent on exploiting illegal labor and the poorest of our working people in this country that they are lobbying for keeping an open border.

Any discussion of legalization usually creates a magnet effect, and we may now experience an even greater influx of aliens wanting to take advantage of proposed legislation. Republican senator John McCain of Arizona is sponsoring the Border Security and Immigration Improvement Act to make entering easier for foreign workers seeking U.S. employment opportunities, and to simplify the permanent-residency application process. Similar legislation, the Agricultural Job Opportunities, Benefits, and Security Act of 2003, was sponsored by Republican senator Larry Craig of Idaho and Democratic senator Edward Kennedy of Massachusetts. It would have allowed undocumented farmworkers and their families to qualify for permanent residency after a specific tenure of work. It failed the first time, but supporters are determined to bring it back.

And Republican senator Orrin Hatch of Utah introduced a bill called the Dream Act that would allow states to grant in-state tuition rates to children of illegal aliens. Meanwhile, out-of-state parents of legal residents would get no such break. Look at that carefully: People who are here illegally would be entitled to a lower-cost education, while the vast majority of American citizens would not.

Each of these politicians is doing nothing more than pandering to the business and agricultural lobbies, and none of these legislative initiatives addresses the economic and social impact of their passage. The discussion no longer turns on what is good for Americans. It has become a venue for name-calling and race-baiting. Proponents of illegal immigration, who find themselves unable to deny that this form of immigration is unlawful, charge that their opponents are simply racists. They lump any attempt to control illegal immigration as being virulently anti-immigration and restrictionist and an affront to the immigrants who built this country. None of this is true, but it does serve to distract attention from the facts of the issue. The rhetoric and the attempt to control language are, in my judgment, part of the whole political correctness movement in this country, which is insidiously fostered by corporate America and many academic institutions. The idea that the media, politicians, and special interest groups would use the term "restrictionist" to describe those who would enforce our laws, and who demand legal and not illegal immigration while calling for border security, is remarkable. If those of us interested in immigration reform want to restrict something, it is simply the prospect of terrorism and those who would violate our laws. This is one country where we should be focusing on commonality and similarities rather than differences, and we should be looking to the national interest, not special interests.

Five years after 9/11, our borders are still wide open. The U.S. Congress, along with a Republican administration, has not aggressively pursued border and port security, which is part and parcel of national security. The American people are left vulnerable. It's time for business and government leaders to end the practice of hiring illegal aliens. It's time to form a national policy on immigration and border security that effectively reduces the threat of terrorism and stops the drain on our economy. It's time to take our borders seriously.

— *Chapter 9* —

A Generation of Failure

One out of every three students in our public high schools will drop out this year. Half of our black students will drop out. Half of our Hispanic students will drop out.

High school dropout rates have been rising steadily for over thirty years, after having reached their low in 1969. Yet neither Congress nor the president is talking about our failure to educate nearly two generations of Americans. That failure is creating a new underclass of citizens, not to mention making liars out of entire education departments, both state and federal. Most local school districts must contend with community apathy, teachers union intransigence, a sizable number of poorly trained and educated teachers, administrative incompetence, and too many parents who neither discipline nor nurture their children, encourage learning, or care enough to meet with teachers and other parents to assure quality instruction in even the basic skills of reading and mathematics.

We try to come up with solutions to the decline in public education but find ourselves in constant battle with school districts, the teachers unions, and national and local political officials—elected officials who are seemingly lacking in a commitment to excellence in our public school system. I find it mind-boggling to consider the number of people who seem indifferent to an educational system that is failing, a public education system that to me is the bedrock of what has been the American Dream, offering millions and millions of people an opportunity to move from the so-called working class into the middle class and beyond.

Today we're spending $8,287 annually for each child in our public schools. Thirty years ago, we were spending less than half that amount. The cost of education has outpaced almost every other economic benchmark for more than a generation. Politicians are finding reasons not to put money into schools, not to pay teachers, and not to improve the education offered to every kid in every school. It's going to the bureaucracy. And it shows.

We've ceded our children's future to the public school system—a faceless bureaucracy that has proven time and time again that it can't change. A 2005 report released by the Department of Education showed no progress in the reading skills of fourth and eighth graders. Math scores were up slightly. The national average eighth-grade reading score was, in point of fact, a point lower than in 2003.

The United States is no longer the most educated country in the world—it's not even close. Canada, Finland, Japan, South Korea, Norway, and Switzerland top the list. We're down at seventh place, tied with Belgium, Australia, and Denmark. An Academies of Science study reported U.S. twelfth-graders performed below the international average for twenty-one countries on general knowledge in math and science. Results of the Third International Math and Science Study showed that U.S. eighth-graders received lower science and math scores than their peers from fourteen other nations. Overall, the U.S. is twenty-fifth out of forty-one industrialized nations in math and science. We're on the verge, scholastically, of being a third-world country.

It gets worse. Only about 40 percent of U.S. high school seniors were qualified to take college-level algebra. Half of 2005's high school graduates do not have the reading skills necessary to succeed in college. Shockingly, their math and science preparation is even worse—barely one quarter were ready for college-level science. Only 56 percent of all high school students take or exceed the recommended core curriculum for college-bound students. That number is the same as it was a decade ago. Just look at the impact of globalization and how high-tech jobs are leaving the United States. This crisis in math and science education not only threatens our position as a leading global innovator but raises concern over our national security. Technological innovation has allowed the United States to be the global leader that it is. That is quickly going down the drain.

Richard L. Ferguson, the CEO of ACT, the college testing firm, told me, "Our really serious problem has mostly to do with the absence of the course taking in math and science in the high school years. We're simply seeing a decline in the number of students who are taking those higher courses which are so key to their readiness for college and, ultimately, their readiness for careers in those high-tech fields. We have, unfortunately, far too many young people who are in classrooms, particularly in the math and science areas, where often the teachers are not certified in those fields. That is a challenge that our schools face."

Michael Petrilli of the Thomas B. Fordham Foundation said on the show, "We've known this for years and years. It's like someone's pulling a fire alarm but nobody's moving. This is very serious. We have greater and greater competition from around the world. Other countries are taking academics very seriously. They're making sure that their students are taking rigorous courses, and we're simply not doing enough."

Even more disturbing was the assessment from Paul Peterson of Harvard University: "There is a shortage of talent in the United States today of top-level talent. There's a big shortage. We need to bring people in from around the world. And now after 9/11, with all the concern about passports and visas and all of that, it's getting harder to bring people in from abroad, and so business is feeling very pinched. It's really time for our educational system to step up."

To me, this comment betrays a suggestion that our institutions of higher education have been depending on foreign students to make up for the failure of American students.

States are failing in their efforts to teach students science skills that children elsewhere in the world are mastering. According to the Thomas Fordham Institute, when it comes to setting K–12 science standards—expectations of student performance—there are only seven states earning an A grade; twenty-two other states got a D or an F. The Fordham study found that state standards were carelessly written and difficult to navigate, lacked detail and content, and included vague teaching activities, like one used in Mississippi that urges students to watch ice cubes melt. Not surprisingly, the Texas Education Agency, which received an F, dismissed the Fordham report as more science fiction than science, and questioned its methodology. But the Fordham group, made up of scientists and teachers, say there's plenty of evidence to support their conclusions.

Add to these statistics the fact that those charged with the responsibility for schools have consistently misrepresented how well their schools are doing. Studies show that high school dropout rates are far higher than educational institutions had been reporting. Schools and administrators have lied, cheated, or invented more positive graduation figures out of thin air. These people keep their jobs, meet federal statutes like No Child Left Behind, and keep their federal funding when they can demonstrate success. States like Alabama, California, and Florida report one set of numbers; researchers estimate the graduation rates are actually much lower. A Harvard study showed that almost 50 percent of African American and Hispanic kids who enter southern California high schools were dropping out, while the state education department was reporting 80 percent graduation rates.

Some states count GEDs earned in their graduation numbers. In others, kids who go to jail or become too old for high school are not counted as dropouts. Gary Orfield of the Civil Rights Project at Harvard University told our broadcast that kids stop "attending classes, they start flunking, and nobody does anything about them, and they just disappear. And from the high school standpoint, since they're only being evaluated on their test scores and not [on] whether they graduate anybody, if kids with low test scores leave, they look like they are more successful." This is deception at its worst. If the kids who aren't scoring well leave the school, the school doesn't have to worry about their failing grades dragging down their overall performance.

The dropout rate in America is not a secret. Even Tom Luce, the assistant secretary of education, admitted, "We have a problem. Of about every hundred students that enter ninth grade, only about sixty-seven graduate. And we've got to correct the problem." It's been established that high school dropouts have much higher rates of poverty, imprisonment, and welfare enrollment. Today's high school dropouts, even with a GED, will make at least 35 percent less than high school dropouts of a generation ago.

The state of school performance is all the more sordid given our huge education budgets. New York City spends $11,172 per kid in its school system. Do you think each kid is getting that full $11,172? Not even close. New York admits that only 40 percent of its education budget—which is over $16 billion—actually ends up in the classroom. Where does the remaining 60 percent go? Into the bureaucracy to pay for administrators and infrastructure. The budget for the bureaucracy is bigger than the budget for actual classroom and teaching resources.

The New York City Department of Education employs more than 140,000 people, making it one of the biggest organizations in the world. It employs more people than IBM does worldwide. I think that IBM is getting more out of its workforce than the New

York City Department of Education is. But the school bureaucracy is so entrenched that even tough mayors like Rudolph Giuliani and Michael Bloomberg have butted their heads against its walls, with only headaches to show for it.

New York is not alone. Washington, D.C., schools spend roughly twelve thousand dollars a year per kid. Its schools have deteriorated to the point that they had to be taken away from the city and put into the care of a congressional financial oversight board. When the federal government has to take control of schools that spend twelve thousand dollars a year on each student, we're in serious trouble. It's obvious that no one in the system is taking responsibility or being held accountable.

The bulk of education spending goes to the bureaucracy because no one's watching where the money goes. That money serves the people who are more interested in making the system work for them than they are about serving the needs of students and teachers. Jay P. Greene, author of *Education Myths: What Special Interest Groups Want You to Believe About Our Schools and Why It Isn't So,* told me, "What people don't realize when they say schools need more money is, first, how much we spend. It's almost ten thousand dollars per child per year now on average in the United States. And people don't realize that we've doubled per-pupil spending, adjusted for inflation, over the last three decades. And what have we gotten for the increase? What we've gotten is flat outcomes. Student achievement has not gotten better. Graduation rates have actually declined. So if spending money alone were the answer, things would be better already. Clearly we need to do something more than just give schools more money. We've detached the money that schools get from their performance. And so what we have to do is, we have to give schools better incentives to use their money well to improve student achievement."

Look at California. California is twenty-fifth in education funding, yet it's forty-ninth when it comes to student achievement. As we reported on the show, Jefferson High School in Los Angeles has over thirty-eight hundred students, more than double its size in the 1980s. There are more than four times as many students per acre at this school than the state recommends. Jefferson also has a teacher shortage, and of the teachers it does have, a third lack proper state credentials. Here's what happens to students when you have this kind of situation: Fewer than one third of Jefferson students graduate; only one in eight meet the requirements to get into a state college.

Nearly every state has cut funding for public schools. In 2004, state tax appropriations for higher education experienced their steepest decline since tracking began in 1958. At the college level, this is forcing students to pay out more every year for public education—and four out of five college-age students in this country attend our public universities. In Colorado, the state covers only 8 percent of its university's operating budget, while in Michigan the state pays for just 7 percent. The schools have to make up the difference, and that's creating more hardship for working men and women trying to provide for their kids' educations. The university systems in Colorado, Kentucky, and Michigan all announced double-digit tuition increases in 2005. In general, the cost of tuition, in good times and bad, has been rising faster than the inflation rate. There's absolutely no excuse for that.

As Sarah Flanagan of the National Association of Independent Colleges and Universities succinctly put it on the show, "There are very few families out there, whether they're lower income or moderate income or upper income, that can afford to just write a check for college tuitions." And Richard Kahlenberg of the Century Foundation added, "We are cheating our low-income and working-class kids. And we'll have a society where the very well off, the children of the very well off become highly educated, and then the rest of us don't have those same opportunities." Seventy-four percent of all kids in college come from the top one-quarter income group.

Public colleges in need of funds—and nearly all are—often sacrifice their independence in exchange for private funding or corporate sponsorship. Such "donors" expect something in return for their money, and not just buildings and sports complexes with their names on them. It is an opportunity for them to place their "brands" prominently on campus and insinuate those brands into student life. But corporate America is downright subtle compared to the often heavy hand of government, which routinely subverts the process of getting an education. The House and Senate cut $12 billion from the Federal Student Loan Program when the Deficit Reduction Act was signed into law on February 8, 2006. They did this even as our middle-class students fall further behind the rest of the world in educational excellence. The law will prevent students from consolidating college loans, while raising the maximum cap on student-loan interest rates to 8.5 percent, further squeezing families faced with rising tuition costs. It's the largest cut in the history of the Federal Student Loan Program, one of the primary sources of financing for middle-class and working-class kids in this country who want a college education.

Bill Moyers and I discussed this on the show. Bill's story is telling: "My parents worked hard all their lives and never had much money, but my brother went to school on a GI Bill. I went to a public school, hitchhiked down a public highway, stopped and rested in a public park. I mean, I was the beneficiary of what we used to call the common wealth. And all of us pitched in to make opportunity available to everyone. With the loss of that, a lot of working-class families today cannot afford to send their kids to college. Tuition is zooming out of sight."

The first line of education is teachers, so the ability to attract good ones must be one indicator of why schools do well, no matter where they are. Compare our country's teachers' pay against those of other countries. Germany's teachers earn a starting salary of nearly $37,000, which goes up to more than $44,000 after fifteen years. Korea's start at about $27,000, increasing to $46,000 after fifteen years. Switzerland's teachers go from roughly $35,000 to almost $47,000 in the same period. In the United States, teachers are paid an average of $29,000 their first year and don't quite reach $43,000 by the fifteenth year. We pay our teachers less than other countries by almost a tenth. Our salaries for schoolteachers are downright embarrassing. I think our position as the world's most powerful nation presupposes that we should at least be paying our teachers what they're making in other countries around the world. You get what you pay for, whether it's for minimum wage at McDonald's or $100,000 for a good software programmer. Teaching is no different. Any business without competitive pay attracts those who don't have the skills to go elsewhere.

Unfortunately, even the teachers we do have don't always have the right qualifications. Too many are teaching subjects in which they've not been adequately trained. For instance, less than 40 percent of public school math teachers have an academic major in the field. More than half of middle school math teachers have never even had a calculus course. Nobody should expect great math and science minds to emerge from a classroom where the teacher doesn't have specific training in math and science.

Teachers are aware of this problem, and many don't like it any more than you and I. Scott Corwin, a math teacher in Fort Worth, Texas, told me that teacher pay is indeed part of the problem. "As a certified math teacher with a PhD, married to a certified chemistry teacher with nineteen years of experience, we are frequently tempted to 'jump ship' and get into a different profession that pays. We are part of the middle class that is getting squeezed. Many of our certified experienced colleagues are leaving the profession to chase better salaries. In their place are less experienced and sometimes uncertified teachers. Pay teachers what we're worth. We're making an investment in today's youth but are not getting appropriate return for our investment."

A study by the Glenn Commission, a group chaired by former senator John Glenn and designed to study the scientific education crisis in America, found that there will be an enormous shortfall of new science and math teachers over the next decade. We don't have enough who are qualified at the elementary or high school level now.

It's not just about having enough teachers, however. With U.S. corporations outsourcing technical work to cheaper overseas foreign labor, hundreds of thousands of high-paying, high-value technology jobs have been lost to foreign markets. Because of this, Americans have diminished incentives to pursue careers in math or the natural sciences. As of mid-2004, computer hardware engineers were experiencing 6.9 percent unemployment, and electrical engineers were at 6.7 percent. By contrast, only about 1 percent of lawyers were unemployed. This does not bode well for our country's prospects in science and technology, which are the foundations of the extraordinary economic growth Americans have enjoyed for more than half a century. Unless these trends are reversed, the next half century could be one of national decline.

Teachers overall are not paid as well as they should be, even though they are represented by powerful unions. The National Education Association (NEA) represents 2.7 million teachers, and the American Federation of Teachers (AFT) represents another 1.3 million. These unions spend millions of dollars lobbying Washington on behalf of their members. In the 2003–2004 election cycle, for example, the NEA spent $1,841,500, while the AFT spent $1,729,872. So what exactly are these unions doing on behalf of their members, and what does their lobbying achieve? Even Enron got the government to look the other way when it spread its lobbying dollars around. What has lobbying gotten for our teachers? Seemingly, not very much, although we know that it's keeping the unions in business. Approximately 91 percent of the NEA's and 97 percent of the AFT's money goes to Democrats. Here's a question: If the Democrats are getting all this money from the teachers' union, where is the liberal support for our schools? Democrats routinely claim that private schools are mainstays of elitism. If private schools are only for the rich and conservative, explain why Bill Clinton sent Chelsea to a private school. Or why the Kennedy kids go to private schools. Democratic support has obviously not improved schools in liberal havens like New York or Boston.

Studies say that teachers hit their peak around the fourth year of teaching. What they don't say is that half of all teachers leave before they have taught five years. The reason? Low pay. The teachers' unions obviously aren't coming through for their dues-paying members.

Where the unions are failing the entire middle class, though, is in their stance on *how* teachers are paid. Most people in this country are paid based on job performance. Not teachers, who have long been paid on the seniority system. The longer you're in, no matter how good you are, the more you get paid. Better teachers are not singled out for better pay, nor are substandard teachers demoted or given pay cuts.

Teachers' unions like this system. They are dead set against any form of merit-based pay, and have fought it tooth and nail on every front. For decades they have defeated the notion that people should be paid based on their performance. Union leaders like Barbara Kerr of the California Teachers Association have insisted on my show that paying for performance won't help schools, and argue that the key issues all boil down to school overcrowding, safe and secure classrooms, and more textbooks. But even though there are states where all of these elements are in place, the United States still lags behind other countries.

As author Jay Greene told me, "We have more resources in school. Unfortunately, we're just not using them well. So kids are not much worse off, they're just not any better off. Any time you spend twice as much money, though, to get the same result, there's a big problem. And one of the biggest changes from fifty years ago is, we did not have a unionized teacher workforce fifty years ago. And so schools had greater flexibility in who they hired, how they paid people, and who they got rid of if they weren't good."

Merit-based pay would allow local governments to reward teachers who excel, and to get rid of bad or incompetent teachers—just like every other enterprise. But because of seniority, tenure, and union rules, bad teachers cannot be removed from their jobs for months, even years. Some call this system "jobs for life," while the unions defend it as the best way to apply due process. Never mind that the group getting hurt most by this archaic practice are the kids.

As well as poor grades, poor student performance, poor funding, poor teacher pay, and poor union representation, there are a host of other issues that assail our public education, many of them foisted upon us by our elected officials. Consider the issue of English proficiency, something that should be expected of every student in the United States. Currently, almost ten million of our students speak a foreign language at home, nearly a fifth of the total student population, which is of concern to numerous school districts trying to teach English proficiency.

Yet some politicians want schools to handle not only the language needs of the students, but also the incredibly diverse needs of their parents. The Dallas school board voted to force many of its principals to learn and speak Spanish. Dallas school board trustee Joe May said it started with an award presentation at Sam Houston Elementary School. Spanish-speaking parents who attended were upset that the ceremony was conducted only in English. He decided that Spanish-speaking administrators could communicate better with parents, which would improve children's education. May wants principals in schools with a majority of Hispanic students to become proficient in Spanish in three years—or else they can start looking for another job. However, this district is home to people speaking seventy different languages, Spanish being just one of dozens, including various Asian and South American dialects.

This logic is absolutely upside down. English is the language of this nation. The suggestion that students not learn English, or not help in translating for their parents, is utter madness. What about the teachers? Must all our teachers also now learn to speak Spanish, since kids learn from teachers, not the administrators? It would make more sense for the parents to learn English to help with their children's bilingual education.

The chairman of the organization U.S.ENGLISH, Mauro Mujica, said on the show, "This is sort of a bad national trend, that we're trying to teach foreign languages to Americans so that they can communicate with immigrants that are supposed to be learning English anyway. It's going to slow down the assimilation of those immigrants. Second, there's no way that adult administrators are going to learn the nuances of Spanish, or any language, in three years in order to be able to communicate with parents on very sensitive issues."

As a practical matter, where are these principals going to find the time every week—many hours every week—to learn a new language? Is that supposed to come out of their workday, or their own time, or are they going to be given time off? And if they don't learn it well enough, who is the district going to find to replace them? And how long before they also have to speak Cantonese or Portuguese?

The absurdity isn't limited to Dallas. Hiram Monserrate (D-New York City Council) introduced a proposal to require public schools to translate report cards and other school documents into nine languages. He says it will help parents who don't speak English get involved in their kids' education. Never mind that it will cost the city some $20 million per year, and that it will entail changing the entire way that report cards are drawn up, printed up, and administered throughout the city. Never mind that these new citizens, kids and parents, need to be learning English as a way to become engaged in this society. We do them a disservice by giving them a reason not to immerse themselves in the language, not to mention the culture, of the city in which they've chosen to live.

Monserrate's opponent on this, Dennis Gallagher (D-New York City Council), summed it up to me perfectly: "Great nations, no matter how ethnically diverse, have always had a common bond that unites their people socially, politically, economically, and that common bond has always been language. And we should do everything that we can to really take that commonality of language and push it forward, not destroy it."

Supporters of the bill say that since New York is one of the world's great melting pots, it needs to reach out linguistically to its citizens. In the past, when people came to a city, they met with a common purpose, common goals, and a common language. When you start changing the way the city is run, allowing ethnic groups to remain isolated because they are unable to speak the common language of the city, you no longer have a melting pot: You have a city with multiple communities that don't have to learn to communicate with one another, and thus won't interact.

Not to mention that in a plan like this, money that should be going to classrooms goes to more administration and bureaucratic overhead.

Even corporate America itself acknowledges that the public education system is failing students. The National Association of Manufacturers says U.S. workers can't keep up with new technology. Its study recommends that companies spend at least 3 percent of their payroll on training. Three quarters of the surveyed companies are not meeting that mark.

Richard Kleinert of Deloitte Consulting told my show that his company's survey of companies showed that "84 percent of respondents say that K-to-twelve schools do not do a good job of preparing individuals for the workplace."

This is a misguided attack on middle-class workers trying to earn a livable wage rather than an indictment of a broken system of education. Big business is saying it won't hire Americans because they aren't smart enough or aren't well prepared for the rigors of the job market. If corporate America is really concerned about our schools, why isn't the business community on the front line, fighting proposed cuts in student loan aid and worker-training programs? Business leaders used to be among the most important benefactors to schools; now they have all but disappeared.

At the same time, the Bush administration has pushed for federal cuts in programs that provide training to disadvantaged workers and match Americans with jobs, while the government proposes making it more expensive for college students to take out federal loans. Where is the outcry from big business? If corporate America is so concerned that American school systems aren't turning out the right kinds of students, it should use its lobbying dollars to persuade Congress to invest heavily in education and training, and to not continue their budget cuts.

The fact is that by 2008 a third of American jobs will need high-tech skills. There will be another six million job openings for scientists, engineers, and technicians. The U.S. Department of Labor states that we'll need 260,000 new math and science teachers by the 2008–2009 school year to keep up with demand. And those teachers will have a lot of work to do, with American students ranking twenty-eighth in the world for math preparedness, after China, Finland, and South Korea. In science, our kids are twenty-second, after Finland, Japan, and China. Urban schools, the fastest growing in America, have dramatically worse math and science performance than other schools. In the next decade and a half, communist China's Academy of Sciences will increase GDP spending on technology and science from 1.5 percent to 2.5 percent, encourage Chinese scientists abroad to return to their home country, and invest in education to turn out even more scientists and engineers.

As part of their war on the middle class, our government and our large corporations have no plans to help working men and women compete against other countries and their increasingly better educated citizens. Instead, corporate America will turn to these countries for future generations of employees.

— *Chapter 10* —

Health Care: It's Enough to Make You Sick

Health care—and the ability to afford it—is something we used to take for granted. Now it is so expensive that even our biggest companies are trying to get out of providing basic coverage to their employees. Those people who do have health care coverage recognize that it costs too much; those who don't have it know they can't afford to get sick.

A CNN/*USA Today*/Gallup poll conducted in early 2005 asked people to rate the issues that were most important to them. The cost of health care came in second, right after terrorism. That means Americans put health care costs ahead of their concerns about the economy and gas prices. Farther down on the list were Social Security and the way federal courts handle moral matters—two issues the Bush administration seems to think are more compelling to the American people than their health and well-being.

The United States is one of the only industrialized nations that doesn't provide health care to all its citizens, yet we still spend more on it than any other country. Right now, forty-six million people in this country do not have health insurance, meaning that they literally cannot afford to have a baby or a heart attack. The number of workers who get health insurance from their employers is dropping quickly—today it is only 60 percent; four years ago it was 69 percent. Six million workers have lost health insurance coverage since the turn of this century. That statistic is astounding when you consider that in 1991—barely fifteen years ago—80 percent of all companies provided health insurance to their employees.

In the past five years company premiums for family coverage increased by 73 percent. Inflation only grew at 14 percent, and wages increased 15 percent. It now costs companies an average of $10,880 to offer family coverage. Employee contributions have nearly doubled since 2002, and most employees pay 20 percent of the premium themselves. That takes the average employee's total health care costs, including out-of-pocket expenses, up over $3,100 per year.

Skyrocketing health care costs are having an effect on the standard of living of American workers. As we have seen, out-of-control payments for health care and treatment are at the root of many of the personal bankruptcies filed in the United States by members of the middle class. This finding has been verified by researchers at Harvard University, who examined seventeen hundred bankruptcy cases in five states. They found that nearly half of the filers said that out-of-pocket medical expenses played a role in their financial troubles. Most of those individuals were working men and women with health insurance. The Harvard study also found that medical-related bankruptcies are up thirtyfold since 1981.

According to Harvard's findings, the average person with insurance who declared bankruptcy paid more than thirteen thousand dollars in medical copayments, with insured cancer patients facing out-of-pocket expenses topping thirty-five thousand dollars. Harvard's Dr. David Himmelstein told us on our broadcast, "I think it tells us no one in this country is safe, other than maybe Bill Gates. But if you're sick enough long enough, even if you have coverage, if you have a good job, you could be bankrupted by the cost of your care or the severity of your illness."

That conclusion is evident in stories like that of Stephanie Birket, a woman we interviewed on the show. In the process of changing jobs, there was a three-day period when she was without health care insurance. In that seventy-two hours, her son Christopher had a seizure. After taking him to see several neurologists, she ended up with thirty thousand dollars in medical bills—none of them covered. With these expenses—on top of her normal expenses, like car payments, car insurance, and utilities—Stephanie found that there was no way she could meet all her financial commitments. She decided she had to file for Chapter 7 bankruptcy. As she told us, "You're stuck with medical bills. I mean, there's no way you can get around them, and they get really expensive. And it's not something that you just decide to go out and get. It's not a choice."

If she was in a similar situation today—after President Bush signed the new bankruptcy law—Stephanie might have found that bankruptcy was not an option, no matter how dire her circumstances. Judges now have less leeway to forgive debt, and individuals are subjected to stricter means tests to determine payment options.

America has wrestled with the problems of how to provide its citizens with affordable health care over the course of several decades and several White House administrations. There have been several high-profile attempts to address the situation, including a national health insurance plan proposed by President Truman, the development of Medicare during the early 1960s, President Nixon's plan to establish national health insurance, and the Clinton administration's efforts to initiate health care reform. Only President Johnson's efforts to expand coverage through Medicare and Medicaid achieved any degree of success.

Bill Clinton promised to make health care reform a hallmark of his presidency. Voters in 1992 ranked health care in their top three concerns, as the number of uninsured was rising dramatically. And with both the Senate and House controlled by Democrats, it appeared as if he would be able to make good on his promise. But President Clinton made a number of political missteps, including having his wife direct the development of the White House–led reform package and not pushing for swift legislation. There was a significant amount of antipathy toward having the First Lady take such a prominent role in the program, and the delay allowed opponents to mount an effective campaign against the president's plan.

More than $100 million was spent to convince the American public that the proposed reform was a bad idea. The Health Insurance Association of America alone spent $20 million on an advertising campaign that featured an elderly couple bemoaning the plan as unworkable and ineffective. President Clinton and his supporters found themselves defending the program instead of advocating its benefits. When many of its supporters couldn't even agree on what the proposal should include, the result was congressional infighting and a confused public. Unable to articulate exactly how reform would benefit the people of the United States, the plan lost public support, and many disparaged it as an example of Democrats trying to add too much bureaucracy and regulation to an obvious problem. In the end President Clinton's health care effort was so disastrous that it almost derailed his presidency—and it certainly set back the course of health care reform for years.

The state of affairs has fared no better under the current administration. The Medicare Prescription Drug, Improvement, and Modernization Act of 2003, signed into law by President Bush, has met with resistance from the very people it should be helping. Known as Medicare Part D, the program is comprised of various plans offered by different insurers that have different cost structures and cover different medications. This has created a bewildering array of options that participants, many of them low income and elderly, had to wade through and sign up for before the May 15, 2006, deadline. Almost no one found it easy to understand. The president acknowledged this when he told a group of people in a retirement community, "We fully realize that for some seniors, this is a daunting task. . . . When you give people choice and options, it can be a situation where people say, 'I don't really—this is something I may not want to do.' . . . There are people around who are willing to help explain the program for you."

That last statement may be true, but the Government Accountability Office determined that those willing to help explain the program weren't very reliable. In a May 2006 report, the office stated that the accuracy rate for information given to callers trying to determine the least costly drug plan was only 41 percent. In addition, the office also found that the basic enrollment documents were flawed in two areas: "First, although about 40 percent of seniors read at or below the fifth-grade level, the reading levels of these documents ranged from seventh grade to postcollege. Second, on average, the six documents did not comply with about half of 60 common guidelines for good communication. For example, the documents used too much technical jargon and often did not define difficult terms, such as formulary."

American citizens who need health care assistance shouldn't need a postcollege education to figure out how to enroll in Medicare. It's little wonder that many of those eligible for the program have been hesitant to sign up, especially when they can't be sure exactly what it is they're signing up for. This, of course, didn't stop the president from ruling out an extension to the May 15 deadline.

One aspect of the new plan that *is* easy to figure out is who the real beneficiaries are: the big insurers administering the Medicare drug plans. Insurance giant UnitedHealth Group alone enrolled nearly four million new customers under Part D by the deadline. When you add UnitedHealth's numbers to the customers signed up by rivals Humana and WellPoint, these three companies account for two thirds of all the early participants in Medicare's prescription-only programs. By contrast, the not-for-profit Blue Cross and Blue Shield plans account for less than 10 percent of the enrollees. If nothing else, Medicare Part D is keeping corporate America healthy.

There are currently 1,162 congressional bills that contain the words "health insurance." A number of them are intended to assist small businesses in offering benefits to employees. They range in scope from creating association plans for small firms to making some costs tax-deductible. None of these, however, is a full-on effort at reform. The exception is a national health plan sponsored by Senator Barbara Boxer (D-California), and she has no cosponsors on the bill.

Across the board, our elected officials have either turned their backs on health care concerns or have botched their opportunities to make a real difference for the working men and women in this country. Not coincidentally, health care has become increasingly crucial in the war on the middle class because of its value as a bargaining chip that this country's elites can use to line their own pockets. Large corporations like General Motors, which used to be this country's biggest provider of health benefits, now point to that same coverage as one of the anchors dragging down their bottom line—claiming a direct cause and effect between their expenditures for employee health insurance and their withering profit margins. Mention is not made of inferior products or bad management; it is the employees' health that is the culprit.

Corporate America complains about insurance companies, health maintenance organizations (HMOs), and doctors that charge them ever higher rates to provide coverage and medical treatment. Insurers, HMOs, and doctors' groups in turn point to the trial lawyers of America, who stand to gain billions of dollars in legal fees and punitive damages generated by medical lawsuits. The lawyers disingenuously claim they're just protecting—or compensating—those individuals who have been harmed by substandard care, malpractice, faulty drugs and machinery, and inept medical professionals.

Through it all, as the working American spends more for health care and more for insurance coverage, the pharmaceutical companies, the HMOs, and the insurers make bigger profits, year after year. Trial lawyers get bigger slices of bigger payouts when they win their cases—typically a third of whatever the poor victim of our medical profession's ineptitude receives. In no case is the interest of our nation served by any of this finger-pointing or the popular pursuit of suing doctors.

It's an ongoing cycle. Lawsuits are filed so that lawyers can get paid. Insurance premiums go up so that insurers can show a hefty profit. HMOs charge more for their services to report a healthy bottom line. And big business, which has gotten tired of paying for any of this in the name of its workers, has decided that workers can take care of themselves. There are plenty of other workers—like so much cannon fodder—waiting to take their turn in the trenches.

Unfortunately, health care, despite being an issue that intimately affects each and every American, is tangled up with even more elitist interests than most of us can imagine. There are the pharmaceutical companies, and insurance companies, which pay huge money for lobbyists. The pharmaceutical companies, as a point of fact, spend more on lobbying than any other industry in America. The Trial Lawyers Associations lobby our elected officials to make sure they can continue to bombard health care providers with huge lawsuits—and not be limited to how much their clients can be awarded by a sympathetic jury. Politicians stand to get big paychecks from these lobbying groups and professional associations once they leave office.

While much of corporate America has been cutting the level of benefits provided to employees, some businesses have simply stopped offering health insurance coverage altogether, or offer so little as to make it meaningless. That puts the burden of getting coverage on the employee, or even on the state. A prime example is Wal-Mart, which has been under fire from its employees all over America. The company, the largest private employer in the United States, with more than a million employees, insures less than half of its workforce. It has major restrictions on who is eligible for health insurance, which family members are eligible, and how long employees have to work to be eligible for coverage.

Critics of Wal-Mart have accused the company of using taxpayer money to underwrite employee health care. Because it pays less than 10 percent of its employees' health care costs, many are forced to seek coverage through Medicaid. In effect, Wal-Mart is holding on to its dollars and making you and me responsible for its employees' coverage. In Florida, in the middle of 2006, Wal-Mart has more employees and family members eligible for Medicaid than any other company in the state.

Some states are beginning to fight back. In Maryland, where only half of Wal-Mart's employees are enrolled in the company-provided health insurance program, the state legislature has passed a bill requiring any company that has ten thousand or more employees to pay at least 8 percent of its payroll into health insurance coverage or into a Medicaid fund.

Another way that corporate America gets around the entire issue of health care is by employing illegal immigrants who don't, and can't, demand health benefits from them. This is why big business backs illegal immigration: It provides a cheap workforce with negligible ancillary expenses. But immigrants do get sick, they get pregnant, and they need medical attention. And illegal immigrants tend to make very expensive patients, given that they have no health insurance, no preventive health care, and are often working jobs that are dangerous. Since they aren't getting coverage from their employers in corporate America, they do the only thing they can do when they require medical attention—they head to the local emergency room. Very few hospitals will turn away a sick patient in the ER; many hospitals must by law treat anyone who enters their ERs. When the illegal immigrants can't pay, the hospitals just send the bill for services rendered to the government. And the government pays the bill for treating illegal workers with your taxes.

Rick Pollack, the executive vice president of the American Hospital Association, appeared on the show and told us that his organization found that "in the twenty-four counties that border Mexico, over $200 million dollars has been spent on care for illegal immigrants. We know in the state of New Jersey alone, $200 million dollars has been spent for that purpose. New York City's Health and Hospitals Corporation alone, one hospital system, spent $225 million in taking care for illegal immigrants." In Los Angeles County, the number is $340 million. In Harris County, Texas, $80 million. In Maricopa County, Arizona, $60 million to $80 million.

The problem is epidemic, to put it mildly. In California, eighty-four hospitals have closed, victims of the very real costs of providing free health care to illegal aliens. Across the country, at Jackson Memorial Hospital in Florida, 90 percent of the patients are illegal. For every $1.00 of taxpayer funding, Jackson Memorial spends $1.66 in charity care. It also spends $1 million a year on translators so its staff can communicate with the people who are coming into its emergency room. Jackson CFO Frank Barrett explained on the show, "We have a burden that we clearly didn't ask for, but we're taking it on. We're treating everybody that comes through our door, and we treat everybody the same."

Those are the economic ramifications of illegal immigration on our health care system. But with the treatment of ever more illegals, there is the rising fear that once-eradicated diseases are now returning to this country through our open borders, diseases that are threatening the health of nearly every American as well as illegal aliens themselves. And they are diseases we thought had been consigned to our history books. As Dr. Ken Castro of the Centers for Disease Control told the show, "Those persons who enter the country illegally are often at risk for tuberculosis, don't necessarily have access to the necessary medical services, and would potentially pose a threat to others." And medical lawyer and author Dr. Madeleine

Cosman told our viewers, "We have some enormous problems with horrendous diseases that are being brought into America by illegal aliens. Some of these diseases we had already vanquished, such as tuberculosis, and other diseases we have only rarely had here in America, such as Chagas disease, leprosy, malaria."

Over the last forty years, there have been just under a thousand cases of leprosy in the United States—a disease that most people felt had disappeared in this country. Yet there have been seven thousand cases reported in just the past three years. Obviously, leprosy, which still affects third-world countries, did not just spring back to life in America of its own accord. It's obvious we're not checking people for diseases at our borders, because we aren't checking these people at all.

Hospitals don't need the additional burden of combating rare diseases. They have enough trouble keeping their patients from contracting new ones, let alone infections developed while those patients are in their care. Every year, two million people in the United States contract dangerous infections during their stay in our nation's hospitals. As many as ninety thousand people die every year from those infections. This is a staggering number: Health care-associated infections kill more than two hundred people a day. In fact, you could say that the diseases people catch while in hospitals constitute the eighth leading cause of death in this country. These diseases add more than twelve days to an infected patient's hospital stay. And they add up to medical costs of $4.5 billion a year, according to the CDC.

The failing of our health care system is not limited to the quality of our treatment, or lack thereof, or to the high cost of coverage. It extends to those organizations that exist specifically to safeguard public welfare and the common good. One such organization, the National Institutes of Health, recently admitted that over the last several years it was working too closely with big business. Internal audits found that drug companies were paying top NIH scientists hundreds of thousands of dollars in consulting contracts. Even worse, these scientists were being paid by companies that were trying to obtain NIH grants. For example, investigations revealed that the NIH panel that wrote the guidelines on the use of cholesterol drugs had financial ties to the makers of those drugs. Over the last five years, thanks in part to institute guidelines, sales of cholesterol drugs have risen by two thirds, to more than $15 billion.

The problem is not limited to NIH's cholesterol panel, however, for some two hundred of its scientists have relationships with private industry. The institute admitted that its staff members were being paid to help big business, but has promised to implement reforms. Maybe we should be thinking about better pay for the people who research and provide the bulk of the knowledge that we employ in the war against disease in this country. Maybe they should make a better living so they aren't so easily susceptible to the cash proffered by big business.

Collusion between government agencies and corporate America is especially disconcerting when it affects the decision-making process by which medications are approved for our use. The Food and Drug Administration often relies on the National Institutes of Health for scientific information and research, but the NIH's relationship with industry makes those recommendations suspect. Not that the FDA itself is above suspicion. In 2004, the FDA's safety officer, Dr. David Graham, testified before Congress that America faced what he called the single greatest drug safety catastrophe in our history. His testimony blew the whistle on the dangers of Vioxx—the arthritis medicine implicated in nearly 150,000 heart attacks. Graham testified that the FDA is not doing enough to protect the health and lives of Americans, and claimed that the agency simply cannot protect the American people from dangerous drugs. When Graham called for pulling Vioxx off the market—as he had done with other unsafe drugs—he was castigated by his management, which attempted to smear his reputation and his career.

Most of us look upon the FDA as an agency set up to serve us—the consumers, the patients, those who require prescription drugs. We consider ourselves to be the FDA's primary constituency. Yet, as Dr. Graham told Congress, "I would argue that the FDA as currently configured is incapable of protecting America against another Vioxx. . . . The scientific standards [the FDA] applies to drug safety guarantee that unsafe and deadly drugs will remain on the U.S. market."

Later he told me, "Most of the scientists who work at FDA are very conscientious, very dedicated, and are trying to do the right thing by the American people. I think the problem is with the management of FDA and the culture that management has created. That basically, at least in the Center for Drugs where I work, the industry is the client, first and foremost. And that the public, if they're a client at all, if they're a customer at all, is kind of a distant second. . . . This is institutional, and it's long term, and it's taken a generation, probably, to develop. But the culture now is well established, and it feeds on itself."

So where in this scenario are our elected officials, the people we pay to protect us from such bureaucratic nightmares? Many of them are too busy benefiting from the largesse given to them by the pharmaceutical lobby. And they continue to benefit even after they've served their stint on Capitol Hill. As noted earlier, former congressman Billy Tauzin, who helped craft our nation's Medicare drug bill, now heads the Pharmaceutical Research and Manufacturers of America, the drug companies' lobbying arm. Tom Scully, former head of the Medicare program, is now a lobbyist working on Medicare issues. Former congressman Bob Walker is a lobbyist who represents Wyeth Pharmaceuticals.

These representatives were once in office presumably looking after the interests of the middle class. However, it's arguable that their true constituents have remained the same throughout. At least now the influence of the pharmaceutical and health care industries, their real constituency, is obvious to all who will look and see. It is certainly clear that the health and well-being of our middle class is not at the top of their agenda.

— Chapter 11 —

The Best of Intentions

I am certainly not the only person who takes objection and offense to way this country is being run. There are a lot of concerned citizens. There are even a few concerned lawmakers, and—amazingly—a handful of concerned CEOs.

All of these individuals have made some efforts at reform, and those efforts should be lauded. Anyone who stands up to the juggernaut that is our bought and paid-for government and its corporate sponsors is doing work that this country desperately needs. These glimmers of hope are occurring across party lines and across state lines, proving that the problems we face aren't limited to any particular locale or any partisan ideology.

Take the exporting of American jobs to other countries. A few CEOs have stood up to outsourcing. Dan Dimicco, the CEO of steel producer Nucor Corporation, has been on a mission to save American jobs. He's conducted town hall meetings to educate people on exactly what is going on with outsourcing and bad trade agreements—especially those where we let trade partners such as China dictate how our industries are run. According to Dimicco, "There's nothing wrong with the rest of the world rising up. But it shouldn't be done at the detriment of our leadership position and our ability to provide for ourselves. Shame on our politicians, shame on us for not doing what's necessary to keep a level playing field so we give our workers and our companies a chance to compete."

He's joined by Bill Hickey, the president of Lapham-Hickey Steel, who asked, "Where do we go? Do we just give away all these manufacturing jobs, and we have higher poverty rates, and we have less and less disposable income, we have less tax base? This is what's going to happen. Less innovation. Manufacturing is the iron of the engine of the United States. It's going to go away."

It doesn't have to go away if we can get more and more CEOs to realize that what is at stake is nothing less than the destruction of the American middle class. Every single effort counts, be it from large businesses or small. Our broadcast featured Dov Charney, the CEO and founder of American Apparel, another executive who is bucking the trend. His company employs thirteen hundred people in Los Angeles to make quality swimwear, T-shirts, and other garments. All of American Apparel's operations are in one building, and its employees are paid an average of $12.50 an hour. As Charney told us, "A lot of people misunderstand it and think it was a moral decision. I think there is some morality to it. I mean, it is more fun to pay people well than pay people poorly. But it's also an economic one." That economic decision has resulted in a doubling of revenues for three straight years, and a waiting list of more than one thousand applicants hoping to work at American Apparel.

A few politicians have also begun to recognize the damage inherent in outsourcing—perhaps as they realize that angry voters without jobs are not inclined to vote for the status quo. In December 2005, the Burlington, Vermont, city council passed a law banning outsourcers from doing business with the city. Under the new ordinance, Burlington will not award service contracts over fifty thousand dollars to firms that outsource work abroad. According to Burlington City Council member Phil Fiermonte, passing the law was "a modest but important step that our city can take to help protect workers in Burlington. And to send a message [from] Burlington public officials [that] they are not going to stand by idly as corporations ship jobs overseas."

Over the course of 2005, forty-one states considered outlawing the outsourcing of state contract work overseas. Seven states now limit outsourcing. For now it's only a small effort—but it's a start.

Immigration concerns, which many people believe are limited to those states that border Mexico, are problems for our entire country. A few congressmen appreciate the magnitude of the problem and are trying to propose solutions to fix it. Representative James Sensenbrenner (R-Wisconsin) is fighting the administration to pass necessary reforms as part of the intelligence overhaul bill signed this year. "I think that you can't have homeland security without border security," Sensenbrenner says. "And obviously this is a place that smugglers use not only to bring people across the border, but to bring drugs across the border, and gang members across the border. This is a public safety problem that impacts every American, even Americans who live as far away from the Mexican border as my constituents in Wisconsin."

State governments have been forced to take an active role in battling our nation's illegal alien crisis since the federal government has failed to take action. In the first month of 2006, nearly thirty states introduced legislation to combat the border emergency. From New Hampshire to South Carolina, Virginia to Arizona, at least twenty-eight states have introduced seventy-one new bills. Another seventy-three bills written last year remain on the agenda. These include legislation on everything from employer sanctions for hiring illegal aliens, to criminalizing trafficking of illegals, to mandatory immigration checks during every street arrest. In Indiana, one bill restricts public assistance, allowing it for legal immigrants only. It requires schools to verify the legal status of all students, prohibits the state from issuing IDs or driver's licenses, and makes document forgery a class C felony. In New Hampshire, there are eight bills under consideration; one targets coyotes, the people who transport illegal aliens.

The National Conference of State Legislatures reports that in 2005, legislatures considered three hundred bills and approved thirty-six. That figure is expected to be surpassed in 2006. Such measures are a forceful expression of the degree of frustration with a do-nothing Congress and White House that have all but ignored the issue, and with a federal government that is not enforcing existing laws.

Local officials from New York and Connecticut are joining forces to stop illegal aliens from looking for work on their streets, work that should be going to American citizens. Illegal immigrant day laborers are part of the landscape in Suffolk County, New York, and Danbury, Connecticut, communities one hundred miles apart. According to Suffolk County executive Steve Levy, a Democrat, "We estimate, and this is very speculative, over forty thousand illegal immigrants in Suffolk County today. And that puts tremendous stress on our local infrastructure. Our emergency rooms get overwhelmed. We have a large number of people in our school districts we don't know, you know, where their parents came from."

Levy and Mark Boughton, Danbury's Republican mayor, have teamed up to start Mayors and Executives for Immigration Reform, a group made up of city and county executives. Through their efforts and their Web site, SupportReform.org, they have found a lot more officials with the exact same concerns across the country. As Levy told the show, "We're saying, federal government, it's your responsibility. Deal with it. Step up to the plate, because ignoring this problem for the last several decades has placed tremendous pressure on local governments. . . . We think we have a coalition that's very broad-based, from Maine to California, from executives and mayors alike, who are going to be pressuring their congressional delegation to give us some type of break, because our property taxpayers are bearing the brunt. . . . [T]he pressure that illegal immigration is having on our schools, on our jails, on our health care services, and on the housing market, where we see thirty, forty, fifty people in one single-family home turning neighborhoods upside down. Over the last ten years, we have seen more and more instances of, in one specific case, sixty people in a nine-hundred-square-foot house. This was a tinderbox ready to explode. And it takes months and months to get the search warrants that gather the evidence. We're not against immigration. We like immigration. We understand the benefits, culturally and economically, but it has to be done controlled, orderly, and legal."

Representatives in Maryland are considering a bill that would make it a crime to drive a car without a valid driver's license. In the last three years the number of unlicensed drivers in the state has increased nearly 60 percent. Immigrant groups like CASA Maryland protest that the measure will impact a disproportionate number of illegal aliens. Under Maryland law, aliens are able to get a driver's license, but the Motor Vehicle Administration has strict rules requiring proof of identity, state residency, and age. Under the new law, many illegal aliens will not qualify.

The frustration with our government's failure to act has prompted American citizens to find their own ways to deal with illegal immigration. The Minuteman Project was founded in April 2005 as "a citizens' Neighborhood Watch on our border"; they are, they claim, "Americans doing the jobs that Congress won't do." The project spread more than one thousand volunteers along the Arizona border in an effort to report suspected illegal aliens to the border patrol. Their mission has helped bring national attention to the crisis, yet the group has come under fire. A group representing dozens of open borders advocates, religious groups, and human rights organizations delivered a letter to the office of California governor Arnold Schwarzenegger and demanded he withdraw his public support for the Minutemen. Nonetheless, scores of elected officials in California and across the nation have endorsed them. And the actions of the Minutemen are legal, unlike those of the millions of aliens and smugglers who cross our borders each year.

In response to the Minuteman Project, President Bush said, "I am against vigilantes in the United States of America. I am for enforcing law in a rational way." There's tremendous irony in the president's declaration that it's the Border Patrol's job to enforce laws in a rational way. In his budget, he provided for only 210 additional Border Patrol agents this year, even though the National Intelligence Reform Act mandated ten thousand over the next five years. If the president wants to enforce the law in a rational way, he might start by enforcing the laws already on the books. Until Bush can find it in his budget, for example, to fund an adequate number of Border Patrol agents requested by Congress, concerned private citizens and state governments will continue to take action.

Those who rail against the Minuteman Project denounce what they call acts of violence against immigrants by armed vigilantes, though there have been no documented instances of a Minuteman harming anyone. The *Wall Street Journal* assailed this group (and me) in an editorial in which it managed in limited space to confuse illegal immigration and legal immigration, and to dismiss the significance of border security altogether. In case the *Journal* left any doubts, I want to be clear that I support the Minuteman Project and the fine Americans who are its members in all they've accomplished fully, relentlessly, and proudly.

The Minuteman idea has spread to other parts of this nation. The town council of Herndon, Virginia, approved building a work center for illegal aliens using taxpayer money—over the loud objections of its citizens. Residents felt betrayed by what they viewed as their town's complete lack of concern over illegal day laborers, so they began their own movement. A group of sixty volunteer Minutemen take pictures of day laborers and record the license plate numbers of employers who hire them. While some in town raised privacy concerns over the photos, their actions are all perfectly legal. George Taplin, who organized the group, explained that citizens were conscientiously taking a nonconfrontational approach, simply recording what goes on and reporting on it.

Many corporations skirt our tax and immigration laws by hiring illegal immigrants, but some companies have taken a stand and decided not to employ them. AMC Entertainment, which has more than four hundred movie theaters across the country, employs some twenty-four thousand people and is committed to hiring American citizens. It sends its payroll data to the Social Security Administration to verify that its entire workforce has valid Social Security numbers. If there is a discrepancy with a number, the employee has three days to validate it. As we reported on the show, nearly a dozen AMC employees in Maryland resigned after not being able to explain why their Social Security numbers weren't valid. Most companies aren't as concerned about who they're hiring as AMC, but since illegal immigrants can't get legitimate numbers—most are obtained fraudulently or are duplicates—any employer could easily verify its employees' status by having the SSA vouch for the numbers. Several immigration reform groups believe that AMC's model should be utilized across the country to ensure that only legal workers are hired.

All of the issues I've discussed in this book are taking their toll on the middle class. But few have the potential to damage future generations as seriously as the decline of our public education system. While it needs an overhaul, there have been several success stories of attempts to try and redress the abject failures of our schools. The first is in the area of pay for performance, making sure teachers are remunerated for doing their jobs—or are gotten rid of when they don't do their jobs. Both Colorado and Michigan have had notable victories in the drive toward pay for performance. Douglas County, Colorado, in particular has one of the most comprehensive such plans in the country, rewarding teachers using a results-oriented compensation system. This reward also considers involvement in group activities, individual achievement, and student performance. And teachers can receive additional pay for extra work.

As Colorado governor Bill Owens told the show, "We are excited in Colorado with choice, with reforms, with compensation based on performance. It's what the rest of the private sector, including you, get paid based on. We ought to be able to pay teachers the same way. I hope that we're able to start to move toward rewarding those outstanding teachers and perhaps incentivizing those who aren't up to par, doing the things that do work in the private sector in the most important thing we do, which is educate our children."

In Minnesota, concern over teacher accountability resulted in a merit-based system for teacher compensation. Passed in 2005, it was not an easy process, and the unions were reluctant participants in the program. As Governor Tim Pawlenty told me, "They're such an instrumental part of the whole system. They're very powerful. If they're not brought into the reform or the change, it's not going to be successful. Minnesota leads the nation, or very close to it, in almost every measure of standardized education performance, but we need to raise the bar even on ourselves for a whole variety of reasons. . . . I have to say candidly they were skeptical at first, and many of them still are. But after they have some experience with this, they become our best proponents and advocates for the change."

Governor Mitt Romney (R-Massachusetts) is trying to establish a pay for performance program in Massachusetts. He states, "We'd like to see the very best teachers promoted, given responsibility to mentor other teachers, train other teachers. We'd like advanced placement teachers to get an extra bonus. Math and science teachers, and those that are willing to go into our toughest schools, get extra pay. . . . I think teachers' union members, particularly the teachers themselves, want to see higher pay. They want to get better pay, and I want to give more pay. That's why I proposed hundreds of millions of dollars more in funding. But I don't want better pay just for showing up. I want better pay for being excellent."

I would think that top-quality teachers would be excited to be told they're going make a lot more money if, in fact, they can teach so well that their students will do better on national standardized tests. Something is fundamentally askew if the teachers' unions can't see how much sense that makes.

There are some educators who realize that the situation isn't going to get better unless they take it upon themselves to enact change. One such individual is Truett Abbott, the principal of Warren County Middle School in Georgia. He turned one of Georgia's worst-performing public middle schools into one of Georgia's best, and he accomplished it with little money and very few resources. In 2000, 28 percent of the school's students passed the state writing test, and only 14 percent of his eighth-graders passed the state math test. In 2005, 86 percent passed the writing test and 88 percent passed the math. That's remarkable progress by any measure. I asked principal Abbott to join me on the broadcast to discuss his school's turnaround. He described the problems that the school had faced: "We have a student population that's 92 percent African American, and all of our students are on 100 percent free and reduced lunch, which indicates that it's not a high-income neighborhood. . . . The state has reduced the funding in all the counties in Georgia for three years in a row. So we haven't had more money; we've had to do with less money. The significant changes have been that we discovered that our students coming into the middle school could not read higher than a third-grade level—and they were coming to sixth grade. So we found a phonetic program that we could use in the classrooms to remediate the students, so they could begin to read the textbooks all across the curriculum."

Abbott's program entailed a nine-week intensive review of phonics, and it included more at-home reading. In fact, kids were required to read twenty-five books, and were tested on each one to ensure that they had read them. The school also reduced discipline problems by separating middle schoolers from high school students, who all share one building. As Abbott told me, "I felt that if our teachers were good in doing the right things in the classrooms—we increased the core class time by 50 percent—that we would obviously make great gains. And that's proven to be true. We involved our parents, especially, to help us to make discipline work. And that was a big part of it: making discipline work."

Today Warren County Middle School beats the state average for math by fifteen points, and has eliminated the achievement gap between students in suburban wealthy school districts and minority rural areas. The change was brought about by—and praise must be given to—Abbott, his teachers, and the parents of Warren students. They achieved this despite a lack of assistance (and, one could surmise, interest) from the state or the federal governments.

Some elected officials, and even corporations, have come to realize that we must not only fix the classroom, but also provide a long-term system of preparing our citizens for the future. Congressman George Miller (D-California) is calling for urgent action to restore America's competitiveness by making science and technology top priorities. He believes that America's global leadership is being challenged as never before by countries such as China, South Korea, and India, and says that the country must graduate one hundred thousand additional scientists, engineers, and mathematicians over just the next four years. As he told me on the show, "This is going to cost—if you've taken its entirety, and it's larger than just what we put down in the innovation challenge—you're talking about hundreds of millions of dollars over the next five to ten years, maybe billions of dollars. But what's interesting is when you talk to those who are betting their money, their shareholders' money, their personal money, their venture capital money, they tell us that we have no alternative. We have no alternative to making this kind of investment in better math and science teachers, better math and science students, graduate schools and obviously research opportunities in the private sector and in the public sector."

In a demonstration that corporate America can address the needs of the middle class when it so desires, IBM announced its Transition to Teaching program in September 2005, in which its veteran employees are asked to consider becoming math and science teachers. The pilot program will assist employees in getting their teacher accreditation after they've left the company, and IBM will offer online mentoring and course work, as well as reimbursement for as much as fifteen thousand dollars for tuition and stipends while the former employees student teach.

These are only a few significant examples of work being done to try to stem the assault on the middle class. There are more, but not nearly enough. And some of these examples, for all their best intentions, are really operating at the margins, because the efforts are little more than quick fixes to the issues that are undermining our nation. Unfortunately, at the margins they will remain until we directly address—and change—the fundamental flaws in the way this country is being run.

Doing that will be the only way we can take back America. For the sake of our future, I don't think we have any choice.

— *Chapter 12* —

Taking Back America

Every working man and woman in this country must fight back against the powerful forces—political, economic, and social—that threaten our way of life. If we are to preserve the American Dream for future generations, we must find common cause in the common good and in our national interest. To do so requires that we celebrate our similarities rather than differences, demand both economic and educational opportunity for every American, and invigorate participatory democracy in our communities, states, and nation.

No one will give us our country back, not without a fight. Congress will not suddenly take seriously its responsibilities to represent the will and interests of its largest constituency, the middle class. Corporations will not abandon business practices and goals that are antithetical to the well-being of working men and women. And our public schools will not restore the promise of quality education unless you and I take seriously our duties as engaged citizens.

You and I must work to change a social order that is in disrepair, a body politic that is fractured, and a government that is dysfunctional. We must begin with ourselves as individuals. A good starting point for each of us is to read the two most important documents that govern our lives as individuals and as a nation.

Years ago, Senator Robert Byrd (D-West Virginia) gave me a little paperback pamphlet of the Constitution and the Declaration of Independence. I admit I was taken aback when he handed it to me, and it sat on my desk for weeks before I picked it up. I realized that I hadn't read the Constitution in its entirety since college. But I've read it countless times since. I've started giving it out to viewers whose e-mails are read on my broadcast, and to the guests we interview on the program, as well.

Pick up a copy of the Declaration of Independence and the Constitution, or turn to them in the back of this book. As you read these two documents, consider how far we've moved from the basic tenets and principles on which our democracy was established. Our Constitution begins with the purest statement of the source of our government's foundation and its legitimacy: "We the people . . ." The Declaration asserts as the first self-evident truth in the creation of our nation that all men are created equal. We must acknowledge that we as a society have drifted too far from that fundamental American value.

I fully acknowledge that we are all too busy, work too hard, and are faced with numerous distractions in our daily lives. But I believe we must commit ourselves to involvement in our communities and local governments, to taking the time and effort to attend school board and city hall meetings, and to express our views to state legislators and congressional delegations. We need to understand the positions of our elected officials on the issues that matter most, and remember that the goal of government at all levels is to work for the common good and the national interest.

"We get the government we deserve" is a frequent refrain following elections, and it may well be that you and I do deserve what this "best government that money can buy" is delivering. We've failed to vote, and have allowed corporations and organizations that we once trusted to take control of our political process. But the next generation of Americans certainly deserves better from us, and from our government. Whatever you and I deserve, I believe we've gotten a government that we've tolerated for too long. And we've tolerated for far too long elected officials who are committed to, and have represented, privileged and special interests rather than you and me.

I believe we've failed to achieve equality of educational and economic opportunity for every American because we've failed to become engaged in our political life, ignoring something even as basic as our responsibility to vote. We can change that, and we must. And yes, that change entails your resolution and mine to cast a fully informed vote in every election, whether for school board, mayor, state representative, congressman, or president. While four out of ten of us haven't bothered to vote for president, eight out of ten of us don't vote in school board elections. That has to change, and change will take great effort on our part, and it will take time.

However, we can't wait for elections to begin to engage in our new political life. There are steps all of us can take that will have an immediate impact and send a powerful message to both of the political parties and our elected officials in Washington. Elected officials in both parties have been working against the interests of the middle class for so long that they take our votes for granted, or they take advantage of the fact that a sizable number of us don't vote at all.

What if we all resolved that we would not permit either the Republicans or the Democrats to waste their time and ours with campaigns that focus on "wedge" issues? Both parties love to excite their bases by focusing on controversial topics like gay marriage, the pledge of allegiance, school prayer, judicial appointments, gun control, stem cell research, and welfare reform. Each of these is important to varying degrees to large numbers of us, but none of them rises to the level of urgency or the requirement of immediate attention in public policy. These issues are raised by both political parties to distract and divert public attention from the profound issues that affect the American way of life. John D. Donahue, professor at Harvard's Kennedy School of Government, has stated that politicians "have seen the advantages of cultural wedge issues and seek to inflame them." In nearly every case, the politicians who drive wedge issues in their rhetoric avoid the subjects that are most important to voters, but that require thoughtful campaigns and taking positions that often can't be advanced with a simple sound bite.

What if a sizable number of us decided to walk into our town and city halls all over the country and change our party affiliation from Republican or Democrat to Independent? I believe that for the first time in decades, working middle-class Americans might just get the attention of our elected officials. Imagine the consternation in Washington if both parties had to contend with a national electorate whose political affiliation had dramatically changed within a matter of weeks or months. What would happen if partisan Republicans and partisan Democrats actually did something to demand that their respective parties begin to represent the public interest instead of special interest? What would happen if there were as many registered Independents as registered Republicans and registered Democrats?

I truly believe that changing our registration from the Republican and Democratic parties to that of Independent would be a more powerful demonstration of middle-class determination to have its interests represented in government than massive rallies or street protests of any kind.

Registering as an Independent would serve notice to both parties that they can no longer take votes for granted. It would serve notice that they would have to earn our votes in each and every campaign and election. And if large numbers of us were to register as Independents, I believe that the tenor of politics and the quality of governance in our country would be elevated almost immediately. I have changed my registration to Independent, and hope you will, too. I hope you agree with me that it's a step that's worth a try, but we also need to do much more.

As I said at the outset of this book, our political system is now owned by corporate and special interests, and it's time to return ownership of our government and our political system, including our elections, to working men and women and the middle class.

Neither the Republicans or the Democrats, nor the House or the Senate, have proved themselves capable of reforming what has become a culture of corruption. So long as corporate America and special interests maintain their stranglehold on the electoral and legislative processes, the middle class will remain without representation in Washington.

The McCain-Feingold bill to reform campaign finance was introduced in 1997 and became law five years later. It has failed miserably in light of the Abramoff and Cunningham scandals, prompting Congress to promise substantive reform of both lobbying and its own rules yet again. But as expected, little has been accomplished, and the culture hasn't changed. As of this writing, we have too many elected officials in both parties being investigated for engaging in improper financial transactions.

Over the years I've examined dozens of ideas and proposals to weaken the grip of big money and special interests in our electoral and legislative processes. I've come to the conclusion that the only way we'll ever see their power substantially diminished, and the common good and national interest fully represented in Washington, is through the complete public financing of all elections.

Lobbying, campaigns, and elections are all about money. And in this case, we have to meet power with power. Only one group of people has more money than corporate America and special interests: taxpayers. I love the idea of our elected officials being beholden to public money and the public interest rather than to corporate America and special interests.

Complete public financing, also called "clean elections," means that candidates cannot accept private money for their campaigns. Clean elections were first adopted by Maine in 1996. Arizona followed with a clean election mandate in 1998. Vermont took a partial step toward complete public financing in 1998 by stipulating that races for governor and lieutenant governor be clean. The most recent state to follow this path is Connecticut, which will have clean elections in 2008. Right now, these states allow for candidates to opt in to the program. Those who do are entitled to state funding of their campaigns. Those who choose not to opt in can raise private and special interest money, but are not given any state money. This is not yet a perfect solution, but it's heading in the right direction.

Of course, many politicians in both parties will struggle mightily to preserve the status quo, and will resist change for the common good. I believe they can be beaten in elections for their offices, but there is another way to assert the public interest over special interest, and that is through initiatives and referendums.

An initiative is a process whereby citizens gather enough signatures, using a petition, to get an issue placed on the ballot—without the legislature's ever becoming involved. Initiatives are typically grassroots movements, generated by concerned citizens who are tired of their elected officials not listening to them. Once it's on the ballot, voters can accept or reject it.

A referendum is a direct vote. This means that each person gets to vote on whether or not a proposal should be accepted or rejected. The legislature puts it on the ballot—in effect, referring it back to the voters—and citizens decide whether it's a good idea or not. It is a vote that represents the actual will of every person who votes. When voting for a candidate, voters expect that the candidate will represent them when voting on such issues. Of course, the candidate promises to represent the will of the voters, but Congress is rife with broken promises.

The important element of an initiative or referendum is that the voter is casting his or her vote directly to adopt or reject a particular issue: changes to the state constitution, bond issues, a new law, etc. They allow citizens to overrule and override their representatives, and it's possible that simply the threat of being overruled will make legislators pay closer attention to the jobs they're doing.

Initiatives and referendums have been responsible for some of the most important changes to our system of government. They have dealt with a wide range of subjects: the end of government contracting and hiring based on racial preferences; the abolishment of poll taxes; allowing theaters and stores to open on Sundays; placing term limits on local and state officials; the creation of the eight-hour workday; giving women the right to vote; and electing politicians through direct primaries. The initiative process was used by the people of California in 1978 to cap the property tax at 1 percent. Under Proposition 13, voters literally struck back against laws that they felt were fiscally irresponsible. The passage of Prop 13 presaged the national "taxpayer revolt" that ushered in Ronald Reagan's presidency in 1980.

Arizona's Proposition 200, passed in 2004, was the result of an electorate confounded by both the governor and state officials, who refused to do anything to stem the tide of illegal immigration and the hemorrhaging of local and state budgets that were providing services to illegal aliens. Proposition 200 requires that all state residents must prove that they are American citizens in order to vote and to receive public services such as welfare. And public employees are required to ask for ID from people requesting these services. Prop 200 was the first confirmation that the people's will could be successfully asserted in the illegal immigration crisis.

Through independent registration we can gain the attention and respect of our politicians and elected officials. That's the first step. Through the public financing of elections we will roll back the influence of corporate America. And through referenda and initiatives we can directly assert the will of the people. That would be a great beginning in the fight to take back America.

On some of the most troubling issues facing the nation, our elected officials excuse apathy and their failure to serve the public interest by regaling us with assertions of the complexity of the problems that face us, and by extolling the virtues of delay in confronting and resolving those issues.

Citizens are under no illusion of the need to reform the relationship between lobbyists and our representatives and senators. More than 80 percent of us surveyed recently responded that it would be a "very serious" or "moderately serious" ethical breach if our congressmen took a trip paid for by a lobbyist, according to a 2005 *USA Today*/CNN/Gallup poll. The conclusion to be drawn is obvious. Any congressional trip should be paid for by the federal government. No elected officials should be allowed to accept gifts of any kind, shape, or size.

We should extend the "cooling off" period between the time our senators and representatives leave office to the time they can become lobbyists to five years, a minimum that I believe would be appropriate. The current one-year period allows officials to return too quickly to lobby their former colleagues. And there is no reason to continue floor privileges for former representatives and senators who are now allowed access to the Capitol.

These standards should be strictly applied to all who serve in the federal government. Our trade officials should not be allowed to leave the U.S. government and then go to work as lobbyists for foreign governments. These people spent their public service careers working on trade policy and on agreements to benefit the United States, their salaries paid by our tax dollars. They should not take their knowledge, expertise, and sense of public service to serve another nation and another government. I'm often told that such a limitation would make it difficult if not impossible to recruit the highest quality talent for government service. After thirty consecutive years of trade deficits and $4.5 trillion in trade debt, I don't believe we can afford such talented people much longer, at any rate. And if the basis for their government service is the opportunity to serve another nation, then a simple "go to hell" is a more appropriate response than "you're hired," anyway.

Similar restrictions should apply to our military. No military officer at the rank of colonel or higher should be permitted to work in a lobbying, contracting, procurement, or sales capacity for any corporation doing business with the U.S. government. Our retired senior officers are bright and talented enough to work in any number of areas in any other industry.

Not only do we have to radically change the way our politicians and lobbyists conduct themselves, we have to change the way our government does business with other nations. Our trade agreements first need to be reciprocal and fair, based on mutuality of trade. We need to have justifications for each and every agreement, and those justifications need to be based on economic benefit. The Bush administration couldn't rationalize the economics of CAFTA, so it sought congressional support for the agreement based on arguments of regional security and stability. Why not instead insist that every so-called free trade agreement be accompanied by an economic impact statement that would assure Congress and the American people of the specific benefits to both American labor and American business, as well as the mutual benefits to our trading partners?

We also need to get rid of something called "fast track." So-called fast-track authority gives the president the authority to negotiate all trade deals. Section 8 of the Constitution specifically assigns Congress the authority and responsibility "to regulate commerce with foreign nations." But in 1976, Congress ceded that authority to the president, and they renewed fast-track authority in the Trade Act of 2002, which continues to allow the president to negotiate trade deals, with Congress only allowed to offer a straight up-or-down vote on those agreements, without the power to amend them. When fast-track authority expires in July of 2007, Congress under no circumstance should permit it to be renewed. Our trade agreements have been negotiated disastrously, and the only way these agreements can be considered "free trade" would be in application to our trading partners, who have free access to the world's richest consumer market without reciprocity.

Those trade deals have benefited U.S. multinationals and our trading partners with little or no benefit for our working men and women. In fact, most of them have been injurious to the middle class, especially in how they facilitate the outsourcing of American jobs to cheap foreign labor markets, and devastate our manufacturing industry. I strongly believe that U.S.-based companies should be subjected to tariffs, duties, and fees on any product and service they produce overseas for consumption in the U.S. market. If the only way a U.S. company can compete effectively in the American economy is to offshore production and outsource American jobs, then it should be abundantly clear to even a politician that our so-called free trade agreements are exacting too high a price on the American economy and American workers.

Corporate America is quick to defend the high prices of gasoline and heating oil by insisting that they simply reflect the law of supply and demand at work. Unfortunately, they're as quick to deny the same law of supply and demand when discussing the impact of the loss of American jobs to outsourcing and the impact of illegal immigration on wages.

Every reputable nonpartisan economist acknowledges that pay wages for those who work at the lower end of the pay scale are adversely affected by the flood of illegal aliens into this country. As open border and illegal immigration advocates urge for immigration reform by Congress, they ignore the fundamental fact of the economics: Wage levels are dropping, not soaring, for unskilled labor, which is a clear indication that we have too many, not too few, workers at the lower end of the wage scale.

As to reforming our immigration laws, I would urge first that we enforce the ones Congress has already passed. I believe we need to ensure that our government exacts heavy penalties and fines upon illegal employers of illegal aliens. And I believe that HR-98, sponsored by Congressmen Silvestre Reyes of Texas, a former Border Patrolman, and Congressman David Dreier of California, chairman of the House Rules Committee, comes closest, by imposing jail sentences of five years and fines of fifty thousand dollars on employers for each illegal alien hired. Other nations have successfully implemented solutions to their own security and immigration problems. France, Germany, and Belgium penalize employers with imprisonment, confiscation of equipment, and threats to close the company.

The exploitation of illegal workers must end. Any employer, whether an individual or a corporation, who does not pay workers at least minimum wage should be subjected to additional fines. And this would be a good time to raise the minimum wage to a living wage and to establish heavy penalties for those who violate that standard. By doing so we benefit American workers and legal immigrants alike by removing a rationale for the demand for illegal labor, and simultaneously improve their living conditions.

But if we are to reform our immigration laws, we must first secure and control our borders. Without control of our borders, we cannot control immigration. And if we cannot control immigration, we certainly cannot reform it.

I believe that before Congress takes any action on immigration reform, it must demonstrate to the American people that our government has taken command of our borders and our ports, not only to control immigration, but to assure the safety and security of the American people. Until our borders and ports are secure, it's counterproductive to the national interest to discuss the particular elements of immigration reform. But I do believe that once our borders and ports are secure, any reform of our immigration laws and policies must be rational, humane, and effective, and they must benefit, not burden, American citizens.

In a post–September 11 world, safeguarding our borders and our ports should not be considered, as some elected officials have suggested, an impossibility. It should be considered an absolute necessity and essential to our national security. Unless the U.S. government can persuade the Mexican government to become a partner in shutting down all illegal immigration across our southern border, we should begin building a fence there immediately. We need to put as many agents along this border as we have in the Transportation Security Administration protecting our airports, at least forty thousand. Then we must increase the number of enforcement personnel across the nation to at least fifty thousand for our borders and ports. And we need to double the size of the Coast Guard, which not only secures our ports but also patrols our coastline.

In addition, all containers and cargo entering the United States, regardless of country of origin, should be inspected. As of this writing, only 5 percent of the goods and containers entering the United States are examined. All containers should be inspected upon embarkation from their country of origin, without exception. If they're not, they should be turned back. And no shipments should be allowed into our ports without U.S. Customs being part of the process in every case. Granting a foreign company the authority to sign off on what does and does not enter this country is foolhardy and potentially disastrous.

Instead of committing to establishing true security of our borders and ports, our elected officials focus instead on the difficulties and the cost. They need to understand that Americans want a return to a determinist and confident government, not one that is incompetent and failing, and one that understands there is no price too high to pay for our sovereignty and our security.

I believe the following quotation is the best expression of the American view of the issue of immigration and of our history and tradition of being a land of both laws and immigrants. It was written by President Theodore Roosevelt in a letter to the American Defense Society in 1919, ten years after he left the White House:

> In the first place we should insist that if the immigrant who comes here in good faith becomes an American and assimilates himself to us, he shall be treated on an exact equality with everyone else, for it is an outrage to discriminate against any such man because of creed, or birthplace, or origin. But this is predicated upon the man's becoming in very fact an American, and nothing but an American. . . .
>
> There can be no divided allegiance here. Any man who says he is an American, but something else also, isn't an American at all. We have room for but one flag, the American flag, and this excludes the red flag, which symbolizes all wars against liberty and civilization, just as much as it excludes any foreign flag of a nation to which we are hostile. . . . We have room for but one language here, and that is the English language . . . and we have room for but one sole loyalty and that is a loyalty to the American people.

That loyalty is best demonstrated by our commitment to our participatory democracy, and by our commitment to focus on our responsibilities as well as on the privileges and benefits of citizenship.

If we are to succeed in making our demands known to Washington, we must demand more of ourselves, whether we vote for president or mayor, or attend school board meetings. The state of our public schools is deplorable. Leaving aside the intense debate as to whether the highly publicized and often criticized No Child Left Behind program is working or not, it is clearly not working well enough for all students and all schools, and it is not working fast enough.

We need to make improvements, and make them quickly, before we fail another generation of Americans. We should begin with national standards and national tests for both students and teachers. We should establish a national core curriculum and standards of discipline in the classroom. And our national standards for math, science, and English should be raised, not lowered. If we are serious about preserving the American way of life, and assuring educational and economic opportunity, our educational standards should be the highest in the world.

We should also set standards for class size, length of school year, teacher qualifications, and pay. An optimal student-to-teacher ratio ensures that our children receive the education they both need and deserve. The establishment of discipline will maintain order in the classroom, and minimize the disruptions to the educational process. And we must lengthen the school year to make certain our children are receiving the full value of their education.

It is past time to cut through the petty politics of education at both the local and national level. We need to test teachers. Teachers who do not want to be tested are probably not as good as their unions claim. Every teacher should be tested for proficiency in the subjects he teaches. Those with outstanding results on their tests will get bonuses. And the school districts that hire them will get additional funds for hiring these exceptional teachers. Likewise, those administrators who can't achieve excellence in their schools need to be replaced.

Districts should also be rewarded for maintaining optimum class sizes and graduating students with satisfactory grades in the required curriculum. That core curriculum of reading, writing, mathematics, and science should be bolstered by civics. Civics and understanding of our government are, to my mind, as critically important as math and science. Our public schools are not succeeding if students are not taught the basic values of our society, the rules of citizenship, the working of our government, and the history of our nation.

In our high schools, I believe we should focus on reward at a time when we have the highest dropout rate in our history. The top 10 percent of every high school graduating class, based on grades, should be guaranteed admission to state colleges and universities, regardless of financial circumstance. The federal government should create a fund for the specific purpose of providing scholarship and financial aid for tuition, and room and board for all students in the top 10 percent of their classes who require financial aid.

In addition to good education, the people of this country should have access to adequate health care. The few attempts our legislators have made to rein in health care costs have been failures. Only the recently signed health care bills in Massachusetts and Vermont have tackled the problem substantively. In particular, the Massachusetts bill is designed to cover all residents, using a three-point plan. First, get those people who are eligible for Medicaid, but have not yet enrolled, to sign up. Second, allow small businesses and working people with moderate incomes to buy medical insurance from private insurers at a special rate with reduced premiums. The state doesn't subsidize this level of insurance. And third, make those living at or just above the poverty line eligible for subsidized insurance such that they would pay only a fraction of their income, between 1 and 6 percent, for their premiums. The Massachusetts program also requires that all citizens obtain health insurance, just as they are required to get car insurance.

Vermont's plan is to make coverage available to more than 90 percent of its residents, primarily the half million people who are currently uninsured. The subsidized health care plan will be offered by insurance companies, but will be paid for in part by a fee levied on employers who do not offer health insurance to their workers, as well as by an increase in Vermont's cigarette tax.

I believe these programs could serve as models for the nation, yet I think they should go even further. We should provide complete coverage for those who suffer a catastrophic illness. As I pointed out earlier in this book, the repercussion from these illnesses are responsible for the majority of personal bankruptcies in this country. Insurance coverage for catastrophic illnesses will help to protect families from financial catastrophe.

There must also be complete portability of health plans, meaning that when working men and women change jobs or employers they don't suffer any loss of or reduction in coverage. Coverage should be uniform and constant throughout an individual's working life, regardless of employer.

Our health care system would be of little value without the highly trained and skilled doctors and nurses who provide care. We should, through tax incentives and funding, support outstanding medical students by financing their education and training.

All of these goals and possible solutions may seem unattainable given our current state of politics and government. We're a nation desperate for leadership in our communities, cities, states, and Washington. We need leaders capable of fostering the energy and public commitment to not only overcome our problems, but to restore to primacy our national values of equality, liberty, and individual responsibility. They need to articulate a clear vision of our national purpose to fulfill the ideals that shaped America's founding, and to inspire us to achieve that bright future, a future that will restore a strong and binding contract between working men and women and business, and between the people and our government, and reasserts a commitment to public policy that ensures the strength and survival of both contracts. We must all acknowledge that we are, first and foremost, Americans committed to the values embodied in the Declaration of Independence and our Constitution. And that we are foremost neither Republican nor Democrat, conservative nor liberal, but American.

The Declaration of Independence

The Constitution of the United States

The Bill of Rights

The Constitution: Amendments 11–17

THE DECLARATION OF INDEPENDENCE

Action of Second Continental Congress, July 4, 1776

The unanimous Declaration of the thirteen united States of America

WHEN in the Course of human events, it becomes necessary for one people to dissolve the political bands which have connected them with another, and to assume among the powers of the earth, the separate and equal station to which the Laws of Nature and of Nature's God entitle them, a decent respect to the opinions of mankind requires that they should declare the causes which impel them to the separation.

We hold these truths to be self-evident, that all men are created equal, that they are endowed by their Creator with certain unalienable Rights, that among these are Life, Liberty and the pursuit of Happiness.—That to secure these rights, Governments are instituted among Men, deriving their just powers from the consent of the governed,—That whenever any Form of Government becomes destructive of these ends, it is the Right of the People to alter or to abolish it, and to institute new Government, laying its foundation on such principles and organizing its powers in such form, as to them shall seem most likely to effect their Safety and Happiness. Prudence, indeed, will dictate that Governments long established should not be changed for light and transient causes; and accordingly all experience hath shewn, that mankind are more disposed to suffer, while evils are sufferable, than to right themselves by abolishing the forms to which they are accustomed. But when a long train of abuses and usurpations, pursuing invariably the same Object evinces a design to reduce them under absolute Despotism, it is their right, it is their duty, to throw off such Government, and to provide new Guards for their future security.—Such has been the patient sufferance of these Colonies; and such is now the necessity which constrains them to alter their former Systems of Government. The history of the present King of Great Britain is a history of repeated injuries and usurpations, all having in direct object the establishment of an absolute Tyranny over these States. To prove this, let Facts be submitted to a candid world.

He has refused his Assent to Laws, the most wholesome and necessary for the public good.

He has forbidden his Governors to pass Laws of immediate and pressing importance, unless suspended in their operation till his Assent should be obtained; and when so suspended, he has utterly neglected to attend to them.

He has refused to pass other Laws for the accommodation of large districts of people, unless those people would relinquish the right of Representation in the Legislature, a right inestimable to them and formidable to tyrants only.

He has called together legislative bodies at places unusual, uncomfortable, and distant from the depository of their public Records, for the sole purpose of fatiguing them into compliance with his measures.

He has dissolved Representative Houses repeatedly, for opposing with manly firmness his invasions on the rights of the people.

He has refused for a long time, after such dissolutions, to cause others to be elected; whereby the Legislative powers, incapable of Annihilation, have returned to the People at large for their exercise; the State remaining in the mean time exposed to all the dangers of invasion from without, and convulsions within.

He has endeavoured to prevent the population of these States; for that purpose obstructing the Laws for Naturalization of Foreigners; refusing to pass others to encourage their migrations hither, and raising the conditions of new Appropriations of Lands.

He has obstructed the Administration of Justice, by refusing his Assent to Laws for establishing Judiciary powers.

He has made Judges dependent on his Will alone, for the tenure of their offices, and the amount and payment of their salaries.

He has erected a multitude of New Offices, and sent hither swarms of Officers to harrass our people, and eat out their substance.

He has kept among us, in times of peace, Standing Armies without the Consent of our legislatures.

He has affected to render the Military independent of and superior to the Civil power.

He has combined with others to subject us to a jurisdiction foreign to our constitution, and unacknowledged by our laws; giving his Assent to their Acts of pretended Legislation:

For Quartering large bodies of armed troops among us:

For protecting them, by a mock Trial, from punishment for any Murders which they should commit on the Inhabitants of these States:

For cutting off our Trade with all parts of the world:

For imposing Taxes on us without our Consent:

For depriving us in many cases, of the benefits of Trial by Jury:

For transporting us beyond Seas to be tried for pretended offences:

For abolishing the free System of English Laws in a neighbouring Province, establishing therein an Arbitrary government, and enlarging its Boundaries, so as to render it at once an example and fit instrument for introducing the same absolute rule into these Colonies:

For taking away our Charters, abolishing our most valuable Laws, and altering fundamentally the Forms of our Governments:

For suspending our own Legislatures, and declaring themselves invested with power to legislate for us in all cases whatsoever.

He has abdicated Government here, by declaring us out of his Protection and waging War against us.

He has plundered our seas, ravaged our Coasts, burnt our towns, and destroyed the lives of our people.

He is at this time transporting large Armies of foreign Mercenaries to compleat the works of death, desolation and tyranny, already begun with circumstances of Cruelty & perfidy scarcely paralleled in the most barbarous ages, and totally unworthy the Head of a civilized nation.

He has constrained our fellow Citizens taken Captive on the high Seas to bear Arms against their Country, to become the executioners of their friends and Brethren, or to fall themselves by their Hands.

He has excited domestic insurrections amongst us, and has endeavoured to bring on the inhabitants of our frontiers, the merciless Indian Savages, whose known rule of warfare, is an undistinguished destruction of all ages, sexes and conditions.

In every stage of these Oppressions We have Petitioned for Redress in the most humble terms: Our repeated Petitions have been answered only by repeated injury. A Prince whose character is thus marked by every act which may define a Tyrant, is unfit to be the ruler of a free people.

Nor have We been wanting in attentions to our British brethren. We have warned them from time to time of attempts by their legislature to extend an unwarrantable jurisdiction over us. We have reminded them of the circumstances of our emigration and settlement here. We have appealed to their native justice and magnanimity, and we have conjured them by the ties of our common kindred to disavow these usurpations, which would inevitably interrupt our connections and correspondence. They too have been deaf to the voice of justice and of consanguinity. We must, therefore, acquiesce in the necessity, which denounces our Separation, and hold them, as we hold the rest of mankind, Enemies in War, in Peace Friends.

We, therefore, the Representatives of the united States of America, in General Congress, Assembled, appealing to the Supreme Judge of the world for the rectitude of our intentions, do, in the Name, and by Authority of the good People of these Colonies, solemnly publish and declare, That these United Colonies are, and of Right ought to be Free and Independent States; that they are Absolved from all Allegiance to the British Crown, and that all political connection between them and the State of Great Britain, is and ought to be totally dissolved; and that as Free and Independent States, they have full Power to levy War, conclude Peace, contract Alliances, establish Commerce, and to do all other Acts and Things which Independent States may of right do. And for the support of this Declaration, with a firm reliance on the protection of divine Providence, we mutually pledge to each other our Lives, our Fortunes and our sacred Honor.

THE CONSTITUTION OF THE UNITED STATES

We the People of the United States, in Order to form a more perfect Union, establish Justice, insure domestic Tranquility, provide for the common defence, promote the general Welfare, and secure the Blessings of Liberty to ourselves and our Posterity, do ordain and establish this Constitution for the United States of America.

Article. I.

Section. 1. All legislative Powers herein granted shall be vested in a Congress of the United States, which shall consist of a Senate and House of Representatives.

Section. 2. The House of Representatives shall be composed of Members chosen every second Year by the People of the several States, and the Electors in each State shall have the Qualifications requisite for Electors of the most numerous Branch of the State Legislature.

No Person shall be a Representative who shall not have attained to the Age of twenty five Years, and been seven Years a Citizen of the United States, and who shall not, when elected, be an Inhabitant of that State in which he shall be chosen.

[Representatives and direct Taxes shall be apportioned among the several States which may be included within this Union, according to their respective Numbers, which shall be determined by adding to the whole Number of free Persons, including those bound to Service for a Term of Years, and excluding Indians not taxed, three fifths of all other Persons.]* The actual Enumeration shall be made within three Years after the first Meeting of the Congress of the United States, and within every subsequent Term of ten Years, in such Manner as they shall by Law direct. The Number of Representatives shall not exceed one for every thirty Thousand, but each State shall have at Least one Representative; and until such enumeration shall be made, the State of New Hampshire shall be entitled to chuse three, Massachusetts eight, Rhode-Island and Providence Plantations one, Connecticut five, New-York six, New Jersey four, Pennsylvania eight, Delaware one, Maryland six, Virginia ten, North Carolina five, South Carolina five, and Georgia three.

When vacancies happen in the Representation from any State, the Executive Authority thereof shall issue Writs of Election to fill such Vacancies.

The House of Representatives shall chuse their Speaker and other Officers; and shall have the sole Power of Impeachment.

Section. 3. The Senate of the United States shall be composed of two Senators from each State, [chosen by the Legislature thereof]† for six Years; and each Senator shall have one Vote.

Immediately after they shall be assembled in Consequence of the first Election, they shall be divided as equally as may be into three Classes. The Seats of the Senators of the first Class shall be vacated at the Expiration of the second Year, of the second Class at the Expiration of the fourth Year, and of the third Class at the Expiration of the sixth Year, so that one third may be chosen every second Year; [and if Vacancies happen by Resignation, or otherwise, during the Recess of the Legislature of any State, the Executive thereof may make temporary Appointments until the next Meeting of the Legislature, which shall then fill such Vacancies.]‡

*Changed by section 2 of the Fourteenth Amendment.

†Changed by the Seventeenth Amendment.

‡Changed by the Seventeenth Amendment.

No Person shall be a Senator who shall not have attained to the Age of thirty Years, and been nine Years a Citizen of the United States, and who shall not, when elected, be an Inhabitant of that State for which he shall be chosen.

The Vice President of the United States shall be President of the Senate, but shall have no Vote, unless they be equally divided.

The Senate shall chuse their other Officers, and also a President pro tempore, in the Absence of the Vice President, or when he shall exercise the Office of President of the United States.

The Senate shall have the sole Power to try all Impeachments. When sitting for that Purpose, they shall be on Oath or Affirmation. When the President of the United States is tried, the Chief Justice shall preside: And no Person shall be convicted without the Concurrence of two thirds of the Members present.

Judgment in Cases of Impeachment shall not extend further than to removal from Office, and disqualification to hold and enjoy any Office of honor, Trust or Profit under the United States: but the Party convicted shall nevertheless be liable and subject to Indictment, Trial, Judgment and Punishment, according to Law.

Section. 4. The Times, Places and Manner of holding Elections for Senators and Representatives, shall be prescribed in each State by the Legislature thereof; but the Congress may at any time by Law make or alter such Regulations, except as to the Places of chusing Senators.

The Congress shall assemble at least once in every Year, and such Meeting shall be [on the first Monday in December,]* unless they shall by Law appoint a different Day.

Section. 5. Each House shall be the Judge of the Elections, Returns and Qualifications of its own Members, and a Majority of each shall constitute a Quorum to do Business; but a smaller Number may adjourn from day to day, and may be authorized to com-

*Changed by section 2 of the Twentieth Amendment.

pel the Attendance of absent Members, in such Manner, and under such Penalties as each House may provide.

Each House may determine the Rules of its Proceedings, punish its Members for disorderly Behaviour, and, with the Concurrence of two thirds, expel a Member.

Each House shall keep a Journal of its Proceedings, and from time to time publish the same, excepting such Parts as may in their Judgment require Secrecy; and the Yeas and Nays of the Members of either House on any question shall, at the Desire of one fifth of those Present, be entered on the Journal.

Neither House, during the Session of Congress, shall, without the Consent of the other, adjourn for more than three days, nor to any other Place than that in which the two Houses shall be sitting.

Section. 6. The Senators and Representatives shall receive a Compensation for their Services, to be ascertained by Law, and paid out of the Treasury of the United States. They shall in all Cases, except Treason, Felony and Breach of the Peace, be privileged from Arrest during their Attendance at the Session of their respective Houses, and in going to and returning from the same; and for any Speech or Debate in either House, they shall not be questioned in any other Place.

No Senator or Representative shall, during the Time for which he was elected, be appointed to any civil Office under the Authority of the United States, which shall have been created, or the Emoluments whereof shall have been encreased during such time; and no Person holding any Office under the United States, shall be a Member of either House during his Continuance in Office.

Section. 7. All Bills for raising Revenue shall originate in the House of Representatives; but the Senate may propose or concur with Amendments as on other Bills.

Every Bill which shall have passed the House of Representatives and the Senate, shall, before it become a Law, be presented to the President of the United States: If he approve he shall sign it, but if not he shall return it, with his Objections to that House in which it shall have originated, who shall enter the Objections at large on their Journal, and proceed to reconsider it. If after such Reconsideration two thirds of that House shall agree to pass the Bill, it shall be sent, together with the Objections, to the other House, by which it shall likewise be reconsidered, and if approved by two thirds of that House, it shall become a Law. But in all such Cases the Votes of both Houses shall be determined by yeas and Nays, and the Names of the Persons voting for and against the Bill shall be entered on the Journal of each House respectively. If any Bill shall not be returned by the President within ten Days (Sundays excepted) after it shall have been presented to him, the Same shall be a Law, in like Manner as if he had signed it, unless the Congress by their Adjournment prevent its Return, in which Case it shall not be a Law.

Every Order, Resolution, or Vote to which the Concurrence of the Senate and House of Representatives may be necessary (except on a question of Adjournment) shall be presented to the President of the United States; and before the Same shall take Effect, shall be approved by him, or being disapproved by him, shall be repassed by two thirds of the Senate and House of Representatives, according to the Rules and Limitations prescribed in the Case of a Bill.

Section. 8. The Congress shall have Power To lay and collect Taxes, Duties, Imposts and Excises, to pay the Debts and provide for the common Defence and general Welfare of the United States; but all Duties, Imposts and Excises shall be uniform throughout the United States;

To borrow Money on the credit of the United States;

To regulate Commerce with foreign Nations, and among the several States, and with the Indian Tribes;

To establish an uniform Rule of Naturalization, and uniform Laws on the subject of Bankruptcies throughout the United States;

To coin Money, regulate the Value thereof, and of foreign Coin, and fix the Standard of Weights and Measures;

To provide for the Punishment of counterfeiting the Securities and current Coin of the United States;

To establish Post Offices and post Roads;

To promote the Progress of Science and useful Arts, by securing for limited Times to Authors and Inventors the exclusive Right to their respective Writings and Discoveries;

To constitute Tribunals inferior to the supreme Court;

To define and punish Piracies and Felonies committed on the high Seas, and Offences against the Law of Nations;

To declare War, grant Letters of Marque and Reprisal, and make Rules concerning Captures on Land and Water;

To raise and support Armies, but no Appropriation of Money to that Use shall be for a longer Term than two Years;

To provide and maintain a Navy;

To make Rules for the Government and Regulation of the land and naval Forces;

To provide for calling forth the Militia to execute the Laws of the Union, suppress Insurrections and repel Invasions;

To provide for organizing, arming, and disciplining, the Militia, and for governing such Part of them as may be employed in the Service of the United States, reserving to the States respectively, the Appointment of the Officers, and the Authority of training the Militia according to the discipline prescribed by Congress;

To exercise exclusive Legislation in all Cases whatsoever, over such District (not exceeding ten Miles square) as may, by Cession of particular States, and the Acceptance of Congress, become the Seat of the Government of the United States, and to exercise like Authority over all Places purchased by the Consent of the Legislature of the State in which the Same shall be, for the Erection of Forts, Magazines, Arsenals, dock-Yards, and other needful Buildings;—And

To make all Laws which shall be necessary and proper for carrying into Execution the foregoing Powers, and all other Powers vested by this Constitution in the Government of the United States, or in any Department or Officer thereof.

Section. 9. The Migration or Importation of such Persons as any of the States now existing shall think proper to admit, shall not be prohibited by the Congress prior to the Year one thousand eight hundred and eight, but a Tax or duty may be imposed on such Importation, not exceeding ten dollars for each Person.

The Privilege of the Writ of Habeas Corpus shall not be suspended, unless when in Cases of Rebellion or Invasion the public Safety may require it.

No Bill of Attainder or ex post facto Law shall be passed.

No Capitation, or other direct, Tax shall be laid, unless in Proportion to the Census or enumeration herein before directed to be taken.*

No Tax or Duty shall be laid on Articles exported from any State.

No Preference shall be given by any Regulation of Commerce or Revenue to the Ports of one State over those of another; nor shall Vessels bound to, or from, one State, be obliged to enter, clear, or pay Duties in another.

No Money shall be drawn from the Treasury, but in Consequence of Appropriations made by Law; and a regular Statement and Account of the Receipts and Expenditures of all public Money shall be published from time to time.

No Title of Nobility shall be granted by the United States: And no Person holding any Office of Profit or Trust under them, shall, without the Consent of the Congress, accept of any present, Emolument, Office, or Title, of any kind whatever, from any King, Prince, or foreign State.

Section. 10. No State shall enter into any Treaty, Alliance, or Confederation; grant Letters of Marque and Reprisal; coin Money;

*See the Sixteenth Amendment.

emit Bills of Credit; make any Thing but gold and silver Coin a Tender in Payment of Debts; pass any Bill of Attainder, ex post facto Law, or Law impairing the Obligation of Contracts, or grant any Title of Nobility.

No State shall, without the Consent of the Congress, lay any Imposts or Duties on Imports or Exports, except what may be absolutely necessary for executing it's inspection Laws: and the net Produce of all Duties and Imposts, laid by any State on Imports or Exports, shall be for the Use of the Treasury of the United States; and all such Laws shall be subject to the Revision and Controul of the Congress.

No State shall, without the Consent of Congress, lay any Duty of Tonnage, keep Troops, or Ships of War in time of Peace, enter into any Agreement or Compact with another State, or with a foreign Power, or engage in War, unless actually invaded, or in such imminent Danger as will not admit of delay.

Article. II.

Section. 1. The executive Power shall be vested in a President of the United States of America. He shall hold his Office during the Term of four Years, and, together with the Vice President, chosen for the same Term, be elected, as follows:

Each State shall appoint, in such Manner as the Legislature thereof may direct, a Number of Electors, equal to the whole Number of Senators and Representatives to which the State may be entitled in the Congress: but no Senator or Representative, or Person holding an Office of Trust or Profit under the United States, shall be appointed an Elector.

[The Electors shall meet in their respective States, and vote by Ballot for two Persons, of whom one at least shall not be an Inhabitant of the same State with themselves. And they shall make a List of all the Persons voted for, and of the Number of Votes for each; which List they shall sign and certify, and transmit sealed to the Seat of the Government of the United States, directed to the President of the Senate. The President of the Senate shall, in the Presence of the Senate and House of Representatives, open all the Certificates, and the Votes shall then be counted. The Person having the greatest Number of Votes shall be the President, if such Number be a Majority of the whole Number of Electors appointed; and if there be more than one who have such Majority, and have an equal Number of Votes, then the House of Representatives shall immediately chuse by Ballot one of them for President; and if no Person have a Majority, then from the five highest on the List the said House shall in like Manner chuse the President. But in chusing the President, the Votes shall be taken by States, the Representation from each State having one Vote; A quorum for this purpose shall consist of a Member or Members from two thirds of the States, and a Majority of all the States shall be necessary to a Choice. In every Case, after the Choice of the President, the Person having the greatest Number of Votes of the Electors shall be the Vice President. But if there should remain two or more who have equal Votes, the Senate shall chuse from them by Ballot the Vice President.]*

The Congress may determine the Time of chusing the Electors, and the Day on which they shall give their Votes; which Day shall be the same throughout the United States.

No Person except a natural born Citizen, or a Citizen of the United States, at the time of the Adoption of this Constitution, shall be eligible to the Office of President; neither shall any Person be eligible to that Office who shall not have attained to the Age of thirty five Years, and been fourteen Years a Resident within the United States.

[In Case of the Removal of the President from Office, or of his Death, Resignation, or Inability to discharge the Powers and Duties of the said Office, the Same shall devolve on the Vice President,

*Changed by the Twelfth Amendment.

and the Congress may by Law provide for the Case of Removal, Death, Resignation or Inability, both of the President and Vice President, declaring what Officer shall then act as President, and such Officer shall act accordingly, until the Disability be removed, or a President shall be elected.]*

The President shall, at stated Times, receive for his Services, a Compensation, which shall neither be increased nor diminished during the Period for which he shall have been elected, and he shall not receive within that Period any other Emolument from the United States, or any of them.

Before he enter on the Execution of his Office, he shall take the following Oath or Affirmation:—"I do solemnly swear (or affirm) that I will faithfully execute the Office of President of the United States, and will to the best of my Ability, preserve, protect and defend the Constitution of the United States."

Section. 2. The President shall be Commander in Chief of the Army and Navy of the United States, and of the Militia of the several States, when called into the actual Service of the United States; he may require the Opinion, in writing, of the principal Officer in each of the executive Departments, upon any Subject relating to the Duties of their respective Offices, and he shall have Power to grant Reprieves and Pardons for Offences against the United States, except in Cases of Impeachment.

He shall have Power, by and with the Advice and Consent of the Senate, to make Treaties, provided two thirds of the Senators present concur; and he shall nominate, and by and with the Advice and Consent of the Senate, shall appoint Ambassadors, other public Ministers and Consuls, Judges of the supreme Court, and all other Officers of the United States, whose Appointments are not herein otherwise provided for, and which shall be established by Law: but the Congress may by Law vest the Appointment of such inferior

*Changed by the Twenty-fifth Amendment.

Officers, as they think proper, in the President alone, in the Courts of Law, or in the Heads of Departments.

The President shall have Power to fill up all Vacancies that may happen during the Recess of the Senate, by granting Commissions which shall expire at the End of their next Session.

Section. 3. He shall from time to time give to the Congress Information of the State of the Union, and recommend to their Consideration such Measures as he shall judge necessary and expedient; he may, on extraordinary Occasions, convene both Houses, or either of them, and in Case of Disagreement between them, with Respect to the Time of Adjournment, he may adjourn them to such Time as he shall think proper; he shall receive Ambassadors and other public Ministers; he shall take Care that the Laws be faithfully executed, and shall Commission all the Officers of the United States.

Section. 4. The President, Vice President and all civil Officers of the United States, shall be removed from Office on Impeachment for, and Conviction of, Treason, Bribery, or other high Crimes and Misdemeanors.

Article. III.

Section. 1. The judicial Power of the United States shall be vested in one supreme Court, and in such inferior Courts as the Congress may from time to time ordain and establish. The Judges, both of the supreme and inferior Courts, shall hold their Offices during good Behaviour, and shall, at stated Times, receive for their Services a Compensation, which shall not be diminished during their Continuance in Office.

Section. 2. The judicial Power shall extend to all Cases, in Law and Equity, arising under this Constitution, the Laws of the United States, and Treaties made, or which shall be made, under their Authority;—to all Cases affecting Ambassadors, other public Ministers and Consuls;—to all Cases of admiralty and maritime

Jurisdiction;—to Controversies to which the United States shall be a Party;—to Controversies between two or more States;—[between a State and Citizens of another State;—]* between Citizens of different States;—between Citizens of the same State claiming Lands under Grants of different States, [and between a State, or the Citizens thereof, and foreign States, Citizens or Subjects.]†

In all Cases affecting Ambassadors, other public Ministers and Consuls, and those in which a State shall be Party, the supreme Court shall have original Jurisdiction. In all the other Cases before mentioned, the supreme Court shall have appellate Jurisdiction, both as to Law and Fact, with such Exceptions, and under such Regulations as the Congress shall make.

The Trial of all Crimes, except in Cases of Impeachment, shall be by Jury; and such Trial shall be held in the State where the said Crimes shall have been committed; but when not committed within any State, the Trial shall be at such Place or Places as the Congress may by Law have directed.

Section. 3. Treason against the United States, shall consist only in levying War against them, or in adhering to their Enemies, giving them Aid and Comfort. No Person shall be convicted of Treason unless on the Testimony of two Witnesses to the same overt Act, or on Confession in open Court.

The Congress shall have Power to declare the Punishment of Treason, but no Attainder of Treason shall work Corruption of Blood, or Forfeiture except during the Life of the Person attainted.

*Changed by the Eleventh Amendment.
†Changed by the Eleventh Amendment.

Article. IV.

Section. 1. Full Faith and Credit shall be given in each State to the public Acts, Records, and judicial Proceedings of every other State. And the Congress may by general Laws prescribe the Manner in which such Acts, Records and Proceedings shall be proved, and the Effect thereof.

Section. 2. The Citizens of each State shall be entitled to all Privileges and Immunities of Citizens in the several States.

A Person charged in any State with Treason, Felony, or other Crime, who shall flee from Justice, and be found in another State, shall on Demand of the executive Authority of the State from which he fled, be delivered up, to be removed to the State having Jurisdiction of the Crime.

[No Person held to Service or Labour in one State, under the Laws thereof, escaping into another, shall, in Consequence of any Law or Regulation therein, be discharged from such Service or Labour, but shall be delivered up on Claim of the Party to whom such Service or Labour may be due.]*

Section. 3. New States may be admitted by the Congress into this Union; but no new State shall be formed or erected within the Jurisdiction of any other State; nor any State be formed by the Junction of two or more States, or Parts of States, without the Consent of the Legislatures of the States concerned as well as of the Congress.

The Congress shall have Power to dispose of and make all needful Rules and Regulations respecting the Territory or other Property belonging to the United States; and nothing in this Constitution shall be so construed as to Prejudice any Claims of the United States, or of any particular State.

Section. 4. The United States shall guarantee to every State in this Union a Republican Form of Government, and shall protect

*Changed by the Thirteenth Amendment.

each of them against Invasion; and on Application of the Legislature, or of the Executive (when the Legislature cannot be convened), against domestic Violence.

Article. V.

The Congress, whenever two thirds of both Houses shall deem it necessary, shall propose Amendments to this Constitution, or, on the Application of the Legislatures of two thirds of the several States, shall call a Convention for proposing Amendments, which, in either Case, shall be valid to all Intents and Purposes, as Part of this Constitution, when ratified by the Legislatures of three fourths of the several States, or by Conventions in three fourths thereof, as the one or the other Mode of Ratification may be proposed by the Congress; Provided that no Amendment which may be made prior to the Year One thousand eight hundred and eight shall in any Manner affect the first and fourth Clauses in the Ninth Section of the first Article; and that no State, without its Consent, shall be deprived of its equal Suffrage in the Senate.

Article. VI.

All Debts contracted and Engagements entered into, before the Adoption of this Constitution, shall be as valid against the United States under this Constitution, as under the Confederation.

This Constitution, and the Laws of the United States which shall be made in Pursuance thereof; and all Treaties made, or which shall be made, under the Authority of the United States, shall be the supreme Law of the Land; and the Judges in every State shall be bound thereby, any Thing in the Constitution or Laws of any State to the Contrary notwithstanding.

The Senators and Representatives before mentioned, and the Members of the several State Legislatures, and all executive and judicial Officers, both of the United States and of the several States, shall be bound by Oath or Affirmation, to support this Constitution; but no religious Test shall ever be required as a Qualification to any Office or public Trust under the United States.

Article. VII.

The Ratification of the Conventions of nine States, shall be sufficient for the Establishment of this Constitution between the States so ratifying the Same.

The Word, "the," being interlined between the seventh and eighth Lines of the first Page, the Word "Thirty" being partly written on an Erazure in the fifteenth Line of the first Page, The Words "is tried" being interlined between the thirty second and thirty third Lines of the first Page and the Word "the" being interlined between the forty third and forty fourth Lines of the second Page.

Attest William Jackson Secretary

Done in Convention by the Unanimous Consent of the States present the Seventeenth Day of September in the Year of our Lord one thousand seven hundred and Eighty seven and of the Independence of the United States of America the Twelfth In witness whereof We have hereunto subscribed our Names, . . .

THE BILL OF RIGHTS

Amendment I

Congress shall make no law respecting an establishment of religion, or prohibiting the free exercise thereof; or abridging the freedom of speech, or of the press; or the right of the people peaceably to assemble, and to petition the Government for a redress of grievances.

Amendment II

A well regulated Militia, being necessary to the security of a free State, the right of the people to keep and bear Arms, shall not be infringed.

Amendment III

No Soldier shall, in time of peace be quartered in any house, without the consent of the Owner, nor in time of war, but in a manner to be prescribed by law.

Amendment IV

The right of the people to be secure in their persons, houses, papers, and effects, against unreasonable searches and seizures, shall not be violated, and no Warrants shall issue, but upon probable cause, supported by Oath or affirmation, and particularly describing the place to be searched, and the persons or things to be seized.

THE BILL OF RIGHTS

Amendment I

Congress shall make no law respecting an establishment of religion, or prohibiting the free exercise thereof; or abridging the freedom of speech, or of the press; or the right of the people peaceably to assemble, and to petition the Government for a redress of grievances.

Amendment II

A well regulated Militia, being necessary to the security of a free State, the right of the people to keep and bear Arms, shall not be infringed.

Amendment III

No Soldier shall, in time of peace be quartered in any house, without the consent of the Owner, nor in time of war, but in a manner to be prescribed by law.

Amendment IV

The right of the people to be secure in their persons, houses, papers, and effects, against unreasonable searches and seizures, shall not be violated, and no Warrants shall issue, but upon probable cause, supported by Oath or affirmation, and particularly describing the place to be searched, and the persons or things to be seized.

Amendment V

No person shall be held to answer for a capital, or otherwise infamous crime, unless on a presentment or indictment of a Grand Jury, except in cases arising in the land or naval forces, or in the Militia, when in actual service in time of War or public danger; nor shall any person be subject for the same offence to be twice put in jeopardy of life or limb; nor shall be compelled in any criminal case to be a witness against himself, nor be deprived of life, liberty, or property, without due process of law; nor shall private property be taken for public use, without just compensation.

Amendment VI

In all criminal prosecutions, the accused shall enjoy the right to a speedy and public trial, by an impartial jury of the State and district wherein the crime shall have been committed, which district shall have been previously ascertained by law, and to be informed of the nature and cause of the accusation; to be confronted with the witnesses against him; to have compulsory process for obtaining witnesses in his favor, and to have the Assistance of Counsel for his defence.

Amendment VII

In Suits at common law, where the value in controversy shall exceed twenty dollars, the right of trial by jury shall be preserved, and no fact tried by a jury, shall be otherwise re-examined in any Court of the United States, than according to the rules of the common law.

Amendment VIII

Excessive bail shall not be required, nor excessive fines imposed, nor cruel and unusual punishments inflicted.

Amendment IX

The enumeration in the Constitution, of certain rights, shall not be construed to deny or disparage others retained by the people.

Amendment X

The powers not delegated to the United States by the Constitution, nor prohibited by it to the States, are reserved to the States respectively, or to the people.

THE CONSTITUTION: AMENDMENTS 11–27

Constitutional Amendments 1–10 make up what is known as The Bill of Rights, ratified December 15, 1991. Amendments 11–27 are listed below.

Amendment XI[1]

The Judicial power of the United States shall not be construed to extend to any suit in law or equity, commenced or prosecuted against one of the United States by Citizens of another State, or by Citizens or Subjects of any Foreign State.

Amendment XII[2]

The Electors shall meet in their respective states and vote by ballot for President and Vice-President, one of whom, at least, shall not be an inhabitant of the same state with themselves; they shall name in their ballots the person voted for as President, and in distinct ballots the person voted for as Vice-President, and they shall make distinct lists of all persons voted for as President, and of all persons voted for as Vice-President, and of the number of votes for each, which lists they shall sign and certify, and transmit sealed to the seat of the government of the United States, directed to the President of the Senate;—the President of the Senate shall, in the presence of the Senate and House of Representatives, open all the

1. Passed by Congress March 4, 1794. Ratified February 7, 1795. Article III, section 2, of the Constitution was modified by amendment 11.

2. Passed by Congress December 9, 1803. Ratified June 15, 1804. A portion of Article II, section 1, of the Constitution was superseded by the 12th amendment.

certificates and the votes shall then be counted;—The person having the greatest number of votes for President, shall be the President, if such number be a majority of the whole number of Electors appointed; and if no person have such majority, then from the persons having the highest numbers not exceeding three on the list of those voted for as President, the House of Representatives shall choose immediately, by ballot, the President. But in choosing the President, the votes shall be taken by states, the representation from each state having one vote; a quorum for this purpose shall consist of a member or members from two-thirds of the states, and a majority of all the states shall be necessary to a choice. [And if the House of Representatives shall not choose a President whenever the right of choice shall devolve upon them, before the fourth day of March next following, then the Vice-President shall act as President, as in case of the death or other constitutional disability of the President.—][3] The person having the greatest number of votes as Vice-President, shall be the Vice-President, if such number be a majority of the whole number of Electors appointed, and if no person have a majority, then from the two highest numbers on the list, the Senate shall choose the Vice-President; a quorum for the purpose shall consist of two-thirds of the whole number of Senators, and a majority of the whole number shall be necessary to a choice. But no person constitutionally ineligible to the office of President shall be eligible to that of Vice-President of the United States.

Amendment XIII[4]

Section. 1. Neither slavery nor involuntary servitude, except as a punishment for crime whereof the party shall have been duly convicted, shall exist within the United States, or any place subject to their jurisdiction.

3. Superseded by section 3 of the 20th amendment.

4. Passed by Congress January 31, 1865. Ratified December 6, 1865. A portion of Article IV, section 2, of the Constitution was superseded by the 13th amendment.

Section. 2. Congress shall have power to enforce this article by appropriate legislation.

Amendment XIV[5]

Section. 1. All persons born or naturalized in the United States, and subject to the jurisdiction thereof, are citizens of the United States and of the State wherein they reside. No State shall make or enforce any law which shall abridge the privileges or immunities of citizens of the United States; nor shall any State deprive any person of life, liberty, or property, without due process of law; nor deny to any person within its jurisdiction the equal protection of the laws.

Section. 2. Representatives shall be apportioned among the several States according to their respective numbers, counting the whole number of persons in each State, excluding Indians not taxed. But when the right to vote at any election for the choice of electors for President and Vice-President of the United States, Representatives in Congress, the Executive and Judicial officers of a State, or the members of the Legislature thereof, is denied to any of the male inhabitants of such State, being twenty-one years of age,[6] and citizens of the United States, or in any way abridged, except for participation in rebellion, or other crime, the basis of representation therein shall be reduced in the proportion which the number of such male citizens shall bear to the whole number of male citizens twenty-one years of age in such State.

Section. 3. No person shall be a Senator or Representative in Congress, or elector of President and Vice-President, or hold any office, civil or military, under the United States, or under any State, who, having previously taken an oath, as a member of Congress, or as an officer of the United States, or as a member of any State

5. Passed by Congress June 13, 1866. Ratified July 9, 1868. Article I, section 2, of the Constitution was modified by section 2 of the 14th amendment.

6. Changed by section 1 of the 26th amendment.

legislature, or as an executive or judicial officer of any State, to support the Constitution of the United States, shall have engaged in insurrection or rebellion against the same, or given aid or comfort to the enemies thereof. But Congress may by a vote of two-thirds of each House, remove such disability.

Section. 4. The validity of the public debt of the United States, authorized by law, including debts incurred for payment of pensions and bounties for services in suppressing insurrection or rebellion, shall not be questioned. But neither the United States nor any State shall assume or pay any debt or obligation incurred in aid of insurrection or rebellion against the United States, or any claim for the loss or emancipation of any slave; but all such debts, obligations and claims shall be held illegal and void.

Section. 5. The Congress shall have the power to enforce, by appropriate legislation, the provisions of this article.

Amendment XV[7]

Section. 1. The right of citizens of the United States to vote shall not be denied or abridged by the United States or by any State on account of race, color, or previous condition of servitude—

Section. 2. The Congress shall have the power to enforce this article by appropriate legislation.

Amendment XVI[8]

The Congress shall have power to lay and collect taxes on incomes, from whatever source derived, without apportionment among the several States, and without regard to any census or enumeration.

7. Passed by Congress February 26, 1869. Ratified February 3, 1870.

8. Passed by Congress July 2, 1909. Ratified February 3, 1913. Article I, section 9, of the Constitution was modified by amendment 16.

Amendment XVII[9]

The Senate of the United States shall be composed of two Senators from each State, elected by the people thereof, for six years; and each Senator shall have one vote. The electors in each State shall have the qualifications requisite for electors of the most numerous branch of the State legislatures.

When vacancies happen in the representation of any State in the Senate, the executive authority of such State shall issue writs of election to fill such vacancies: *Provided*, That the legislature of any State may empower the executive thereof to make temporary appointments until the people fill the vacancies by election as the legislature may direct.

This amendment shall not be so construed as to affect the election or term of any Senator chosen before it becomes valid as part of the Constitution.

Amendment XVIII[10]

Section. 1. After one year from the ratification of this article the manufacture, sale, or transportation of intoxicating liquors within, the importation thereof into, or the exportation thereof from the United States and all territory subject to the jurisdiction thereof for beverage purposes is hereby prohibited.

Section. 2. The Congress and the several States shall have concurrent power to enforce this article by appropriate legislation.

Section. 3. This article shall be inoperative unless it shall have been ratified as an amendment to the Constitution by the legislatures of the several States, as provided in the Constitution, within seven years from the date of the submission hereof to the States by the Congress.

9. Passed by Congress May 13, 1912. Ratified April 8, 1913. Article I, section 3, of the Constitution was modified by the 17th amendment.

10. Passed by Congress December 18, 1917. Ratified January 16, 1919. Repealed by amendment 21.

Amendment XIX[11]

The right of citizens of the United States to vote shall not be denied or abridged by the United States or by any State on account of sex.

Congress shall have power to enforce this article by appropriate legislation.

Amendment XX[12]

Section. 1. The terms of the President and the Vice President shall end at noon on the 20th day of January, and the terms of Senators and Representatives at noon on the 3d day of January, of the years in which such terms would have ended if this article had not been ratified; and the terms of their successors shall then begin.

Section. 2. The Congress shall assemble at least once in every year, and such meeting shall begin at noon on the 3d day of January, unless they shall by law appoint a different day.

Section. 3. If, at the time fixed for the beginning of the term of the President, the President elect shall have died, the Vice President elect shall become President. If a President shall not have been chosen before the time fixed for the beginning of his term, or if the President elect shall have failed to qualify, then the Vice President elect shall act as President until a President shall have qualified; and the Congress may by law provide for the case wherein neither a President elect nor a Vice President shall have qualified, declaring who shall then act as President, or the manner in which one who is to act shall be selected, and such person shall act accordingly until a President or Vice President shall have qualified.

11. Passed by Congress June 4, 1919. Ratified August 18, 1920.

12. Passed by Congress March 2, 1932. Ratified January 23, 1933. Article I, section 4, of the Constitution was modified by section 2 of this amendment. In addition, a portion of the 12th amendment was superseded by section 3.

Section. 4. The Congress may by law provide for the case of the death of any of the persons from whom the House of Representatives may choose a President whenever the right of choice shall have devolved upon them, and for the case of the death of any of the persons from whom the Senate may choose a Vice President whenever the right of choice shall have devolved upon them.

Section. 5. Sections 1 and 2 shall take effect on the 15th day of October following the ratification of this article.

Section. 6. This article shall be inoperative unless it shall have been ratified as an amendment to the Constitution by the legislatures of three-fourths of the several States within seven years from the date of its submission.

Amendment XXI[13]

Section. 1. The eighteenth article of amendment to the Constitution of the United States is hereby repealed.

Section. 2. The transportation or importation into any State, Territory, or Possession of the United States for delivery or use therein of intoxicating liquors, in violation of the laws thereof, is hereby prohibited.

Section. 3. This article shall be inoperative unless it shall have been ratified as an amendment to the Constitution by conventions in the several States, as provided in the Constitution, within seven years from the date of the submission hereof to the States by the Congress.

Amendment XXII[14]

Section. 1. No person shall be elected to the office of the President more than twice, and no person who has held the office of President, or acted as President, for more than two years of a term

13. Passed by Congress February 20, 1933. Ratified December 5, 1933.
14. Passed by Congress March 21, 1947. Ratified February 27, 1951.

to which some other person was elected President shall be elected to the office of President more than once. But this Article shall not apply to any person holding the office of President when this Article was proposed by Congress, and shall not prevent any person who may be holding the office of President, or acting as President, during the term within which this Article becomes operative from holding the office of President or acting as President during the remainder of such term.

Section. 2. This article shall be inoperative unless it shall have been ratified as an amendment to the Constitution by the legislatures of three-fourths of the several States within seven years from the date of its submission to the States by the Congress.

Amendment XXIII[15]

Section. 1. The District constituting the seat of Government of the United States shall appoint in such manner as Congress may direct:

A number of electors of President and Vice President equal to the whole number of Senators and Representatives in Congress to which the District would be entitled if it were a State, but in no event more than the least populous State; they shall be in addition to those appointed by the States, but they shall be considered, for the purposes of the election of President and Vice President, to be electors appointed by a State; and they shall meet in the District and perform such duties as provided by the twelfth article of amendment.

Section. 2. The Congress shall have power to enforce this article by appropriate legislation.

15. Passed by Congress June 16, 1960. Ratified March 29, 1961.

Amendment XXIV[16]

Section. 1. The right of citizens of the United States to vote in any primary or other election for President or Vice President, for electors for President or Vice President, or for Senator or Representative in Congress, shall not be denied or abridged by the United States or any State by reason of failure to pay poll tax or other tax.

Section. 2. The Congress shall have power to enforce this article by appropriate legislation.

Amendment XXV[17]

Section. 1. In case of the removal of the President from office or of his death or resignation, the Vice President shall become President.

Section. 2. Whenever there is a vacancy in the office of the Vice President, the President shall nominate a Vice President who shall take office upon confirmation by a majority vote of both Houses of Congress.

Section. 3. Whenever the President transmits to the President pro tempore of the Senate and the Speaker of the House of Representatives his written declaration that he is unable to discharge the powers and duties of his office, and until he transmits to them a written declaration to the contrary, such powers and duties shall be discharged by the Vice President as Acting President.

Section. 4. Whenever the Vice President and a majority of either the principal officers of the executive departments or of such other body as Congress may by law provide, transmit to the President pro tempore of the Senate and the Speaker of the House of Representatives their written declaration that the President is unable to discharge the powers and duties of his office, the Vice Pres-

16. Passed by Congress August 27, 1962. Ratified January 23, 1964.

17. Passed by Congress July 6, 1965. Ratified February 10, 1967. Article II, section 1, of the Constitution was affected by the 25th amendment.

ident shall immediately assume the powers and duties of the office as Acting President.

Thereafter, when the President transmits to the President pro tempore of the Senate and the Speaker of the House of Representatives his written declaration that no inability exists, he shall resume the powers and duties of his office unless the Vice President and a majority of either the principal officers of the executive department or of such other body as Congress may by law provide, transmit within four days to the President pro tempore of the Senate and the Speaker of the House of Representatives their written declaration that the President is unable to discharge the powers and duties of his office. Thereupon Congress shall decide the issue, assembling within forty-eight hours for that purpose if not in session. If the Congress, within twenty-one days after receipt of the latter written declaration, or, if Congress is not in session, within twenty-one days after Congress is required to assemble, determines by two-thirds vote of both Houses that the President is unable to discharge the powers and duties of his office, the Vice President shall continue to discharge the same as Acting President; otherwise, the President shall resume the powers and duties of his office.

Amendment XXVI[18]

Section. 1. The right of citizens of the United States, who are eighteen years of age or older, to vote shall not be denied or abridged by the United States or by any State on account of age.

Section. 2. The Congress shall have power to enforce this article by appropriate legislation.

18. Passed by Congress March 23, 1971. Ratified July 1, 1971. Amendment 14, section 2, of the Constitution was modified by section 1 of the 26th amendment.

Amendment XXVII[19]

No law, varying the compensation for the services of the Senators and Representatives, shall take effect, until an election of representatives shall have intervened.

19. Originally proposed *Sept. 25, 1789*. Ratified May 7, 1992.

NOTES

INTRODUCTION

pg. 3: The Bankruptcy Abuse Prevention; Credit card, banking; As a law: David I. Himmelstein, Elizabeth Warren, Deborah Thorne, and Steffie Woolhandler, "Marketwatch: Illness and Injury as Contributors to Bankruptcy," *Health Affairs,* February 2, 2005.

pg. 6: The American-Arab Anti-Discrimination Committee: Zogby on MSNC's *Hardball,* June 13, 2002.

pg. 7: My position on the issue: U.S. Supreme Court, *Arthur Andersen LLP v. United States,* Certiorari to the United States, Court of Appeals for the Fifth Circuit, No. 04-368. Argued April 27, 2005. Decided May 31, 2005.

pg. 7: In a speech, Castellani said: Castellani in a speech at the Detroit Economic Club, April 26, 2004, quoting a *Wall Street Journal* article from March 5, 2004, by Daniel Henninger, "Dobbs Takes On the World: The Good Thing About His Demagoguery: It Can't Be Taken Seriously."

pg. 7: Gerard Baker of the Financial Times: "An Economist's Ill-Advised Moment of Truth," *Financial Times,* February 19, 2004, p. 17.

pg. 7: James Glassman of the Washington Post: James Glassman, "The Two Faces of Lou Dobbs," American Enterprise Institute for Public Policy Research, posted March 4, 2004.

pg. 8: Columnist Andres Oppenheimer of the Miami Herald: Oppenheimer, "Border Deal Would Counter Terrorists, Isolationists," *Miami Herald,* January 27, 2005, 11A.

CHAPTER 1: WAR ON THE MIDDLE CLASS

pg. 14: The fifty-six men who signed: The National Archives, http://www.archives.gov/education/lessons/constitution-day/signers.html.

pg. 15: While the census's top quintile: U.S. Census Bureau, Historical Income Tables, http://www.census.gov/hhes/income/histinc/ie1.html.

pg. 16: The average U.S. income; In actuality: U.S. Census Bureau, 2004 Current Population Survey, Annual Social and Economic Supplements, Historical Income Tables—Families.

pg. 17: A recent comprehensive series on class: "Class Matters," *New York Times* series, May 15–June 12, 2005.

pg. 19: Warren said to me: Lou Dobbs Tonight interview, May 4, 2005.

pg. 19: The estate tax affects barely; Those who are helping to fund: "Spending Millions to Save Billions: The Campaign of the Super Wealthy to Kill the Estate Tax," Public Citizen and United for a Fair Economy report, April 2006.

pg. 19: In 1996, the organization: "Born on Third Base: The Sources of Wealth of the 1996 *Forbes* 400," 1996, United for a Fair Economy report.

pg. 21: What do you hear: Fiorina Paper, adapted from a speech to the Detroit Economic Forum, May 2005, posted on Washington Speakers Bureau Web site. I was doing a reporters' roundtable in Washington in January 2006 on the subject of competitiveness, and I was quoted as saying, "No American has a God-given right to a job." Now in this case, it was an accurate quote; I said it and I believed it.

pg. 22: You hear Google executices: Lou Dobbs Tonight, January 26, 2006.

CHAPTER 2: CLASS WARFARE

pg. 24: The workers in attendance jeered: Ron Fournier, "Union Leaders Boo McCain on Immigration," Associated Press, April 4, 2004. "McCain responded by saying immigrants were taking jobs nobody else wanted. He offered anybody in the crowd $50 an hour to pick lettuce in Arizona. Shouts of protest rose from the crowd, with some accepting McCain's job offer. "I'll take it!" one man shouted. McCain insisted none of them would do such menial labor for a complete season. "You can't do it, my friends."

pg. 24: The average CEO's pay: Louis Lavelle, "55th Annual Executive Scoreboard," *BusinessWeek,* April 18, 2005.

pg. 24: While the gulf in compensation: Sarah Anderson and John Cavanagh, "Executive Excess 2005," United for a Fair Economy report, August 30, 2005.

pg. 24: Median CEO compensation: Standard & Poors' data, cited by the Conference Board.

pg. 25: CEO pay increased: Lavelle, "55th Annual Executive Scoreboard."

pg. 25: By 2004, the average CEO; In 2005, the median pay for CEOs: USA Today annual analysis of CEO pay, April 11, 2006.

pg. 25: In 2004, Terry Semel, chairman and CEO of Yahoo; Lew Frankfort, head of Coach; Robert Nardelli, who runs Home Depot; Ed Zander, Motorola's chairman and CEO; Meg Whitman, president and CEO of eBay: Lavelle, "55th Annual Executive Scoreboard."

pg. 26: Not exactly. Raymond isn't in it; During his thirteen-year run: Jad Mouawad, "For Leading Exxon to Its Riches, $144,573 a Day," *New York Times,* April 15, 2006.

pg. 26: How, then, do they explain: The Corporate Library, 2006.

pg. 26: The former CEO of Time Warner: AOL Time Warner corporate filings, 2002.

pg. 28: It paid $140 million: Lou Dobbs Tonight, September 12, 2003.

pg. 29: The rationale for creating: Financial Times, February 16, 2006, citation of memo from Steve Baronoff, head of global mergers and acquisitions at Merrill.

pg. 29: As its vice president, David Chavern: Amy Borrus, *BusinessWeek,* March 6, 2006.

pg. 30: For instance, in economic terms, Wal-Mart is bigger than Sweden, Austria, and Norway. ExxonMobil is bigger than Turkey and Denmark. General Electric is bigger than Finland, Thailand, Portugal, and Ireland. Ironically, General Motors is bigger than oil-rich Saudi Arabia.

Countries/Corporations 2002 GDP/sales ($mill)

1 United States: 10,416,820
2 Japan: 3,978,782
3 Germany: 1,976,240
4 United Kingdom: 1,552,437
5 France: 1,409,604
6 China: 1,237,145
7 Italy: 1,180,921
8 Canada: 715,692
9 Spain: 649,792
10 Mexico: 637,205
11 India: 515,012
12 Korea Republic: 476,690
13 Brazil: 452,387
14 Netherlands: 413,741
15 Australia: 410,590
16 Russian Federation: 346,520
17 Switzerland: 268,041
18 Belgium: 247,634
19 Wal-Mart: 246,525
20 Sweden: 229,772
21 Austria: 202,954
22 Norway: 189,436
23 Poland: 187,680
24 General Motors: 186,763
25 Saudi Arabia (2001 data): 186,489
26 ExxonMobil: 184,466
27 Turkey: 182,848
28 Royal Dutch/Shell: 179,431
29 BP: 178,721
30 Denmark: 174,798
31 Indonesia: 172,911
32 Ford Motor: 163,871
33 Hong Kong, China: 161,532
34 Daimler Chrysler: 141,421
35 Greece: 132,834
36 Toyota Motor: 131,754
37 General Electric: 131,698
38 Finland: 130,797
39 Thailand: 126,407
40 Portugal: 121,291
41 Ireland: 119,916
42 Mitsubishi: 109,386
43 Mitsui: 108,631
44 Iran: 107,522
45 South Africa: 104,235
46 Argentina: 102,191
47 Allianz: 101,930
48 Citigroup: 100,789
49 Total: 96,945
50 Malaysia: 95,157
51 Venezuela: 94,340
52 ChevronTexaco: 92,043
53 Egypt: 89,845
54 Nippon Telegraph and Telephone: 89,644
55 ING Group: 88,102
56 Singapore: 86,969
57 Itochu: 85,856
58 IBM: 83,132
59 Volkswagen: 82,203
60 Colombia: 82,194
61 Siemens: 77,205
62 Philippines: 77,076
63 Sumitomo: 75,745
64 Marubeni: 72,165
65 Czech Republic: 69,590
66 Verizon: 67,625
67 American International Group: 67,482
68 Hitachi: 67,228
69 Hungary: 65,843
70 Honda Motor: 65,420
71 Carrefour: 64,979
72 Chile: 64,154
73 Altria Group: 62,182
74 Axa: 62,050
75 Sony: 61,335
76 Nippon Life Insurance: 61,175
77 Matsushita Electric Industrial: 60,744
78 Pakistan: 60,521
79 Royal Ahold: 59,455
80 Conocophillips: 58,384
81 Home Depot: 58,247

Countries/Corporations 2002 GDP/sales ($mill)*

82 New Zealand: 58,178
83 Nestle: 57,279
84 McKesson: 57,129
85 Peru: 56,901
86 Hewlett-Packard: 56,588
87 Nissan Motor: 56,040
88 Algeria: 55,666
89 Vivendi Universal: 54,977
90 Boeing: 54,069
91 Assicurazioni Generali: 53,599
92 Fannie Mae: 52,901
93 Fiat: 52,612
94 Deutsche Bank: 52,133
95 Credit Suisse: 52,122
96 Munich Re Group: 51,980
97 Merck: 51,790
98 Kroger: 51,759
99 Peugot: 51,466
100 Cardinal Health: 51,136

*2001 data.

Sources: Sarah Anderson and John Cavanagh, *Field Guide to the Global Economy,* 2nd ed. (New York: New Press, 2005); World Bank: World Development Indicators Online, 2005, and *Fortune* magazine, July 21, 2003.

pg. 30: Fifty years ago, corporate income taxes made up a third of all federal revenues; now corporations account for just an eighth (Author's note: "eighth" is updated figure as of 2007 budget): Historical tables, Office of the President, Budget of the United States Government, Fiscal Year 2007, http://www.whitehouse.gov/omb/budget/fy2007/pdf/hist.pdf.

pg. 30–31: In 2004, when Congress approved; Twenty-eight of the 275 companies surveyed; more than 80 paid: Citizens for Tax Justice and the Institute on Taxation and Economic Policy report, September 23, 2004.

pg. 31: During that same period: Corporate Profits: Level and Percent Change, Bureau of Economic Analysis, GDP106p, Table 11.

pg. 31: "I think Congress and the administration . . .": Interview for *Dobbs Commentary,* October 5, 2004.

pg. 32: As she told me: Interviewed on *Lou Dobbs Tonight,* July 1, 2005.

pg. 33: According to the government's pension agency: "CBO: Multi-Employer Pension Plans," Pension Benefit Guaranty Corp., Congressional Budget Office, June 28, 2005.

pg. 33: At the same time: Lou Dobbs Moneyline, August 16, 2002.

pg. 35: From 1990 to 1999: Annual Growth Statistics: Dow Jones, Standard & Poors, NASDAQ.

pg. 35: This was due in large part: Roy Talman & Associates, Chicago, 2000.

CHAPTER 3: THE BEST GOVERNMENT MONEY CAN BUY

pg. 37: By the mid-1980s: Jeffrey H. Birnbaum, "The Road to Riches Is Called K Street: Lobbying Firms Hire More, Pay More, Charge More to Influence Government," *Washington Post,* June 22, 2005.

pg. 38: more than a hundred: "Bush, Lawmakers Returning Abramoff Donations," Associated Press, January 5, 2006.

pg. 39: Representative Alan Mollohan: Jonathan Wiseman, "Democrat Leaves Ethics Panel: Financial Reports' Accuracy at Issue," *Washington Post,* April 22, 2006.

pg. 40: They had promised then: Susan Collins, R-Maine, to Jeffrey H. Birnbaum, "Senate Passes Lobbying Bill," *Washington Post,* March 30, 2006.

pg. 40: In March 2006: The Legislative Transparency and Accountability Act, 109th Congress, 2nd Session, S. 2349. Library of Congress, http://thomas.loc.gov/cgi-bin/query/z?c109:S.2349. An act to provide greater transparency in the legislative process.

pg. 41: Yet our government is giving $10 billion in subsidies (Author's Note: $10 billion is updated figure as of June 2006): "Lawmakers Send Mixed Signals on Timing of Medicare Bill," *The Hill,* June 14, 2006.

pg. 42: As Tom Donohue: Lou Dobbs Tonight, January 24, 2005.

pg. 42: Lobbyists have, as John Kenneth Galbraith put it: Gailbraith, *The Affluent Society,* (New York: Houghton Mifflin Co., 1958), p. 84.

pg. 42: Individual firms, corporations: PoliticalMoneyLine, FECinfo.com, Money in Politics Database, 2004 year-end.

pg. 43: there are now 4,755 such firms: Jeffrey H. Birnbaum, "Road to Riches is called K Street," *Washington Post,* June 22, 2005.

pg. 43: DeLay created the PAC: "Texans for a Republican Majority (TRMPAC) is founded. DeLay serves on advisory board along with four other Texas elected officials," www.tomdelay.com.

pg. 44: For example, from 1984 to 1993: Guy Gugliotta, "Sen. Pressler's Rise to Power Is Marked by PAC Generosity; Commerce Panel Chairman Leads Incumbents with $1.1 Million," *Washington Post,* September 21, 1996.

pg. 44: Lobbyists have paid out more than $50 million: "Power Trips Special Report: Privately Sponsored Trips Hot Tickets on Capitol Hill," Center for Public Integrity, Northwestern University's Medill News Service and American Public Media, June 5, 2006, http://www.publicintegrity.org/powertrips/report.aspx?aid=799.

pg. 45: During the Clinton years: Center for Public Integrity.

pg. 46: Since 1998, 273 White House staffers: Center for Public Integrity LobbyWatch, 2005.

pg. 46: And how about Capitol Hill?: Center for Public Integrity, March 2006.

pg. 46: At present, half a dozen: Lou Dobbs Tonight, June 16, 2005.

pg. 47: By the time he left eighteen years later: Congressional Reform Briefings, August 10, 2004; *Roll Call,* January 24, 1994; and Julia Angwin, "Disclosing Dollars," *Arizona Daily Star,* March 24, 1994.

pg. 48: "It's a sad commentary on politics": Public Citizens press release, December 15, 2004.

pg. 49: Walker argues that: Lou Dobbs Tonight, January 13, 2005.

pg. 50: Larry Noble of the Center for Responsive Politics: Lou Dobbs Tonight, May 11, 2005.

pg. 50: It was followed by General Electric: Center for Public Integrity LobbyWatch, Top 100 Companies and Organizations, 2005.

pg. 50: The pharmaceutical industry has: Jim Drinkard, "Drugmakers Go Furthest to Sway Congress," *USA Today,* April 29, 2005.

pg. 51: The organization gave $58 million: AP citation of Center for Responsive Politics and FECinfo, July 10, 2000.

pg. 51: Working on behalf of those foreign interests: Center for Public Integrity LobbyWatch, 2005.

pg. 52: When our legislators began to question: Lou Dobbs Tonight, July 5, 2005.

pg. 52: According to Michael Wessel; And as he told us on the show: Lou Dobbs Tonight, September 13, 2005.

pg. 53: Representative Rahm Emanuel (D-Illinois) said: Lou Dobbs Tonight, May 18, 2005.

pg. 53: In the past seven years: Center for Public Integrity LobbyWatch, 2005.

pg. 53: Congress gave Big Oil a combined $12 billion: "The Best Energy Bill Corporations Could Buy: Analysis of the Domenici-Barton Energy Policy Act of 2005," Public Citizen.

pg. 54: The guest-worker program: News & Alerts, www.lulac.org; News Resources, www.nclr.org.

pg. 55: In a "special report" on his evening program: Greg Hait and Sarah Ellison, "Media Sparked Firestorm as Bush Got Snagged in Bipartisan Criticism," *Wall Street Journal,* March 10, 2006.

pg. 56: Additionally, Mark Dennis: Lou Dobbs Tonight, February 27, 2006.

pg. 56: It also hired one of Carl Icahn's companies: "UAE Company Takes Stake in Time-Warner, Hires Icahn," Reuters, February 16, 2006.

pg. 56: Secretary Robert Kimmitt claimed: "Treasury Criticizes Bills on Foreign Takeovers," *Washington Post* International Briefing, May 25, 2006.

pg. 57: There are no exact numbers: "Industry of Influence Nets More Than $10 Billion: Shadowy Lobbyists Ignore Rules and Exploit Connections," Center for Public Integrity report, April 2006.

pg. 58: Over the course of the decade: "Enron Total Contributions to Federal Candidates and Parties, 1989–2001," The Center for Responsive Politics.

pg. 62: The National Wetlands Coalition's sponsors: http://www.thenwc.org/home.htm (Web site currently suspended).

pg. 62: Similarly, the Foundation for Clean Air Progress: Above paragraphs' info from Integrity in Science, A CSPI Project, www.cspinet.org/integrity.

pg. 62: The Americans for Balanced Energy Choices: http://www.balancedenergy.org/abec/index.cfm?cid=7517.

pg. 62: There is a group called: Lou Dobbs Tonight interview with Richard Trumka, secretary-treasurer, AFL-CIO, March 28, 2005.

pg. 62: But my personal favorite: http:///www.acsh.org, http:www.sourcewatch.org/index.php?title=American_Council_on_Science_and_Health#External_Links.

pg. 63: Among middle-aged and elderly people: Kathleen Meister, "Moderate Alcohol Consumption and Health," American Council on Science and Health Web site, February 1, 1999.

CHAPTER 4: THE POLITICS OF DECEIT

pg. 66: In 2004, more Americans: Committee for the Study of the American Electorate, press release, January 14, 2005.

pg. 66–67: Nearly seventeen million more; It was the largest increase; And despite that improvement: U.S. Elections Project, George Mason University, June 7, 2005; Brian Faler, "Election Turnout in 2004 Was Highest Since 1968," *Washington Post*, January 14, 2005.

pg. 67: His second term agenda; President Bush's approval ratings: Gallup/CNN/*USA Today* poll, February 4–6, 2005.

pg. 67: the lowest historical unemployment rates: Bureau of Labor Statistics, current labor statistics, employment situation, 2006.

pg. 70: When Congressman John Murtha: *Lou Dobbs Tonight*, November 17, 2005.

pg. 70: The Bankruptcy Abuse Prevention: Library of Congress, Thomas Bills and Resolutions, February 1, 2005.

pg. 71: A recent Gallup poll: Gallup Poll, April 10–13, 2006.

pg. 71: Congressional approval ratings: ABC News/*Washington Post* poll results dating back to March 1997.

pg. 71: According to Richard Niemi: Richard Niemi, phone interview, May 8, 2006.

pg. 71: While the average income; The speaker of the House; Of course, because our representatives: CapitolNet, *Congressional Quarterly Today*, January 23, 2006.

pg. 72: In addition to their salaries: Retirement Benefits for Members of Congress, Congressional Research Service report, data updated September 21, 2005.

pg. 72: Pension amounts are determined: Congressional Research Service, January 21, 2005.

pg. 73: Meanwhile, most corporations: Fast Facts, Employee Benefit Research Institute, 2006.

pg. 73: Congress has been in session: *Congressional Record Daily Digest*, December 22, 2005.

pg. 74: More than half of the members; How typical of the population; While one out of every three hundred people; It's somewhat ironic that: Membership of 109th Congress, Congressional Research Service.

pg. 74: with forty-two blacks; Over in the Senate: "Membership of the 109th Congress," Congressional Research Service, January 18, 2006.

CHAPTER 5: HE SAYS, SHE SAYS

pg. 78: "Lou has zero tolerance for B.S.": Michael McCarthy, "Dobbs Fires Away Against Outsourcing," *USA Today*, February 22, 2005.

pg. 78: As Thomas Jefferson wrote: Thomas Jefferson to Edward Carrington, January 16, 1787 (Papers 11:48–49).

pg. 80: It was Ray McGovern: *Lou Dobbs Tonight*, May 4, 2006.

pg. 82: In fact, nearly all of the biggest brands; These are the eight: Corporate 10K filings.

pg. 84: Media research shows that: Nielsen Media Research reported on September 29, 2005, that the average American stayed home and watched more television during the previous TV season than during any previous season. During the 2004–5 TV season (which started September 20, 2004, and ended on September 18, 2005), the average household in the United States tuned into television an average of eight hours and eleven minutes per day. This is 2.7 percent higher than the previous season, 12.5 percent higher than ten years ago, and the highest levels ever reported since television viewing was first measured by Nielsen Media Research in the 1950s. During the September 2004–September 2005 season, the average person watched television four hours and thirty-two minutes each day, the highest level in fifteen years.

pg. 84: New York City, 73: Analysis of data supplied by media sources.

pg. 85: "Everybody knows that": Water Cronkite speech at the March 21, 1996, Radio and TV Correspondents Dinner.

pg. 85: A 1996 Roper Poll: The Freedom Forum/Roper Center Survey of 139 Washington-based bureau chiefs and congressional correspondents, released April 1996.

pg. 86: Going back further: Media Research Center (mediaresearch.org): "In 1985, the Los Angeles Times conducted one of the most extensive surveys of journalists in history."

pg. 88: The U.S.media doesn't do; They don't report that: "Few Protections for Migrants to Mexico," Associated Press, April 19, 2006.

pg. 89: According to Professor Barbie Zelizer: Conversation with author, May 2006.

CHAPTER 6: THE EXORBITANT COST OF FREE TRADE

pg. 93: Our dependence on products manufactured: Joe Carson of Alliance Bernstein, reported by Greg Robb, "Oil One of Many U.S. Addictions," *Marketwatch,* February 4, 2006.

pg. 93: We are borrowing almost $3 billion: Robert Scott, "Current Account Picture," Economic Policy Institute, December 16, 2005.

pg. 94: It's really the "Big Two"; General Motors now proudly claims: Micheline Maynard and James Brooke, "Toyota Closes In on G.M.," *New York Times,* December 21, 2005.

pg. 95: For example, we ship more than $10.5 billion: U.S. Census Bureau, Foreign Trade Statistics, NAICS-910, April 2005.

pg. 95: We're number one; A good portion of that; In fact, our leading exports: Congressional Research Service Issue Brief for Congress, July 1, 2005.

pg. 95: As Tom Nassif: Interviewed on *Lou Dobbs Tonight,* June 30, 2005.

pg. 96: Ford and General Motors will face: Commerce Department, July 1, 2006, www.tariffic.com.

pg. 96: That gap doubled: U.S. International Trade in Foods and Services—Annual Revision for 2005. U.S. Census Department, Foreign Trade Division.

pg. 96: Alan Tonelson, the author of Race to the Bottom: *Lou Dobbs Tonight,* January 30, 2006.

pg. 97: As much as 95 percent: IDC Research cited by *MarketWatch,* John Shinol, *Motion Picture Association of America;* "Bush Says He Nudged China's Hu on Piracy," *MarketWatch,* April 22, 2006.

pg. 97: In all, the Chinese stole an estimated: Congressional International Anti-Piracy Caucus, 2006 Country Watch List.

pg. 98: A report by the OpenNet Initiative: "Internet Filtering in China in 2004–2005: A Country Study," OpenNet Initiative Report, April 14, 2005.

pg. 99: As Bill Clinton said: President Clinton, "America's Stake in China," *DLC Blueprint* magazine, June 1, 2000.

pg. 100: Mexican manufacturing wages: Robert Scott, "The High Price of Free Trade," Economic Policy Institute, November 17, 2003.

pg. 100: But during that period: U.S. International Trade in Foods and Services—Annual Revision for 2005.

pg. 101: Our broadcast featured the story: *Lou Dobbs Tonight*, January 31, 2006.

pg. 102: Representative Jim Kolbe (R-Arizona) told me: Interviewed on *Lou Dobbs Tonight*, July 27, 2005.

pg. 102: And Scott McClellan: Press Briefing by Scott McClellan, Office of the Press Secretary, July 28, 2005.

pg. 102: Congressman Charlie Rangel (D-New York) told: Interviewed on *Lou Dobbs Tonight*, January 2, 2006.

pg. 103: As Congressman Sherrod Brown: Interviewed on *Lou Dobbs Tonight*, July 5, 2005.

pg. 103: Two weeks before the vote was taken: *Lou Dobbs Tonight*, July 28, 2005.

pg. 104: Lori Wallach of Public Citizen's: *Lou Dobbs Tonight*, June 30, 2005.

pg. 104: For example, under WTO rules: Jessica Vaughan, "Trade Agreements and Immigration," Center for Immigration Studies, April 13, 2004.

pg. 105: As California state senator Liz Figueroa: *Lou Dobbs Tonight*, December 14, 2005.

pg. 105: For instance, in 2005, America imported: American International Auto Dealers, February 2, 2006.

pg. 106: The Commerce Department accepted: Doug Struck and Paul Blustein, "U.S. Settles Rift with Canada on Lumber," *Washington Post*, April 28, 2006.

pg. 106: "We have serious concerns about": Department of Commerce statement, November 22, 2005.

pg. 107: As Senator Byron Dorgan: Interviewed on *Lou Dobbs Tonight*, January 25, 2006.

pg. 107: "We have had a 30-year period": Pete Engardio, *BusinessWeek*, "Substantial Benefits From China Trade?," February 8, 2006.

CHAPTER 7: EXPORTING AMERICA

pg. 109: As I reported in 2004; Consulting firm A. T. Kearney estimated: University of California–Berkeley, Haas School of Business, October 29, 2003, news release; A. T. Kearney report, May 1, 2003.

pg. 110: In 2004, Gregory Mankiw: N. Gregory Mankiw White House news briefing on the 2004 economic report of the president, February 9, 2004.

pg. 111: As Ramalinga Raju: *Lou Dobbs Tonight*, June 8, 2005.

pg. 112: An estimate by Forrester Research states: Forrester Research brief, November 11, 2002.

pg. 112: 1. Waiters and waitresses: Bureau of Labor Statistics, February 2004, ten-year projection for American job growth.

pg. 114: As we reported on the broadcast: Lou Dobbs Tonight, December 8, 2005.

pg. 114: Ironically, foreign car makers: Michael Hudson, Inside Line, Edmunds.com, research data May 17, 2006.

pg. 115: Well, GM is investing: Michael Bee, Boyd Watterson Asset Management on *Lou Dobbs Tonight,* June 7, 2005.

pg. 116: As speculation continues about: Maynard and Brooke, "Toyota Closes In on G.M."

pg. 116: I think Steve Macfarlane: Lou Dobbs Tonight, August 22, 2005.

pg. 117: A Department of Transportation Office: Lou Dobbs Tonight, August 22, 2005.

pg. 117: Former National Transportation Safety Board chairman: Lou Dobbs Tonight, August 22, 2005.

pg. 118: According to Ross Eisenberry: Lou Dobbs Tonight, December 22, 2005.

pg. 118: As T. J. Bonner: Lou Dobbs Tonight, November 28, 2005.

pg. 119: Because the average manufacturing wage: Bureau of Labor Statistics, National Wage Data, 2006.

pg. 119: Wachovia's director of corporate development: "Wachovia and Genpact Announce Outsourcing Agreement," corporate press release, November 30, 2005, citing Peter Sidebottom, director of corporate development and strategic initiatives at Wachovia Corporation. Full text: http://www.wachovia.com/inside/page/0,,134_307_348_1270_7455%5E1280,00.html.

pg. 119: Wachovia's chairman, Ken Thompson: Lou Dobbs Tonight, December 1, 2005.

pg. 122: As Daniel Pink: Lou Dobbs Tonight, June 3, 2005.

pg. 124–25: Research firm Datamonitor estimates; Costa Rica has added almost; Nicaragua is hoping to set up; Argentina will add: Datamonitor Report, May 10, 2004.

pg. 125: As an example, the Information Technology of America: "ITAA/Global Insight Study Finds Global Sourcing of Software and IT Services Bolsters Domestic Employment and Wages Across the Entire US Economy," March 30, 2004, press release, http://www.itaa.org/workforce/release.cfm?ID=573.

pg. 127: She cited a McKinsey study: Interviewed on *Lou Dobbs Tonight,* October 10, 2003.

pg. 127: Baucus said: Baucus quoted by the Associated Press, January 13, 2006.

pg. 128: "Unlike the Bush administration": Kerry Campaign press release, Associated Press, February 17, 2004.

pg. 128: But in an interview: Jerry Selb, John Harwood, and Jacob Schlesinger, "Excerpts from an Interview with John Kerry," *Wall Street Journal,* May 30, 2004.

pg. 128: There was no mention of the evils: Boston Capital Web site, NewsMax.com, September 24, 2004.

pg. 128: He also didn't mention that: Jim Vandehei, "Kerry Donors Include 'Benedict Arnolds,'" *Washington Post,* February 26, 2004.

pg. 128: DiamondCluster International found: DiamondCluster 2005 Global IT Outsourcing Study, Spring 2005, http://www.diamondcluster.com/Ideas/Viewpoint?PDF/DiamondCluster2005OutsourcingStudy.pdf.

pg. 128: "while 30 percent of the participants": Deloitte and Touche, "Calling a Change in the Outsourcing Market: The Realities for the World's Largest Organizations," April 2005.

pg. 128: Dun & Bradstreet added: D&B Barometer of Global Outsourcing, February 24, 2000.

CHAPTER 8: BROKEN BORDERS

pg. 131: The United States has more than: Department of Homeland Security Fact Sheet, June 19, 2003.

pg. 131: Each year an estimated twenty thousand; Each year as many as three million: U.S. Customs and Border Protection, direct source.

pg. 131: Nearly ten thousand people: Customs and Border Protection, Arizona congressman J. D. Hayworth, direct source.

pg. 132: Against what has become: Syracuse University TRACfed, http://trac.syr.edu.

pg. 132: Last year, they foiled 1.2 million; Extrapolating from that figure: U.S. Customs and Border Protection, direct source.

pg. 132: the estimates range: Bear Stearns Asset Management, "The Underground Labor Force Is Rising to the Surface," January 3, 2005.

pg. 132: Mexican citizens living in the United States: Washington Times, March 26, 2006.

pg. 132: Mexico itself has a population: WorldBank, "Poverty In Mexico" Fact Sheet.

pg. 132–33: despite an abundance of natural resources: U.S. Census Bureau, Foreign Trade Statistics, 2005 Highlights.

pg. 133: The United States is often depicted: Center for Immigration Studies, Analysis of March 2005 current population survey.

pg. 133: In rural areas, only 58 percent of Mexican citizens have access to drinking water, while only 26 percent have access to sanitation services: WorldBank, "Poverty in Mexico" Fact Sheet.

pg. 133: Seventy-five percent of Guatemalans: CIA World Factbook, June 13, 2006.

pg. 133: If impoverishment is indeed: WorldBank 2005 Development Indicators.

pg. 134: The government's own estimates: Number cited by then Homeland Security Department secretary Tom Ridge, Dade County, Florida, Town Hall meeting, December 9, 2003; reported on *Lou Dobbs Tonight,* December 10, 2003.

pg. 134: Every year, more than a million people: Department of Homeland Security, Office of Immigration Statistics, 2005 yearbook.

pg. 135: Of the million people earning legal status: Department of Homeland Security, Office of Immigration Statistics, 2005 yearbook.

pg. 135: A National Academy of Sciences study: Statistics on U.S. Immigration, 2005; "The New Americans: Economic, Demographic, and Fiscal Effects of Immigration 1997," National Academy of Science.

pg. 135: This is a problem that: White House press release, President Discusses Comprehensive Immigration Reform, April 24, 2006: "Now, the problem we have is, you got some person out there in central Texas needing a worker, and he can't find a worker, an American. So he says, look, anybody help me find somebody, I got something to do. This economy is growing, see—4.7 unemployment rate nationwide. Pretty good numbers. And people are having trouble finding work that Americans won't do. And that's a fact of life."

pg. 137: To my surprise: Interview on *Larry King Live,* May 2, 2006.

pg. 138: On May 25, the U.S. Senate: Senate Bill S.2611: A bill to provide for comprehensive immigration reform and for other purposes, Library of Congress.

pg. 138: Some estimates put the overall: Harvard economist George Borjas.

pg. 140: On the other hand, this increase: Professor Philip Martin, University of California–Davis. *Lou Dobbs Tonight,* on December 23, 2004.

pg. 141: As we reported on our broadcast: *Lou Dobbs Tonight,* April 25, 2006.

pg. 141: The border patrol arrested: U.S. Customs and Border Protection, Fact Sheets: Border 2005.

pg. 142: Steven Camarota: Interviewed July 2004 for *Commentary,* "Enforce the Laws We've Got," CNN.com.

pg. 142: The Farmworker Association of Florida: "Farmworker Groups Sue FEMA Over Hurricane Disaster Aid," Associated Press, February 14, 2006.

pg. 143: The rate of violence there: *Lou Dobbs Tonight,* February 7, 2006.

pg. 143: The Dallas school district: *Lou Dobbs Tonight,* February 8, 2006.

pg. 143: yet law enforcement officials near El Paso: *Lou Dobbs Tonight,* January 24, 2006.

pg. 144: As we reported on our broadcast: *Lou Dobbs Tonight,* January 26, 2006.

pg. 144: "When you have people": *Lou Dobbs Tonight,* February 7, 2006.

pg. 145: According to Reverend Robin Hoover: *Lou Dobbs Tonight,* January 24, 2006.

pg. 146: When Hurricane Mitch struck: "Designation of Nicaragua Under Temporary Protected Status," Department of Justice, INS, January 5, 1999.

pg. 146: We reported that, in 2005: *Lou Dobbs Tonight,* January 31, 2006.

pg. 147: In January 2006, the U.S. shut down: *Lou Dobbs Tonight,* January 26, 2006.

pg. 147: California has an absurd state education policy: *Lou Dobbs Tonight,* December 14, 2005.

pg. 148: The nation's 215 immigration judges: *Lou Dobbs Tonight,* January 12, 2006.

pg. 148: In Burbank, California, residents: *Lou Dobbs Tonight,* January 12, 2006.

pg. 149: He was indignant at the idea: *Lou Dobbs Tonight,* December 15, 2005.

pg. 149: Fox has hired the Dallas-based: *Lou Dobbs Tonight,* December 21, 2005; company Web site http://www.allynco.com/political.html.

pg. 150: He said it was one step closer: *Lou Dobbs Tonight,* March 28, 2006.

pg. 151: Thomas Donohue, president of the U.S. Chamber of Commerce; Mark Franken, of the U.S. Conference of Catholic Bishops; Terry O'Sullivan, head of the Laborers International Union: *Lou Dobbs Tonight,* January 19, 2006.

pg. 153: What's not readily apparent: National Council of la Raza Web site.

CHAPTER 9: A GENERATION OF FAILURE

pg. 157: One out of every three students: Reported on *Lou Dobbs Tonight,* March 24, 2005.

pg. 158: Today we're spending $8,287 annually; Thirty years ago: U.S. Census data, April 2006, "National Spending Per Student Rises to $8,287."

pg. 158: Overall, the U.S. is twenty-fifth out of forty-one; We're on the verge: Trends in International Mathematics and Science Study (TIMSS) 2003, National Center for Education Statistics.

pg. 158: Only about 40 percent of U.S. high school seniors: "College readiness crisis spurs call for change by act in nation's core high school curriculum" press release, Act, Inc., October 14, 2004.

pg. 159: Richard L. Ferguson: Interviewed on *Lou Dobbs Tonight,* August 17, 2005.

pg. 159: Michael Petrilli: Lou Dobbs Tonight, August 17, 2005.

pg. 159: Even more disturbing: Lou Dobbs Tonight, August 17, 2005.

pg. 160: According to the Thomas Fordham Institute; The Fordham study found: Thomas Fordham Institute: The State of State Science Standards, December 7, 2005.

pg. 161: Some states count GEDs: Reported on *Lou Dobbs Tonight,* August 22, 2005.

pg. 161: Even Tom Luce: Lou Dobbs Tonight, August 17, 2005.

pg. 161: New York admits: New York City Department of Education data, 2005–2006.

pg. 162: Jay P. Greene: Interviewed on *Lou Dobbs Tonight,* October 3, 2005.

pg. 163: As we reported on the show: Lou Dobbs Tonight, June 6, 2005.

pg. 163: At the college level: Lou Dobbs Tonight, October 20, 2005.

pg. 163: As Sarah Flanagan: Lou Dobbs Tonight, November 10, 2005.

pg. 163: And Richard Kahlenberg: Lou Dobbs Tonight, October 20, 2005.

pg. 164: Bill Moyers and I discussed: Interviewed on *Lou Dobbs Tonight,* June 20, 2005.

pg. 165: We pay our teachers less: "Education at a Glance," Organization for Economic Co-operation and Development, 2002.

pg. 165: For instance, less than 40 percent; More than half: Horizon-Research, National Science Foundation, Report of the 2000 National Survey of Science and Mathematics Education, grant number REC-9814246.

pg. 166: Approximately 91 percent: PoliticalMoneyLine, phone interview, April 2006.

pg. 168: Yet some politicians want schools: Reported on *Lou Dobbs Tonight,* August 25, 2005.

pg. 169: Hiram Monserrate; Monserrate's opponent: Both interviewed on *Lou Dobbs Tonight,* October 12, 2005.

pg. 170: The National Association of Manufacturers: The 2005 Skills Gap Report, produced by the National Association of Manufacturers, the Manufacturing Institute, and Deloitte Consulting LLP, November 22, 2005.

pg. 170: Richard Kleinert: Interviewed on *Lou Dobbs Tonight,* November 22, 2005.

CHAPTER 10: HEALTH CARE: IT'S ENOUGH TO MAKE YOU SICK

pg. 174: Six million workers; That statistic is astounding: "Facts in Health Insurance Coverage," National Coalition on Healthcare, 2004; "Health Care Expectations: Future Strategy and Direction 2005," Hewitt Associates LLC, November 17, 2004; "The Uninsured: A Primer, Key Facts About Americans Without Health Insurance," Henry J. Kaiser Family Foundation, January 2006.

pg. 174: In the past five years: The Kaiser Family Foundation and Health Research and

Educational Trust, Employee Health Benefits, 2005 Summary of Findings, http://www.kff.org/insurance/7315/sections/upload/7316.pdf.

pg. 174: Most of those individuals; The Harvard study also found: Harvard Law School/Harvard Medical School, "Illness and Injury as Contributors to Bankruptcy," February 2, 2005.

pg. 174: That conclusion is evident in stories: reported on *Lou Dobbs Tonight,* April 20, 2005.

pg. 175: There have been several high-profile; Only President Johnson's efforts: Journal of the American Medical Association, "A Historical Survey of National Health Movements and Public Opinion in the United States," March 5, 2003.

pg. 176: The president acknowledged: "President Participates in Medicare Roundtable with Seniors," Greenspring Village Retirement Community, Springfield, Virginia. White House Press Release, Office of the Press Secretary, December 13, 2005.

pg. 177: One aspect of the new plan; rivals Humana and WellPoint; By contrast, the not-for-profit: Lehman Brothers Equity Research analysis, cited in "AARP Insurance Plan Leads in Medicare Drug Coverage," by Ricardo Alonso-Zaldivar, *Baltimore Sun,* March 4, 2006.

pg. 180: In Florida, in the middle of 2006: Florida Department of Children and Families release, March 24, 2005.

pg. 181: Rick Pollack: Interviewed on *Lou Dobbs Tonight,* April 22, 2005.

pg. 181: Jackson CFO Frank Barrett: Lou Dobbs Tonight, April 8, 2005.

pg. 181–82: As Dr. Ken Castro of the Centers for Disease Control; And medical lawyer and author Dr. Madeleine Cosman; Over the last forty years: Lou Dobbs Tonight, April 14, 2005.

pg. 182: As many as ninety thousand people die: Reported on *Lou Dobbs Tonight,* February 28, 2005.

pg. 182: One such organization: David Willman, "NIH to Ban Deals with Drug Firms," *Los Angeles Times,* February 1, 2005.

pg. 183: Over the last five years: IMS Health Inc., cited on *Lou Dobbs Tonight,* January 11, 2005.

pg. 183: In 2004, the FDA's safety officer: Lou Dobbs Tonight, December 1, 2004.

CHAPTER 11: THE BEST OF INTENTIONS

pg. 186: Dan Dimicco: Lou Dobbs Tonight, November 1, 2005.

pg. 187: Our broadcast featured Dov Charney: Lou Dobbs Tonight, February 9, 2004.

pg. 187–88: According to Burlington City Council member Phil Fiermonte; Representative James Sensenbrenner: Interviewed on *Lou Dobbs Tonight,* March 29, 2005.

pg. 189: Illegal immigrant day laborers: Lou Dobbs Tonight, December 22, 2005.

pg. 190: A group representing dozens of open borders advocates, religious groups, and human rights organizations: The letter was signed by, among others, AFSC U.S.–Mexico Program; San Diego Bay Area Immigrant Rights Coalition; Oakland Center for Human Rights and Constitutional Law; Central American Resource Center, Los Angeles; Coalition for Humane Immigrant Rights of Los Angeles; Filipinos for Affirmative Action; Frente Indígena de Organizaciones Binacionales; International Institute of the East Bay; La Raza Centro Legal, San Francisco; the Interfaith Coalition for Immigrant Rights Migration Policy and

Resource Center/Occidental College National Network for Immigrant and Refugee Rights; Oakland Red Mexicana de Acción frente al Libre Comercio (Mexican Action Network on Free Trade); South Asian Network Shan Cretin; Pacific Southwest Regional Director for AFSC Heba Nimr; Partnership for Immigrant Leadership and Action.

pg. 191: In response to the Minuteman Project: Lou Dobbs Tonight, March 23, 2005.

pg. 191: The Wall Street Journal *assailed:* "Immigration (Spin) Control—A guest-worker program is good politics for the GOP," *Wall Street Journal,* December 9, 2005.

pg. 191: so they began their own movement: Reported on *Lou Dobbs Tonight,* October 31, 2005.

pg. 192: AMC Entertainment: Lou Dobbs Tonight, May 10, 2006.

pg. 193: As Colorado governor Bill Owens: Interviewed on *Lou Dobbs Tonight,* November 2, 2005.

pg. 193: As Governor Tim Pawlenty: Interviewed on *Lou Dobbs Tonight,* December 1, 2005.

pg. 193: Governor Mitt Romney: Interviewed on *Lou Dobbs Tonight,* November 22, 2005.

pg. 194: One such individual is Truett Abbott: Interviewed on *Lou Dobbs Tonight,* May 10, 2005.

pg. 195: Congressman George Miller: Interviewed on *Lou Dobbs Tonight,* December 7, 2005.

CHAPTER 12: TAKING BACK AMERICA

pg. 199: four out of ten of us: Phone interview with Professor William Howell of the Kennedy School of Government at Harvard University.

pg. 200: John D. Donahue: Pam Belluck, "The Not-So United States," *New York Times,* April 23, 2006.

pg. 202: Those who choose not to opt in; This is not yet: National Conference of State Legislatures.

pg. 204: More than 80 percent of us: USA Today/CNN/Gallup, April 29–May 1, 2005.

INDEX